Business Ecosystems

Inspiring the Next Game: Strategy Ideas for Forward Looking Leaders

BCG Henderson Institute

Business Ecosystems

Edited by
Martin Reeves and Ulrich Pidun

DE GRUYTER

ISBN 978-3-11-077504-4
e-ISBN (PDF) 978-3-11-077516-7
e-ISBN (EPUB) 978-3-11-077522-8
ISSN 2701-8857

Library of Congress Control Number: 2022942737

Bibliographic information published by the Deutsche Nationalbibliothek
The Deutsche Nationalbibliothek lists this publication in the Deutsche Nationalbibliografie;
detailed bibliographic data are available on the internet at http://dnb.dnb.de.

© 2022 The BCG Henderson Institute
Cover image: sesame/DigitalVision Vectors/Getty Images
Typesetting: Integra Software Services Pvt. Ltd.
Printing and binding: CPI books GmbH, Leck

www.degruyter.com

Acknowledgments

We would like to acknowledge all of the authors whose work appears on the following pages: Marcos Aguiar, Evangelos Avramakis, Simon Beck, Hans-Paul Bürkner, François Candelon, Rodolphe Charme di Carlo, Hind El Bedraoui, Tian Feng, Jack Fuller, Joël Hazan, Wilderich Heising, Michael G. Jacobides, Julian Kawohl, Andreas Klar, Niklas Knust, Thomas Krüger, Daniel Küpper, Santino Lacanna, Julien Legrand, Hen Lotan, Pierre-François Marteau, David Zuluaga Martínez, Ulrich Pidun, Martin Reeves, Harald Rubner, Massimo Russo, Maximilian Schüssler, Anna Schwarz, Gary Wang, Edzard Wesselink, Matthew Williams, David Young, and Balázs Zoletnik.

We would also like to acknowledge the broader BCG Henderson Institute community: our Fellows, Ambassadors, and operations teams over the years, who have all made invaluable contributions to our research; our academic collaborators, who have expanded our horizons of new ideas; and our BCG practice area partners, who have collaborated with us on several of these articles.

https://doi.org/10.1515/9783110775167-202

About the BCG Henderson Institute

The BCG Henderson Institute is the Boston Consulting Group's think tank, dedicated to exploring and developing valuable new insights from business, technology, economics, and science by embracing the powerful technology of ideas. The Institute engages leaders in provocative discussion and experimentation to expand the boundaries of business theory and practice and to translate innovative ideas from within and beyond business.

https://doi.org/10.1515/9783110775167-203

Contents

Acknowledgments —— V

About the BCG Henderson Institute —— VII

Introduction —— XIII

Part I: **Fundamentals of Business Ecosystems**

Jack Fuller, Michael G. Jacobides, and Martin Reeves
Chapter 1
The Myths and Realities of Business Ecosystems —— 3

Ulrich Pidun, Martin Reeves, and Maximilian Schüssler
Chapter 2
Do You Need a Business Ecosystem? —— 13

Martin Reeves, Hen Lotan, Julien Legrand, and Michael G. Jacobides
Chapter 3
How Business Ecosystems Rise (and Often Fall) —— 27

Ulrich Pidun, Martin Reeves, and Maximilian Schüssler
Chapter 4
Why Do Most Business Ecosystems Fail? —— 35

Ulrich Pidun, Martin Reeves, and Edzard Wesselink
Chapter 5
How Healthy Is Your Business Ecosystem? —— 47

Ulrich Pidun, Martin Reeves, and Niklas Knust
Chapter 6
How Do You Manage a Business Ecosystem? —— 63

Ulrich Pidun, Martin Reeves, and Niklas Knust
Chapter 7
Setting the Rules of the Road —— 79

Ulrich Pidun, Martin Reeves, and Balázs Zoletnik
Chapter 8
How Do You Succeed as a Business Ecosystem Contributor? —— 89

Ulrich Pidun, Martin Reeves, and Balázs Zoletnik
Chapter 9
What Is Your Business Ecosystem Strategy? —— 105

Part II: **Special Topics and Applications of Business Ecosystems**

Section A: **Trust in Business Ecosystems**

Marcos Aguiar, Ulrich Pidun, Santino Lacanna, Niklas Knust,
and François Candelon
Chapter 10
Building Trust in Business Ecosystems —— 127

Marcos Aguiar, Ulrich Pidun, Santino Lacanna, Niklas Knust,
Matthew Williams, and François Candelon
Chapter 11
Discovering the Tools and Tactics of Trust in Business Ecosystems —— 139

Section B: **Data in Business Ecosystems**

François Candelon, Massimo Russo, Rodolphe Charme
di Carlo, Hind El Bedraoui, and Tian Feng
Chapter 12
Simple Governance for Data Ecosystems —— 163

Massimo Russo and Tian Feng
Chapter 13
The New Tech Tools in Data Sharing —— 171

Section C: **Industry Applications**

Ulrich Pidun, Niklas Knust, Julian Kawohl, Evangelos Avramakis,
and Andreas Klar
Chapter 14
The Untapped Potential of Ecosystems in Health Care —— 183

Joël Hazan, Martin Reeves, and Pierre-François Marteau
Chapter 15
Solving the Cooperation Paradox in Urban Mobility —— 199

Massimo Russo and Tian Feng
Chapter 16
The Risks and Rewards of Data Sharing for Smart Cities —— 211

Wilderich Heising, Ulrich Pidun, Thomas Krüger, Daniel Küpper,
and Maximilian Schüssler
Chapter 17
Additive Manufacturing Needs a Business Ecosystem —— 221

Massimo Russo and Gary Wang
Chapter 18
Orchestrating the Value in IoT Platform-Based Business Models —— 237

Section D: **Ecosystems and Sustainability**

David Zuluaga Martínez, Martin Reeves, and Ulrich Pidun
Chapter 19
Ecosystems for Ecosystems —— 251

David Young, Ulrich Pidun, Balázs Zoletnik, and Simon Beck
Chapter 20
**When a Business Ecosystem Is the Answer to Sustainability
Challenges —— 263**

François Candelon, Harald Rubner, Hans-Paul Bürkner, Ulrich Pidun,
Balázs Zoletnik, and Anna Schwarz
Chapter 21
How Public-Private Ecosystems Can Help Solve Societal Problems —— 271

List of Figures —— 277

Index —— 279

Introduction

Business ecosystems are on the rise. We define a business ecosystem as a dynamic group of largely independent economic players that create products or services that together constitute a coherent solution for customers. Think of transaction ecosystems with a central platform that links two sides of a market (such as buyers and sellers on a marketplace, or drivers and riders on a ride-hailing platform), or solution ecosystems where a core firm orchestrates the offerings of several complementors (such as app developers for a mobile operating system, or equipment manufacturers in a smart-home ecosystem).

While most of the best-known ecosystem players are big tech and startup companies, the topic is also high on the agenda of many business leaders of incumbent firms. In a recent BCG survey among multinational companies, 90% of managers indicated that they were planning to expand their activities in this field. More than half of the S&P top 100 global companies have already built or bought into at least one business ecosystem, most of them within the past five years. None of the major industries remains untouched by this wave.

While we don't believe that ecosystems are a panacea, we also don't consider them an ephemeral phenomenon. Managing business ecosystems will become pervasive, and all companies should add the required capabilities to their strategy toolbox.

Is this the right time to write a book about business ecosystems? This was a difficult decision because the field is evolving so fast that any book runs the risk of being outdated quickly. However, after more than three years of intense research into the topic of business ecosystems at the BCG Henderson Institute, we have been approached by many clients who encouraged us to consolidate our insights and make them accessible to a broader audience. So we sat down to take stock and summarize what we have learned so far, based on our research, our work with dozens of companies on their ecosystem strategies, and hundreds of conversations with academics, managers, investors, entrepreneurs, and government employees.

This book is divided into two parts. In Part I we discuss the fundamentals of business ecosystems. Chapter 1 prepares the ground by uncovering the myths and realities of business ecosystems. Chapter 2 establishes some important definitions that will be used throughout the book and explains under which conditions business ecosystems are advantaged business models. The next three chapters introduce our research on ecosystem lifecycles and success factors, and elucidate how ecosystems rise (Chapter 3), why most of them actually fail (Chapter 4), and how you can measure the health of your ecosystem in its different phases of development (Chapter 5). The following two chapters address the important topic of

https://doi.org/10.1515/9783110775167-205

ecosystem governance, introducing a framework for how to manage a business ecosystem (Chapter 6), select the right governance model, and use it to achieve competitive advantage (Chapter 7). Chapter 8 explains how you can benefit from a business ecosystem, even if you are not the orchestrator. The first part of the book ends with a summary of the ecosystem opportunity for incumbent firms and a step-by-step framework for developing a company's ecosystem strategy (Chapter 9).

Part II of the book elaborates on special topics and applications of business ecosystems. It starts with a discussion of the importance of trust in business ecosystems (Chapter 10), and which tools and tactics can be used when designing an ecosystem to foster trust (Chapter 11). The next two chapters investigate the opportunities and challenges of sharing data in business ecosystems. They explain how to overcome barriers to data sharing (Chapter 12) and which new technology solutions are available to mitigate risks and enhance value (Chapter 13). The subsequent five chapters elaborate on the potential of business ecosystems in a variety of industry applications, such as health care (Chapter 14), urban mobility (Chapter 15), smart cities (Chapter 16), additive manufacturing (Chapter 17), and IoT platform-based business models (Chapter 18). The book ends with a discussion of different ways business ecosystems can contribute to fostering sustainability, in particular by leveraging powerful digital platforms to mobilize and orchestrate thousands or millions of contributors (Chapter 19), by addressing six specific barriers to sustainable business model innovation (Chapter 20), and through effective collaboration between governments and private companies in public-private ecosystems (Chapter 21).

As the success factors for creating, managing and participating in business ecosystems are increasingly accepted and understood, many established and emerging companies will be in a position to unlock great innovation and value creation potential by engaging in ecosystem business models. We hope that this book will support them on this journey.

Part I: **Fundamentals of Business Ecosystems**

Jack Fuller, Michael G. Jacobides, and Martin Reeves

Chapter 1
The Myths and Realities of Business Ecosystems

In annual reports, the term *ecosystem* occurs 13 times more frequently now than it did a decade ago.[1] But like any buzzword, it's often overapplied. The term has been used to refer to everything from a country ("China is the second strongest ecosystem . . .") to a support function ("the HR ecosystem"), a portfolio of products ("the Darico ecosystem is made up of 5 products"), and even a bundle of services intended to make people happy ("a happiness ecosystem").[2]

Behind this semantic overstretch, however, lies a substantive new phenomenon: the rise of dynamic, multicompany systems as a new way of organizing economic activity. Seven of the world's 10 largest companies, all using technology to disrupt not only their sectors but broad swaths of the economy, now depend on such systems, and ecosystems thinking is more prominent in faster-growing companies across the S&P 500.[3]

Ecosystems are attractive partly because of the new possibilities they create for products and services spanning traditional boundaries – often using digital platforms, APIs, internet of things technology, and new tools for data gathering and analysis. The growing interest is also driven by necessity: Business environments are evolving more rapidly, requiring the rapid acquisition and coordination of diverse, novel capabilities.

The rise of ecosystems requires a new way of thinking about business – the ecosystems perspective. If we can describe this unique perspective and clear up

---

1 BCG Henderson Institute analysis, based on annual and other SEC filings, for global public companies with sales of more than $10 billion or more than $20 billion in market capitalization.
2 B. Joffe, "Ecosystem 101: The Six Necessary Categories to Build the Next Silicon Valley," *Techcrunch*, Sept. 1, 2012; *Business Wire*, "Accenture Extends Its Partner Cloud to Integrate With 3rd-Party HR Systems," May 15, 2018; Darico, "Following Strong Pre-ICO Investor Interest, Darico Launches an Entire Investment Ecosystem," Jan. 16, 2018; Fosun, "Latest News," June 2018.
3 According to BCG Henderson Institute analysis as of the last quarter of 2018, across the S&P 500, companies that mentioned ecosystems in their annual reporting included Alphabet, Amazon, Apple, Facebook, Microsoft, Alibaba, and Tencent. These companies had annualized revenue growth 1% to 4% higher than those that did not, over two-year periods from 2012 to 2017.

Note: Republished with permission by *MIT Sloan Management Review*.

https://doi.org/10.1515/9783110775167-001

the myths and confusion surrounding the use of the term, we will put ourselves on good footing to design strategy effectively in ecosystems.

The Ecosystems Perspective

The essential characteristics of business ecosystems are the following: They are multi-entity, made up of groups of companies not belonging to a single organization. They involve networks of shifting, semipermanent relationships, linked by flows of data, services, and money. The relationships combine aspects of competition and collaboration, often involving complementarity between different products and capabilities (for instance, smartphones and apps). Finally, in ecosystems, players coevolve as they redefine their capabilities and relations to others over time.[4]

At a fundamental level, ecosystems provide new ways of managing the trade-off between flexibility and commitment. In general, companies can either make flexible decisions, as in launching a pilot project, or they can commit themselves to a particular strategic path, which is often necessary to reach efficient scale and secure competitive advantage. In an ecosystem, a company can commit to building a platform, like Facebook, but remain flexible about the services it will deliver by letting others develop and provide those services. Existing capacities can be combined and recombined without one company having to commit to each specific combination in-house. An ecosystem can also explore various new paths in parallel, creating options across the system that a traditional company might not have the resources, time, or risk tolerance to create alone.

Ecosystems can be compared with more traditional ways of organizing production depending on their degree of fluidity (Figure 1.1). Ecosystems sit between, on one extreme, vertically integrated companies or static supply chains and, on the other extreme, open, competitive markets, in which customers combine various products according to their shifting patterns of need.[5]

---

4 M.G. Jacobides, C. Cennamo, and A. Gawer, "Toward a Theory of Ecosystems," *Strategic Management Journal* 39, no. 8 (August 2018); R. Kapoor and R. Adner, "What Firms Make Versus What They Know," *Organization Science* 23, no. 5 (September–October 2012); and K.M. Eisenhardt and C. Galunic, "Coevolving: At Last, a Way to Make Synergies Work," *Harvard Business Review* 78, no. 1 (January–February 2000).
5 Jacobides, Cennamo, and Gawer, "Toward a Theory of Business Ecosystems."

Different organizational structures, along a spectrum of market fluidity, demonstrate the different kinds of relationships companies can have between their products and consumers.

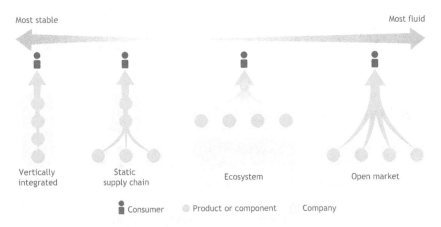

Figure 1.1: Comparing Different Production Structures with Ecosystems.

In order to make use of ecosystems, organizations need to shift from using a traditional, static, company-centric perspective, and instead apply new ways of thinking about strategy from an ecosystems perspective. This perspective is distinctive in multiple ways:

- **Dynamic:** Based on a coevolutionary rather than a static view of relationships and capacities.
- **Collaborative:** Driven by crafting novel product combinations drawing on complementary offerings.
- **Influence based:** Shaped by partial influence rather than full ownership or control.
- **Indirect:** Profits from system transactions or involves cross-subsidies as monetization often occurs indirectly.
- **Emergent:** Generates and embraces unanticipated shifts, reversals, and unintended consequences.
- **Network oriented:** Involves overlapping networks, rather than discrete, linear value chains.
- **Externally focused:** Focuses strongly on activities beyond individual company borders.

Dispelling the 10 Common Ecosystem Myths

A number of sources of misunderstanding can prevent us from framing or using this new perspective effectively. We can identify myths in four areas: (1) when ecosystems are relevant, (2) what they are, (3) what they do, and (4) how to use them.

When Is an Ecosystem Relevant?

Myth 1: You always need an ecosystem. Much of the advice around ecosystems jumps straight to how to build ecosystem engagement into your corporate strategy, without asking if this is actually necessary.[6] Building an ecosystem is a choice; there are many successful companies that do not rely on ecosystems, like EssilorLuxottica, one of the world's largest eyewear companies, which is highly vertically integrated. The choice for companies depends partly on the capabilities of potential collaborators and the cost of developing specialized capacities in-house.[7] The business environment also plays a role. In unpredictable and malleable environments, building an ecosystem can make sense. In more predictable sectors, a classical analyze, plan, and execute approach, relying on static supply chains, is likely a better fit.[8]

Ecosystems are not a solution to every business problem; we should consider what we want an ecosystem to accomplish before setting out to build one.[9] For instance, an ecosystem can be useful when business needs involve:
- Exploring a new area of possibility, conducting parallel experimentation and development with others, especially when you do not possess all the skills to engage in this exploration (for example, groups of companies exploring the possibilities of autonomous vehicles).

---

6 C. Pemberton, "How to Make Ecosystems Part of the Business Strategy," *Gartner*, Oct. 4, 2017; R. Welborn, "4 Ways to Build Your Business Ecosystem (and Why It Matters)," *Business 2 Community*, July 18, 2018; and A. Gale, "The Secret to Growing Your Business Ecosystem," *Management Today*, Jan. 22, 2018.
7 M.G. Jacobides and S.G. Winter, "The Co-Evolution of Capabilities and Transaction Costs: Explaining the Institutional Structure of Production," *Strategic Management Journal* 26, no. 5 (May 2005): 395–413.
8 M. Reeves, K. Haanaes, and J. Sinha, *Your Strategy Needs a Strategy* (Boston: Harvard Business Review Press), 2015.
9 M. Reeves and A. Bernhardt, "Systems Advantage," *Boston Consulting Group*, June 1, 2011.

- Pulling together a complex offering involving multiple complements, especially when you can benefit by co-opting other actors (consider Spotify's ecosystem of musicians and events companies).
- Circumventing distribution complexity and cost by building a new, more effective channel (for example, Alibaba Group's merchants contribute to a shared platform).
- Disrupting an entire industry, giving your model greater scale, scope, and influence by partnering with existing players (for example, PayPal working with established banks).

What Is an Ecosystem?

Myth 2: An ecosystem is a supply chain. "Ecosystem" is often used as a synonym for supply chain. Indeed, a set of relationships with suppliers, if collaborative and dynamic, can be an ecosystem. Apple, for example, has shifting, coevolving relations with multiple suppliers. Rather than just buying standardized parts, Apple pours time and money into codeveloping new kinds of glass or production-line robots, sending its engineers to test new processes in suppliers' factories, which feeds back into its own designs. But ecosystems often extend beyond this kind of partnership. Consider Intel's investments in and relationship with companies that use its microchips – a network extending far beyond its supply chain. We miss the greater value of the ecosystem concept if we restrict our view to suppliers only: An ecosystem can certainly encompass a supply chain and more, or no supply chain at all.

Myth 3: Ecosystems are always maximally open. Discussions of ecosystems often emphasize openness. As a recent Forbes article describes: "Companies that want to spearhead or join . . . ecosystems will aggressively adopt systems that encourage open collaboration."[10]

This emphasis is understandable: All ecosystems are to some degree "open," as they involve interactions across the corporate boundary. But the degree and kind of openness can vary. Any kind of openness comes at the expense of control, and some effective ecosystems are comparatively closed with respect to either new participants or data and intellectual property. For example, Rio Tinto works with an ecosystem of companies to manage its data, including Microsoft, SAP, Accenture, and Avenade – companies the organization has selected to

---

10 D. Wellers, "Beyond Industries: Ecosystems of Co-Innovation Drive the Future," *Forbes*, Feb. 14, 2018.

complement itself. The value here does not come from maximizing the number of participants; data is openly shared, but within a very select group.

To take another example, the Sustainable Fashion Alliance is an ecosystem of companies collaborating to shape one another's sustainability practices. The value they create depends on credibility in this arena – the ecosystem is valuable because it applies strong selection criteria. Openness is a choice: In unpredictable situations when exploration is key, it might make sense to have a more open system. Conversely, it may make sense to have less openness when more control is required for the system to create value.

Myth 4: An ecosystem is a digital platform. In many discussions, ecosystem and digital platform are almost inseparable. Again, it's easy to trace how this myth came to be, as many ecosystems do involve digital platforms – like Spotify, Facebook, or Airbnb. But this shouldn't lead us to equate one with the other and ignore the broader set of options that ecosystems provide. Consider pharma company Novo Nordisk, which entered China in 1994. Novo developed an extensive nondigital ecosystem around diabetes – which was then largely unaddressed in China – by engaging the China Ministry of Health, the Chinese Medical Association, universities, physicians' groups, patients' groups, and nongovernmental organizations, by sending buses of experts to rural areas to educate physicians and patients. The company now has $1 billion in annual diabetes-related sales in China and 60% of market share. A digital platform in this case was not necessary.

Technology can powerfully facilitate the orchestration of multiple players in a complex ecosystem, but successful ecosystems can exist without digital platforms.[11]

What Does an Ecosystem Do?

Myth 5: An ecosystem doesn't change the inner workings of a company. It's possible to think of an ecosystem purely as a structural innovation external to the company. But it would be strange if dependence on an ecosystem didn't have major consequences for how a business runs. Many leading ecosystem players are in fact focused on redesigning their internal processes to be more responsive and adaptive to ecosystem dynamics. For example, one of Alibaba's guiding principles is to "bring the market into the organization." To achieve this, the company uses algorithms, fueled by live data drawn from its ecosystem, to

11 P.C. Evans and A. Gawer, "The Rise of the Platform Enterprise," *The Center for the Global Enterprise*, January 2016.

automate as many operating decisions as possible. Alibaba calls this internal responsiveness the "self-tuning enterprise."[12]

Any company aspiring to manage complex relationships across an ecosystem, like Volkswagen or Alibaba, needs to build the organizational muscle to do so. Many companies still display the hallmarks of 19th-century organizational design, operating as integrated industrial behemoths that attempt to do or control it all. If building or joining an ecosystem makes sense, it requires redesigning internal processes to become much more flexible and responsive.

Myth 6: Ecosystems are constant over time. While designing an ecosystem based on where and how much value each participant adds feels like a natural starting point, this rests on the assumption that we can somehow know this information. But ecosystems are complex; participants have a high degree of autonomy, and roles within ecosystems are not constant. In biological ecosystems, "succession" occurs as one semi-stable configuration gets replaced by the next, like when a grassland ecosystem gets replaced by a forest, held together by a new semi-stable web of relationships. We can see this vividly in business in the case of PayPal. In 2015, PayPal focused on relationships with its 13 million merchants and saw banks as clear competitors. Then banks began pushing into new payment technology, and rival tech giant Amazon began offering payment and banking services. By 2018, the ecosystem dynamics had radically shifted – PayPal was working with multiple previous competitors: Citi, Chase, Barclays, FIS, and Mastercard.[13]

The danger of this myth is that it leads us to adopt static, deductive approaches that are at odds with the dynamic, emergent character of ecosystems. When we assume this kind of approach, we risk being closed to change or not sensing the signs of emerging opportunities fast enough.

How Do You Use an Ecosystem?

Myth 7: Anyone can be the orchestrator. A common assumption around ecosystems is that any company – usually, one's own company – can lead the efforts. Few companies, though, are really in a position to do this. Orchestration requires the possession of several exceptional assets – a powerful brand, an existing platform, the ability to scale, a compelling mutual vision, or cash reserves

---

12 M. Reeves, M. Zeng, and A. Venjara, "The Self-Tuning Enterprise," *Harvard Business Review* 93, no. 6 (June 2015).

13 S. Perez, "PayPal Expands Partnerships With Citi and Chase to Include Reward Points and More," *TechCrunch*, July 20, 2017.

and thus the ability to explore and build patiently. Consider glassmaker Corning, a company that works hard to satisfy Apple's product needs and win investment for joint R&D projects. Corning is successful in the effort but is clearly not the ecosystem leader in this scenario.

Yet, it's easy to lose sight of realism when developing strategy – after all, who wouldn't want their own company to be the central actor? Even industry-leading companies should think carefully about whether they are really in a position to orchestrate new cross-industry ecosystems. All CEOs should consider how their companies would operate in relation to relevant ecosystems, but not every business can or should set out to orchestrate one.

Myth 8: Ecosystems should be controlled or managed. Even orchestrators have limited control over ecosystems. When creating an ecosystem strategy, it's best to err on the side of modesty, with a goal of influence rather than complete control. Successful shaping comes from iteration and coevolution, by updating one's model of the environment and goals continually, alongside others doing the same, rather than pretending that everyone can agree on a single objective and success criterion. This is Alibaba's approach, as colorfully summarized by chief strategy officer Ming Zeng: "Never let an MBA near a marketplace that can run itself."[14] The danger here is using classical plan-and-execute tactics when what we need is adaptation and indirect shaping. In so doing, we delude ourselves and end up unprepared to face the unexpected.

Myth 9: You need only one ecosystem. Most discussions in this space focus on developing a single ecosystem.[15] But companies such as Google, Apple, and Facebook are members of a number of ecosystems. Consider Philips Healthcare, which has an innovation ecosystem involving academic labs, robotics firms, and startups; a delivery ecosystem of suppliers of equipment and software to hospitals; and a third ecosystem, based around a telehealth app supported by multiple digital health care partners. Focusing on just one closes off the possibility of joining or building multiple ecosystems, and it prevents a company from considering how to make best use of the roles it may already be playing in different ecosystems.

Myth 10: If you understand ecosystem strategy, you can do it. Ecosystems require a shaping strategy, which refers to collaborating with others using indirect influence (including being influenced by others), being responsive to

---

14 M. Reeves, "Algorithms Can Make Your Organization Self-Tuning," *Harvard Business Review*, May 13, 2015.

15 "Creating a Connected Data Ecosystem," *AMP Agency*, July 12, 2017; and "5 Building Blocks to an Analytics Culture," *Ellucian*, July 18, 2017.

unpredictable changes, and evolving the ecosystem for mutual benefit. Enacting such a strategy can feel counterintuitive, as we are likely much more familiar and adept with the practices of a classical "plan-and-execute" strategy. To test this, the BCG Henderson Institute research team built a game that simulates different environments and strategies, including the shaping strategy appropriate to ecosystems. Across multiple companies, managers consistently found ecosystem strategy to be the most challenging: Only 18% succeeded versus an AI opponent, versus 71% in the classical strategy. Moreover, both the rate of learning and the proportion of managers who had shaping capabilities as their strongest skill were the lowest among five approaches to strategy.

The shift to ecosystems thinking challenges the very idea of "industry" that we inherited from the industrial revolution – a discrete set of broadly similar players competing to produce a common end product in a vertically integrated fashion. The coming decades will likely see the further spread of ecosystems, with companies coevolving in temporary clusters of semifluid relationships, spanning traditional industry boundaries. We should therefore be wary of inadvertently applying assumptions from more classical environments or overgeneralizing from a handful of well-known precedents. Instead, we should adopt an ecosystems perspective and consider the specific strategic choices we face based on our particular situations, aspirations, and capacities.

Ulrich Pidun, Martin Reeves, and Maximilian Schüssler
Chapter 2
Do You Need a Business Ecosystem?

The term *business ecosystem* has firmly established itself in the dictionary of management buzzwords. All of a sudden, new business ecosystems seem to be popping up all around us. For example, Walgreens Boots Alliance CEO Stefano Pessina declared that his company's partnership with Microsoft will help create an "ecosystem" connecting its drugstores to patients, their insurers, and local medical care providers; SoftBank founder Masayoshi Son announced his ambition to create an "ecosystem" of companies for a second Vision Fund that can collaborate to accelerate growth; and the government of Canada announced support for a new aerospace innovation "ecosystem."

Many managers, fearful of missing out on this trend, feel compelled to come up with their own business ecosystems – or at least to become part of some large emerging ecosystems. But they struggle with the broad scope of the concept, unclear definitions, and the lack of practical advice.

We suggest thinking of a business ecosystem as a solution to a business problem, as a way to organize in order to realize a specific value proposition. To this end, a business ecosystem is a governance model that competes with other ways of organizing the creation of a product or service, such as a vertically integrated organization, a hierarchical supply chain, or an open-market model.

To help managers find their way through the confusing jungle of ecosystem thinking, we aim to address the following questions:
- What is a business ecosystem, and how is it different from other governance models?
- What are the basic types of business ecosystem?
- When is an ecosystem the right governance model?
- What are the benefits and drawbacks of organizing in a business ecosystem?

What Is a Business Ecosystem?

The confusion about ecosystems starts with the question of what they are and how they differ from other forms of organization. We use a simple definition: a business ecosystem is a dynamic group of largely independent economic players that create products or services that together constitute a coherent solution.

https://doi.org/10.1515/9783110775167-002

This definition implies that each ecosystem can be characterized by a specific value proposition (the desired solution) and by a clearly defined, albeit changing, group of actors with different roles (such as producer, supplier, orchestrator, or complementor). The definition excludes some of the more diffuse concepts of ecosystems that describe mere affiliation, such as geographic industry clusters (Silicon Valley or the Boston biotech cluster) or company partnership networks (Toyota and its suppliers or Google and its broad network of partners) without a clear relation to a specific business problem.

Even defined in this stringent way, a business ecosystem is a broad concept and includes, among other things: (1) marketplaces that bring together large numbers of producers of products or services and potential customers, for example, in retail (Amazon, eBay, Taobao), hospitality (Airbnb, TripAdvisor, Open Table), ride hailing (Uber, Lyft, Didi), and freelance labor (Upwork, Croogster, Fiverr); (2) IT systems that integrate components and applications from multiple providers on a common platform (such as Microsoft Windows, Apple iOS, Android, SAP NetWeaver); (3) offerings that integrate components from different players, for example, video games, e-readers, smart home systems, residential solar energy solutions, self-driving vehicles, 3D printing, IoT solutions; and (4) offerings that integrate services from different providers, for example, credit card systems, disease management platforms, smart farming or mining solutions.

Despite the enormous diversity in business ecosystems, several characteristics distinguish them from other governance models:

- **Modularity.** In contrast to vertically integrated models or hierarchical supply chains, in business ecosystems, the components of the offering are designed independently yet function as an integrated whole. In many cases, the customer can choose among the components and/or how they are combined. Think of smartphone apps – some are pre-installed but most are selected by the user and downloaded from an app store.
- **Customization.** In contrast to an open-market model, the contributions of the ecosystem participants tend to be customized to the ecosystem and made mutually compatible. This implies that participation in the ecosystem requires some ecosystem-specific investments. For example, developers of video games need to program their games for a specific console platform.
- **Multilateralism.** In contrast to open-market models, ecosystems consist of a set of relationships that are not decomposable to an aggregation of bilateral interactions. This means that a successful contract between A and B (such as phone maker and app developer) can be undermined by the failure of the contract between A and C (phone maker and telecom provider).
- **Coordination.** In contrast to vertically integrated models or supply chains, business ecosystems are not fully hierarchically controlled, but there is

some mechanism of coordination – for example, through standards, rules, or processes – beyond a simple open-market mechanism. In digital platforms, for instance, access and interaction are generally regulated by a set of application programming interfaces (APIs).

The concept of business ecosystems is not new. Indeed, the large fairs in many medieval cities at which merchants came together and exchanged goods for a given period of time each year can be regarded as early forms of ecosystems. Similarly, as early as the 14th century, the city of Prato, Italy, had established a textile industry as an ecosystem of independent craftsmen specializing in weaving, carding, spinning, fulling, and dyeing; and orchestrated by powerful wool merchants that acted as the trading hubs of the system and provided critical functions of production coordination, quality control, and even financing.[1]

These examples indicate that, while many of today's ecosystems are fostered by digitization, the concept of an ecosystem does not strictly require a digital business model. Many successful ecosystems, such as the Visa payment card platform and the more than 100-year-old Hong Kong-based trading company Li & Fung, which orchestrates the production assets of thousands of manufacturers to serve apparel retailers all over the world, started without a digital backbone. Nor does our definition of a business ecosystem rely on the concept of a platform as an intermediating interface among different kinds of actors. There are many examples of physical ecosystems, such as electric vehicles, solar power systems, and 3D-printing solutions, in which the players interact directly and not through a platform. The concept of business ecosystems is thus more general than the concept of digital platforms, although many of the most successful ecosystems of our time are built on such platforms. Digital technology increases the speed, reach, convenience, efficiency, and scalability of many ecosystems and is thus an important driver of their current growth.

What Are the Basic Types of Business Ecosystem?

There are two basic types of business ecosystem that can be observed in practice: (1) solution ecosystems, which create and/or deliver a product or service by coordinating various contributors, and (2) transaction ecosystems, which match or link participants in a two-sided market through a (digital) platform (Figure 2.1).

---

1 M. Iansiti and R. Levien, *The Keystone Advantage*, Harvard Business School Press, 2004.

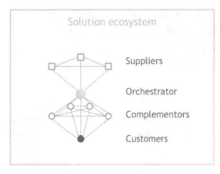
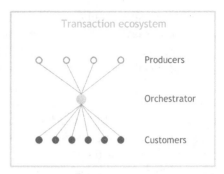

Source: BCG Henderson Institute

Figure 2.1: The Two Basic Types of Business Ecosystem.

Solution Ecosystems

In its most basic form, a solution ecosystem has a core firm that orchestrates the offerings of several complementors. During the development of a new solution, suppliers to the core firm or to important complementors can also be part of the ecosystem because they are independent and their innovation activities must be coordinated with the other players. Once the basic innovation is accomplished, such suppliers may be restricted to a reduced role in a hierarchical supply chain.

In solution ecosystems, the customer is typically not an active member but has a big impact by selecting and combining the offerings of the core firm and the complementors. In addition, intermediaries (such as retailers and other sales agents) may participate in the ecosystem because their activities must be aligned with the other players (not shown in Figure 2.1).

Consider semiconductor lithography – the process by which circuit designs are imprinted on a semiconductor wafer – as a simple example of a solution ecosystem. At the core of the ecosystem is the lithography tool, which includes an energy source and a lens system. For the lithography tool to create value, it needs two complements: a circuit mask, which holds the circuit design to be replicated, and a chemical resist, which reacts when exposed to the energy source to replicate the circuit image on the mask onto the silicon wafer. The enormous advances in semiconductor lithography over the past six decades, which enabled the doubling approximately every two years of the number of transistors that can be placed on a chip, required technology revolutions in all components of the semiconductor lithography ecosystem and close collaboration and co-innovation among the independent companies.[2] Other examples of solution ecosystems include credit card systems (linking merchants, consumers, and banks), smart home solutions (combining climate, lighting, entertainment, and security products and services), and 3D printing (integrating providers of printers, substrates, software, and services).

Transaction Ecosystems

Transaction ecosystems are characterized by a central platform (today in most cases facilitated by digital technology) that links independent producers of products or services with independent customers. Examples of such platform businesses are abundant – think of eBay, which links independent sellers and buyers; Uber, which links drivers and riders; and Upwork, which links freelance workers with companies. Transaction ecosystems are two-sided markets that benefit from direct and indirect network effects. *Direct network effects* occur when participants value the offering more as the number of other participants on their side of the market grows (such as users of fax machines or social networks). More important, *indirect network effects* emerge when the value of the ecosystem for the participants on one side of the market increases with growing numbers of participants on the other side. For example, an increasing number of drivers attracts additional customers to a ride-hailing platform, which in turn will attract even more drivers, resulting in a positive feedback loop. In this way, and in contrast to solution ecosystems, customers are an integral part of transaction ecosystems. They not only create one side of the market but also contribute data and feedback to the ecosystem. Sometimes, customers even switch into the role of producers – for instance, when viewers on YouTube post their own videos or when tenants on Airbnb offer their own homes on the platform.

The two ecosystem archetypes differ not only in their structural form and types of members, but also in their purpose, success factors, and value creation mechanism. The purpose of a solution ecosystem is to create a coherent solution. The core firm is an orchestrator that must motivate and coordinate the innovation activities of the complementors, ensure continuous improvement of the overall product, and safeguard fair value sharing among ecosystem members. Value is

2 R. Adner and R. Kapoor, "Value Creation in Innovation Ecosystems: How the Structure of Technological Interdependence Affects Firm Performance in New Technology Generations," *Strategic Management Journal*, March 2010.

created by identifying and removing bottlenecks in the overall system and by exploiting supermodular complementarities (which exist when more of component B leads to increasing returns for component A). Solution ecosystems typically capture the value they create by selling their solution as a product or service.

By contrast, the purpose of a transaction ecosystem is matchmaking: identifying the best fit between the specific needs of a customer and the specific offering of a producer, and facilitating the subsequent transaction. Value creation in a transaction ecosystem is thus driven by the number of successful transactions and their benefits to both sides of the market. For example, a ride-hailing platform creates value by finding the nearest driver for a given passenger, establishing trust between the two through curation and insurance, and performing financial settlement. In addition to establishing and facilitating the matchmaking mechanism, the role of the platform orchestrator is to manage access to the platform, establish standards and rules, and set incentives for both sides of the market in order to grow the ecosystem and exploit network effects. Monetization of transaction ecosystem value is frequently based on transaction fees, charging for advertising, or both.

When you consider building or joining a business ecosystem, you need to be clear about what type would be the best way to realize your value proposition. Sometimes both solution and transaction ecosystems are viable, and we increasingly see shifts between the models and hybrid forms. For example, the Apple iPhone started as a solution ecosystem, with Apple as core firm coordinating a coherent solution with component suppliers, app developers, and telecom providers, but after the introduction of the App Store, it also became a platform and marketplace for selling apps. On the other hand, Airbnb was established as a transaction ecosystem but has recently started to build a solution ecosystem by inviting outside developers to integrate additional applications and services into the platform (such as tools to make travel arrangements or to simplify guest check-in, cleaning, or linen delivery). Similarly, LinkedIn has moved toward a solution ecosystem model after its acquisition by Microsoft.

When Is an Ecosystem the Right Governance Model?

Let's assume you have identified an attractive business opportunity and are reflecting on the best governance model to realize it. You have multiple options for organizing the required activities:

- *A vertically integrated model*, in which you perform all key activities within your own organization
- *A hierarchical supply chain*, in which you outsource certain activities to suppliers from which you buy and/or intermediaries to which you sell
- *A business ecosystem*, in which you coordinate with other, largely independent economic players in order to create a coherent offering
- *An open-market model*, in which the customer selects and buys the required components from independent and uncoordinated providers in an open, competitive market

Under which conditions is a business ecosystem the most advantageous governance model for your business opportunity? To start with, unpredictable but highly malleable business environments may lend themselves to an ecosystem approach. Such environments enable "shaping" strategies, which define the profile of an industry before its rules have been written or rewritten. Shaping strategies require you to collaborate with others because you cannot shape the industry alone and you need others to share the risk, contribute complementary capabilities, and build the new market quickly, before competitors mobilize. Moreover, business opportunities in such environments are often characterized by both high modularity of the required product or service solution and a high need for coordination among players – ideal conditions for business ecosystems (Figure 2.2).

Source: BCG Henderson Institute

Figure 2.2: Rubric for Choosing a Governance Model.

A product or service solution exhibits high modularity if its components can be combined easily and flexibly and integrated at low (transaction) cost. For example, the production of an iPhone from its components (main I/O, battery, display, camera, and so on) is characterized by low modularity and must be done by the OEM (in this case, in a hierarchical supply chain), while the use of an iPhone by combining the device, the telecom provider, and apps exhibits high modularity and can be done by the individual consumer.

Highly modular offerings lend themselves to an open-market model. However, there are some situations in which the customer clearly benefits from closer coordination among the components, and these are the sweet spots for business ecosystems. Such a need for coordination can have various causes:

- It is not easy to identify and match the required partners, which is the value proposition of most matchmaking platforms.
- The roles and responsibilities of the various partners are not fully specified. For example, effective disease management solutions require a clear definition and division of responsibility for patient treatment and data sharing among insurance companies, individual practitioners, hospitals, labs, pharmacies, and technology companies.
- The interfaces between the components are not well standardized, such as in the competing battery and charging technologies for electric vehicles.
- The specifications of the system or individual components frequently change, such as in many PC and mobile operating systems.
- The change of one component requires changes of other components to realize its value, as illustrated by the coevolution and continuous debottlenecking of the semiconductor lithography system over the past 60 years.

Shifts in the need for coordination, and in the level of modularity, signal the need for a shift in the governance model. The evolution of the governance model for the PC system serves as an illustration. IBM started developing the PC system in the 1970s. In the initial phase, low modularity and high need for coordination between components favored a vertically integrated model, so IBM kept almost all activities in-house, extending its R&D efforts to virtually every technological driver of computing performance – from research on glass ceramics to the design of efficient software algorithms. Once the basic design was established, the need for such close coordination decreased and IBM began to outsource the development and production of some components (such as memory chips, storage devices, the operating system, and software applications), organizing in a hierarchical supply chain. However, IBM had not made exclusive agreements to control the core hardware components (such as the Intel microprocessor) and the core software components (such as Microsoft DOS). IBM's architecture became a common good and the standard for all PCs (except for Apple). The increasing modularity of the PC system enabled an open-market model, in which PC clone makers used the IBM architecture and purchased components directly from Intel, Microsoft, and other suppliers. The open-market model spurred the production, commercialization, and adoption of PCs all over the world.

However, the open-market model restricted innovation. For example, Intel's increasingly powerful microprocessors provided only limited benefit for users as long as the other component players did not redesign their products to take advantage of the new microprocessors. This potential for system-level innovation increased the need for coordination, but the open-market model limited opportunities and incentives for advancing the overall PC system architecture. To fill this gap, Intel created the Intel Architecture Lab (IAL), which set out to drive architectural progress on the PC system, stimulate and facilitate innovation on complementary products, and coordinate outside firms' innovation to drive the development of new system capabilities. An early IAL project was the PCI (peripheral component interconnect) bus initiative, responsible for linking the many components of the PC system. By developing the PCI bus and establishing it as an industry standard, Intel removed an important performance bottleneck in the PC system and grabbed the position as orchestrator of the PC ecosystem.

The PC system example illustrates a pattern evident in many industries. On the one hand, product standardization increases modularity because dominant designs reduce the variety of potential components, and interfaces between components become more clearly defined. Digitization further simplifies these interfaces, lowers transaction costs, and fosters modularity. On the other hand, standardization of the process of combining the components to create the overall solution reduces the need for coordination because there is less variety in activities, more joint experience in aligning activities, and a higher number of suppliers that are able to provide the required components. In this way, many industries naturally converge toward an open-market model, and digital technologies may further support this development. However, as the example of the PC system also illustrates, discontinuous innovation may increase the need for coordination again because it introduces new components or new combinations of existing components, and a change in one component may require changes in other components to fully realize the benefits at a system level.

This observation may also explain the current focus on business ecosystems: on the one hand, digitization facilitates modularity and enables more open governance models, and on the other hand, the resulting boom of business model innovation increases the need for coordination among players, making business ecosystems an advantageous governance model. Many digital platforms have reversed the widespread trend of disintermediation by replacing inefficient and nonscalable intermediaries with automated, data-based algorithms and social feedback. However, further advances in technology (such as blockchain) could conceivably challenge this trend of re-intermediation. As the technology behind many platforms becomes more standardized and commoditized, the need for coordination may decline and, with it, the importance of the orchestrator. Some ecosystems may develop into open-market models. To react to these pressures on their business models, many platform providers have begun to offer services beyond matchmaking on both sides of the market.

Of course, the preferred governance model for a given business opportunity and business environment is often ambiguous. In many industries, we see competing governance models. Think of the classic example of PC operating systems, in which Apple followed a strictly integrated model while Microsoft built an ecosystem of independent software vendors for its Windows platform. Similarly, in electric vehicles, Tesla initially followed an integrated model, even building its own battery production and charging infrastructure, while Better Place tried to establish an ecosystem model by separating car ownership from the battery and offering battery charging and renting as a service. Better Place failed, but probably because of an overly optimistic expansion strategy rather than a flawed business model design. As product and process standards for building and operating electric vehicles are increasingly established, we can expect the usual trend toward higher modularity and lower need for coordination. Indeed, most traditional car OEMs that entered the EV market more recently use a hierarchical supply chain for their batteries, and even Tesla increasingly employs an ecosystem of partners (such as hotels, restaurants, and shopping centers) for its charging infrastructure.

What Are the Benefits and Drawbacks of Organizing in a Business Ecosystem?

If there is a certain flexibility in the choice of governance model for a given business opportunity, our final question is to what extent an ecosystem is an attractive way to organize. What are the advantages of a business ecosystem compared with an integrated model, a hierarchical supply chain, or an open-market model, and what are the potential drawbacks that need to be managed?

The Benefits

Business ecosystems offer three critical benefits: (1) access to a broad range of capabilities, (2) the ability to scale quickly, and (3) flexibility and resilience. In particular during the startup phase, an ecosystem model can provide fast access to external capabilities that may be too expensive or time-consuming to build internally. Bill Joy, a founder of Sun Microsystems, famously said, "Not all smart people work for you." However, while it is hard to find and employ smart people, they might find you if you open up your ecosystem and invite them to participate. This is particularly relevant when it comes to the speed and breadth of "open" innovation. Steve Jobs was initially opposed to opening the iPhone to third-party app developers, but it was only when the App Store was established about eight months after the launch of the iPhone that the ecosystem really took off with the explosion of innovative new applications.

Once launched, ecosystems can scale much faster than other governance models. Their modular structure, with clearly defined interfaces, makes it easy to add participants, and the asset-light business models that underlie many platforms permit rapid growth. Airbnb outperforms most large hotel chains in terms of revenue and market capitalization without owning a single hotel. Moreover, positive network effects can foster explosive growth for transaction ecosystems that solve the chicken-or-egg problem. Airbnb achieved its dominant market position only ten years after its founding, a trajectory that could hardly be imagined in the traditional, asset-intensive hotel business model and can largely be attributed to the self-reinforcing dynamics of growing numbers of guests and beds.

Finally, part of the attractiveness of business ecosystems stems from their flexibility and resilience. Their modular setup, with a stable core or platform and stable interfaces – but highly variable components that can be easily added or subtracted from the system – enable both high variety and a high capacity to evolve. In this way, ecosystems are particularly attractive when consumers' needs and tastes are heterogeneous or unpredictable or when technological trajectories are dynamic or uncertain. Consider the Windows operating system. Owing to its set-up as a flexible ecosystem, Windows managed to remain the dominant PC operating system for more than three decades, despite enormous changes in the underlying technology and in customers' requirements.

The Drawbacks

Of course, there are also drawbacks to the ecosystem model. By definition, an ecosystem consists of largely independent economic players that agree to collaborate, which implies only limited control of the overall system by each participant. Even an ecosystem orchestrator has limited means to enforce or control the behavior of partners, compared with a hierarchical supply chain or an integrated model. Google experienced this in the Open Handset Alliance, where it struggled with several competing forks of its Android operating system – for example, from handset makers Samsung and Xiaomi.

The challenge is to engage and orchestrate external partners without full hierarchical power or control. Such ecosystem governance can be achieved through the architecture of the ecosystem and through clear rules, standards, and norms that are established in a transparent, participative, and fair way that are adjusted as the ecosystem evolves. However, a certain constraint on control is simply the price of open innovation, flexibility, and resilience, so ecosystem governance must be finely balanced, leaving room for serendipitous discoveries and self-organized evolution.

Related to the challenge of limited control is the problem of value capture. It is in the nature of an ecosystem that the total value it creates must be split among its participants. The core firm in a solution ecosystem or the platform orchestrator in a transaction ecosystem is responsible for ensuring that the ecosystem is economically attractive for all its important contributors. An ecosystem has to be a club that others want to join. Achieving this can require huge investments during the startup and scaling phase that can be recouped only once the ecosystem is fully established. Many large digital platforms that have achieved high financial valuations, such as Uber and Lyft, still struggle to earn substantial profits. However, limited initial value capture may be the price of the opportunity to scale fast and grow what can become a powerful oligopolistic position. Companies like Microsoft and Amazon became very profitable after many years of investing in building multiple ecosystems.

The more open the ecosystem, the more difficult it is to capture value, as Google experienced with its open Android ecosystem when compared with the more restrictive Apple iOS. Companies need to come up with new and unconventional ways to monetize the value of their ecosystem beyond charging for access or transaction fees, such as targeted advertising, charging for enhanced access or complementary services, selling data, or expanding into adjacent products or services.

Finally, the enormous success of a few large players should not blind one to the fact that ecosystems can fail. A recent study by the BCG Henderson Institute found that fewer than 15% of the 57 ecosystems investigated were sustainable in the long run (see Chapter 3). And this is probably an optimistic estimate given the impossibility of completely eliminating survivor bias. The odds of succeeding with ecosystems are thus not better than for other governance models, and the gains for those that initially succeed are often temporary, in spite of the impression created by successful incumbents.

The main reason for this mixed performance may be the many new strategic challenges that ecosystems pose: solving the chicken-or-egg problem during launch; ensuring that costs don't explode during scale-up, which can be very fast when positive network effects kick in; preventing the erosion of quality during growth; defending against competitors that use the low entry barriers of many digital business models to copy and improve your model and encourage your complementors or users to multi-home, or even fully switch to their ecosystems. These requirements are new and unfamiliar to many companies. And even if you have established a strong market position, once you start losing share, network effects can quickly reverse and work against you, as illustrated by the fast collapse of the once-dominant BlackBerry and Myspace ecosystems. The dynamism and flexibility of ecosystems cut both ways: the model is evolvable and scalable, but it requires continuous adjustment. Sustainable success calls for permanent engagement with all stakeholders, improvement and expansion of the offering, and innovation and renewal of the ecosystem.

The Business Ecosystem Checklist

When you reflect on the best governance model for a given business opportunity, you should consider building a business ecosystem if:
- you face an unpredictable but highly malleable business environment that requires you to collaborate with others in order to shape or reshape the industry.
- the individual components of the solution can be easily and flexibly combined, but a certain level of coordination is needed to identify the required partners, specify their roles, and align their activities.
- you can benefit from the access to external capabilities, fast scaling, and flexibility and resilience that an ecosystem offers.

If you decide to build you own business ecosystem, make sure that you are prepared for the challenges of limited control and constrained value capture and for the strategic requirements of building, growing, and protecting such an ecosystem.

On the other hand, if your business environment is rather predictable or you cannot really shape it, if your opportunity requires a highly integrated solution or coordination between component providers is not really an issue, or if you can rely on internal capabilities for launching, scaling, and flexibly adjusting your offering, other governance models such as vertical integration, a hierarchical supply chain, or even an open market may be better choices.

There are good reasons for the current hype around ecosystems, but managers should dispassionately evaluate whether a business ecosystem is the best solution to their problem.

Martin Reeves, Hen Lotan, Julien Legrand,
and Michael G. Jacobides

Chapter 3
How Business Ecosystems Rise
(and Often Fall)

Confusion about business ecosystems abounds, and many commonly held beliefs about them simply aren't true (see Chapter 1). To objectively analyze several key details about ecosystems – such as how often they succeed, how important it is to be first, and how long they take to pay off – we conducted a quantitative study of ecosystems over the past four decades. The results show that ecosystems tend to follow one of four paths during their life cycles. Moreover, there are three critical windows during which actions by management can have a disproportionate effect on long-term success.

Ecosystems are tough to analyze due to, among other reasons, a lack of structured data. With so little quantitative analysis, it can be tempting to look at the most conspicuous current examples and believe that ecosystems are wildly successful – but that would be overlooking the much larger number of entrants that failed to take hold. We analyzed the performance of 57 ecosystems in 11 sectors across geographic markets and found that fewer than 15% of the ecosystems studied were sustainable in the long run.

There is no measurable, standard definition of an ecosystem. We focused on multicompany systems cited by at least one academic paper as an ecosystem and then confirmed that they showed several defining characteristics: (1) a large number of partners, (2) diversity across industries, (3) relationships based on collaboration rather than ownership, and (4) the ability for partners to join with limited friction. We then analyzed market share data from IHS, Statista, and other sources to examine ecosystems' life cycles. Because we covered several decades of performance, it is virtually impossible to avoid some survivor bias (we covered all ecosystems that industry analysts would consider when calculating market shares; very early or nonpublic ventures would typically not be covered, hence reducing our visibility on the actual number of failures in early stages). As such, our failure rates are, if anything, conservative.

In addition, our research shows how ecosystems rise and fall. According to the findings, even successful ecosystems often do not last, given their highly

Note: Republished with permission by *MIT Sloan Management Review*.

https://doi.org/10.1515/9783110775167-003

dynamic nature. Therefore, management must continuously reevaluate strategy and adapt it as an ecosystem evolves.

Four Typical Paths for Business Ecosystems

Our research identifies four typical paths for ecosystems (Figure 3.1):

1 Never Took Off

The first, and most common, group includes ecosystems that simply failed to get off the ground (which we define as achieving at least 50% market share). About half of the groups we analyzed followed this path – for example, Microsoft's Windows Phone and BlackBerry's operating system – and most fell far short of the 50% threshold, instead peaking at roughly 15% market share, on average.

2 Won It All . . . Temporarily

The second group includes ecosystems that won significant market share (peaking at an average market share of 80%) but then fell to half that share or less within seven years. This group represented about one-fourth of the ecosystems in our analysis, including Netscape's web browser and Symbian's operating system for mobile devices, among others. Some ultimately exited the market; those that remain have a market share of only about 10% on average.

3 Fork in the Road

In the third trajectory, some ecosystems won it all but have started to lose market share in recent years. This could be a temporary dip or the beginning of a permanent decline. One in 10 ecosystems in our analysis has followed this path, including Uber and Seamless/GrubHub. They peaked on average at roughly 80% market share and subsequently fell to approximately 60% on average in 2018. They still maintain a significant share of their market but need to take critical actions to ensure they hold on to it.

4 Became Sustainable

Finally, the fourth path includes ecosystems that won it all and have sustained their position to date, such as Microsoft Windows and Amazon. This group retained a dominant share of the market for 23 years on average. Critically, this group represented fewer than 15% of the ecosystems in our analysis. There are clear financial rewards for getting to this point, higher profitability levels chief among them. In 2018, sustained ecosystems generated profit margins of 29% on average, while those with an uncertain future are fighting to break even, with profit margins of 1% on average.

The conventional wisdom holds that ecosystems are stable and enduring, yet they are actually highly dynamic, typically following one of four trajectories in terms of their ability to capture and retain market share.

Market Share

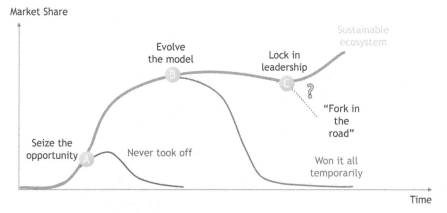

Figure 3.1: The Four Typical Paths of Business Ecosystems.

To put these numbers into perspective, consider that 35% of the ecosystems we examined had already ceased to exist, and an additional 40% had either lost at least half their peak market share or never took off. That total – three-quarters of the ecosystems in our study – is about the same as the failure rate for small businesses in their first 15 years. So while the most successful ecosystems can "win it all" – and earn generous financial rewards – the odds of succeeding with ecosystems are not unequivocally better than for traditional businesses, and the gains for those that initially succeed are often temporary.

Three Critical Windows for Success

By studying the differences among these four groups, we identified three critical windows that make or break ecosystems across their life cycle – and corresponding keys to success for each.

During the first window, companies need to seize the opportunity to capture a large proportion of the market. In the second crucial phase, they need to evolve the model to avoid losing momentum in the face of market saturation and competition. Finally, in the third window, companies must lock in market leadership to maintain their position over the longer term. Each stage requires different actions, underscoring the dynamic nature of ecosystems and the need to evolve strategies over time. This temporal ambidexterity can be tough to master, which explains the relatively low long-term success rate of ecosystems (Figure 3.2).

Successful measures in the early stages of an ecosystem will be far different from those required in later stages, requiring that management teams continuously reassess and adapt their strategy.

		Success rate	
Window	Actions Implemented	In each stage	Cumulative
Seize the opportunity	• Be the first or radically disrupt • Scale fast • Invest persistently and sufficiently	50%[1]	50%
Evolve the model	• Broaden ecosystem scope • Increase engagement	50%	25%
Lock in leadership	• Manage vested interests • Maintain differentiation • Renew the platform	60%	15%

1. This number is most likely an upper limit: While we aimed to be as exhaustive as possible in our ecosystem screening — covering 11 countries and 15 sectors over the past 4 decades, and including dozens of ecosystems that ceased to exist — we still cannot have fully escaped survival bias. We may not have captured some ventures that tried to create ecosystems but failed so early that no data was available.
Source: BCG Henderson Institute Analysis

Figure 3.2: Strategies and Success Rates for the Three Critical Windows in the Ecosystem Life Cycle.

1 Seize the Opportunity

Fewer than half of the ecosystems made it through the first critical window to capture at least half of a given market. Contrary to conventional wisdom, these were not all first movers.[1] By definition, all first movers control the entire market they create, yet almost 50% of the ecosystems that seized the opportunity were disruptive new entrants that came later and overtook the pioneer. For example, Atari pioneered the video game console industry in the late 1970s, but Nintendo redefined video games in the mid-1980s. It gave users a better experience with higher-quality games – in particular, through better in-game stories, more refined graphics, and better game play – both by developing in-house games like Super Mario Bros. and by requiring its third-party developers to meet the same quality standards. As a result, Nintendo overtook Atari and established a dominant position in the industry, with 68% of the market in 1985. In other words, being first does not guarantee long-term success, and entering the market later does not preclude it.

Whether first movers or disrupters, successful ecosystems gained scale fast; roughly 80% garnered more than 50% market share in their first five years. And among those that made it through this first window, the average market share peaked at 80% within seven years. By contrast, those that did not take off earned only 8% market share within five years, and 13% at peak. If scale doesn't come fast, it's very likely not coming at all.

Developing a rapidly scalable model requires attracting users and ecosystem partners simultaneously to capitalize on the network effect: More users attract more partners, who are keen to develop more features to offer to a growing number of users, and so on. For example, IBM's success with the PC in 1981 was driven by drawing interest simultaneously from both users and third-party developers. Users were attracted by IBM's reputation for quality (and reduced prices for PCs), and third-party developers were attracted by IBM's open architecture.

Winning ecosystems are willing to delay profitability to expand quickly. The ecosystems that reached a market share of at least 50% required three years on average to turn profitable, and most of them gained at least 30% market share before turning a profit – reflecting an initial emphasis on growth rather than profitability. These first few years were characterized by a negative profit margin of – 60% on average, highlighting the significant risk involved in scaling up an ecosystem. Although generating a return on the initial investment is far from guaranteed, a willingness to accept significant losses early on appears to be necessary. On average, ecosystems that took off accumulated 130% more in earnings within five years of first turning a profit compared with ecosystems that did not take off. For example, Amazon has long prioritized growth over profits, accumulating

---

1 N. Lang, K. von Szczepanski, and C. Wurzer, "The Emerging Art of Ecosystem Management," Jan. 16, 2019, www.bcg.com; and M.G. Jacobides, N. Lang, N. Louw et al., "What Does a Successful Digital Ecosystem Look Like?" June 26, 2019, www.bcg.com.

more than $3 billion in losses during its first eight years of operation. But thanks to ongoing investments in its platform and processes, it became the clear leader in e-commerce, controlling 52% of U.S. online sales in 2018 – and it continues to gain market share. Now that it has established a strong market position, while constantly evolving its model (as we discuss in the next section), Amazon has improved its operating margin from less than 1% in 2013 to 9% in 2018.

So while timing is important, and first movers can gain an edge, there are no hard and fast rules. Some early movers never reach a dominant position, and others may incur steep losses for a long period before getting there.

2 Evolve the Model

The second critical window occurs once ecosystems have seized the opportunity and captured a substantial share of the market. Only half of the companies reaching this point in our analysis were able to retain their dominant share. Those that did so repeatedly evolved their model in two ways: expanding the scope of the platform and increasing engagement with platform participants.

As initial offerings are often imitated and markets become saturated, ecosystems need to broaden their scope either functionally (by addressing additional customer needs) or organically (by moving into other markets or through acquisitions and strategic partnerships). In fact, our research shows that winning ecosystems implemented these measures more frequently and more quickly than those that ended up failing; they took twice as many actions to broaden their scope, and the vast majority implemented at least one major move every three years on average. Even more than traditional business models, ecosystems must constantly evolve and grow to succeed.

For example, Uber has continuously expanded its offering, from the core UberX service in 2012 to successive services such as UberPool and Uber Eats (in 2014 and 2015, respectively), as well as other market-specific services such as uberMOTO (which allows users in India to book a ride on a motorcycle). And it maintains its forward-looking growth orientation by investing in disruptive technologies such as self-driving cars. By doing so, Uber has been able to protect its leading market position in the United States despite aggressive competition from Lyft and others. Of course, evolving the offering is necessary but not sufficient for long-term, sustainable success, again underlining the challenges and risks of developing ecosystems.

In addition to expanded offerings and markets, winning ecosystems also constantly seek to boost engagement with platform partners through better communication and collaboration. Increased engagement deepens relationships, reducing the chances that partners will jump to the competition. Such measures need to align the ambitions of the ecosystem with those of third-party participants, rather than putting them at cross-purposes – ensuring the ecosystem's continued evolution.

Ecosystems can boost partner engagement and foster greater collaboration in several ways. Netflix, for example, created a program to organize and connect its community of media production service companies. Others facilitated greater flows of information between partners and the ecosystem orchestrator. Google developed communities for its partners to get relevant product and program updates. Google partners can find examples of how to grow their businesses, get advice on Google products, and communicate with Google specialists and thought leaders.

Finally, some orchestrator companies adapt their internal structure to streamline their interactions with partners. In the 1990s, Intel separated the departments that cooperated with hardware PC providers from those that competed with those companies. It also developed new processes to head off potential internal conflicts this approach could lead to,[2] thereby boosting partner engagement.

Our research shows that all these approaches are common among sustainably successful ecosystems, and the majority apply more than one method.

3 Lock in Leadership

Of the companies in our sample that successfully passed the first two stages – one-fourth of the starting sample – only about 60% were able to sustain their success over the longer term, the third critical window in the growth cycle of an ecosystem. A common theme among those that succeeded is the ability to manage vested interests, not only among partners but also with stakeholders such as regulators and customers. Often this entails building communication channels to allow stakeholders to air out issues. For example, Amazon's cloud-computing platform, Amazon Web Services, convenes its third-party developers at free periodic summits in cities around the world where participants can voice concerns and propose solutions. The recent rise of antitrust and privacy concerns in relation to big-tech ecosystems suggests that stakeholder management will be increasingly important in the future.

At the same time, successful ecosystems locked in their market leadership by actively maintaining their differentiation and taking steps to make it hard for competitors to replicate their business models. Some cultivated their unique

---

2 M.A. Cusumano and A. Gawer, "The Elements of Platform Leadership," *MIT Sloan Management Review* (Spring 2002); and M.A. Cusumano, A. Gawer, and D. Yoffie, *The Business of Platforms: Strategy in the Age of Digital Competition, Innovation, and Power* (New York: HarperBusiness), 2019.

internal strengths by building a walled garden for partners. For example, Facebook built an end-to-end suite of tools for advertisers to distribute their content on the platform, effectively requiring them to use it quite separately from competitors' solutions.

Other ecosystems offer dedicated services to partners to help them do business with the platform. For example, Didi Chuxing Technology, the China-based mobility service (similar to Uber), provides its drivers with a range of car-related services, from cheaper gas to car rentals. And some ecosystems have developed industry standards that reinforce the advantages of working within the platform. For example, Intel created standards for the PC hardware architecture that PC hardware manufacturers produce, making it easier to coordinate across the value chain.

Perhaps most important, sustainable ecosystems continuously renew the platforms on which they're based. In today's business environment, competitive disruption is virtually inevitable, and all the ecosystems in our sample started to lose ground to a growing competitor at some point. Yet winners responded with platform redesign – often based on new technology – to regain leadership. Some orchestrator companies developed the new platform in-house; for example, Microsoft redefined its platform based on cloud services under CEO Satya Nadella's leadership.[3] Others acquired business units with the new expertise they needed. When Facebook's initial PC-based service was threatened by mobile-based social networks, it acquired Instagram and WhatsApp. Facebook has thus built a family of apps with a breadth of formats and reach that appeal to marketers, while also streamlining processes and enhancing the customer experience.

Although successful ecosystems can capture and sustain significant market share and generate sizable profits, they are also highly dynamic and require constant renewal. Furthermore, the requirements for renewal are different at each stage of development, requiring ecosystem leaders to be temporally ambidextrous.

The need for a dynamic approach to ecosystem strategy will most likely grow due to the maturation and evolution of the ecosystem space overall. What was once a novel structure is now widespread. Simple two-sided marketplaces are being replaced by nested ecosystems. And the predominantly B2C ecosystems of today will probably soon be supplemented by B2B ecosystems, which may operate on a different logic.

By embracing the dynamic nature of ecosystem strategy and adjusting their approach on the basis of each life cycle stage's requirements, ecosystem leaders can increase their odds of long-term success.

---

3 A. Cave, "How Microsoft Regained Its Crown as the World's Biggest Company," *Forbes*, Nov. 30, 2018.

Ulrich Pidun, Martin Reeves, and Maximilian Schüssler
Chapter 4
Why Do Most Business Ecosystems Fail?

Most of today's business ecosystems are built around digital platforms. Our smartphones, smart cars, and smart homes are powered by ecosystems of hardware suppliers and application developers; we increasingly order our food, transportation, and accommodation on digital marketplaces; and industrial companies are revolutionizing the way they collaborate by moving to IoT platforms. Such collaborative networks are also playing an increasing role in addressing the world's biggest challenges. This was impressively demonstrated during the early days of the COVID-19 crisis, when scores of new ecosystems emerged to coordinate health care services and balance utilization, to offer 3D printing capacity to produce medical equipment, to develop smartphone applications for virus tracking and protection, and more.

There are good reasons for the success of the ecosystem model (see Chapter 2): In the startup phase, this model can quickly provide access to capabilities that may be too expensive or time-consuming to build within a single firm. Once launched, ecosystems can scale much faster than an individual business because their modular structure makes it easy to add partners. Moreover, ecosystems are very flexible and resilient; their modularity enables both high variety and a high capacity to evolve. Given all these advantages, it is no surprise that startups and established companies are rushing to build their own platforms and ecosystems.

However, there is a hidden and inconvenient truth: most business ecosystems fail. Research by the BCG Henderson Institute found that fewer than 15% were sustainable in the long run (see Chapter 3). If we want to harness the power of the ecosystem model, we need to understand not only the reasons for success but also the reasons for failure.

The stakes are high. According to data from Preqin, in recent years $100 billion has been invested annually in venture capital funds. Based on an analysis of individual financing rounds above $250 million, we estimate that 60% of these investments went into digital platforms and ecosystem business models. If we assume a failure rate of 85% for these ecosystem investments, more than $50 billion of capital is lost every year. And this does not include the failed investments of incumbents that try to emulate the ecosystem model.

To understand how to improve the odds of success, we studied more than 100 failed ecosystems in a variety of industries and compared them with their

https://doi.org/10.1515/9783110775167-004

more successful industry peers, using a systematic quantitative and qualitative analysis. We identified an ecosystem as a failure if it was dissolved, shrank to an insignificant market share, or was acquired for an amount substantially below its initial funding. Our database contains B2C, C2C, and B2B ecosystems and includes social networks, marketplaces, and software solutions as well as payment, mobility, entertainment, and health care services. On average, the ecosystems we studied had existed for 6.8 years and had raised funding of $185 million.

Here we summarize the findings and conclusions from our analysis, answering the following questions:

- Why are successful ecosystems so rare?
- How do ecosystems fail?
- When do ecosystems fail?
- What can be done about ecosystem failure?

Why Are Successful Ecosystems So Rare?

Ecosystems and digital platforms challenge traditional ways of thinking about strategy. Boundaries between industries are dissolving as ecosystems span sectors and incumbents are attacked by tech players and platforms that they had never before considered competitors. Boundaries between companies are dissolving, too, as the value the ecosystem creates must be shared among multiple partners and physical assets are increasingly separated from value capture.

Being successful in such a world requires a new mindset. Organizations need to move from controlling internal resources to orchestrating external resources, from erecting competitive barriers to engaging vibrant communities, and from hierarchical control to collaboration and persuasion.

Conventional management education does not prepare us well for success in ecosystems, and experience with traditional business models may be outright misleading. Designing a successful business ecosystem poses multiple challenges. For example, it is not enough to design the value creation and delivery model; the design must also explicitly consider value distribution among ecosystem members, and this requires a systems perspective. At the same time, ecosystems cannot be entirely planned and designed; they also emerge and continuously evolve. This adaptability is one of their major strengths. So ecosystem design must ensure that the basics are in place and strategic blunders are avoided, but it must also leave room for creativity, serendipitous discoveries, and emerging customer needs. Ecosystems that are successful in the long run need to be ready to modify their design in anticipation of shifts in markets, technologies, regulations, and public sentiment.

Managing a business ecosystem also presents distinct strategic challenges: solving the chicken-or-egg problem of building supply or demand during launch; preventing the explosion of costs during scale-up, which can be very fast when network effects kick in; protecting quality during fast growth; and defending against competitors that use the low entry barriers of many digital platform models to copy and improve your model and encourage your complementors or users to multihome or even fully switch their allegiances.

The stakes are high because the failure of ecosystem-based business models tends to be particularly costly. Many ecosystems are driven by strong direct or indirect network effects and have winner-take-all characteristics. They may require substantial upfront investments to build the platform and attract a critical mass of suppliers and customers, but once they take off, they can scale very fast and at low marginal cost. Focusing on scale before focusing on profitability, then, can be justified, but this means that failure becomes apparent only after a significant delay. According to PitchBook, out of the more than 100 companies worth more than $1 billion that have gone public since 2010, 64% were unprofitable at the time of listing, including ecosystems such as Uber, Lyft, Snapchat, and Spotify.

These challenges are exacerbated by the current hype around ecosystems. Herd behavior fosters shallow imitation and the transfer of successful models to locations or domains where they do not apply. And the abundance of cheap venture capital has perhaps supported some questionable investments in zombie businesses that have no inherent right to survive.

Given all these factors, it is no surprise that most ecosystems fail, destroying much value along the way. To address these challenges, we need to learn from failure, better understand its root causes, and identify the traps.

How Do Ecosystems Fail?

Of course, business failure is always the consequence of a multitude of external circumstances and internal decisions. When we analyzed in detail the failed ecosystems in our database, we could identify patterns that allowed us to assign a primary root cause to each failure. In this way, we uncovered seven fundamental failure modes (Figure 4.1).

Remarkably, six of the seven failure modes – and 85% of observed failures – related to weaknesses in ecosystem design, while only 15% were attributable to

Relative share of primary failure modes of the investigated business ecosystems

Insufficient problem to solve — 10%
Wrong ecosystem configuration — 18%
Wrong governance choices — 34%
Inadequate monetization — 5%
Weak launch strategy — 8%
Weak defensibility — 10%
Bad execution — 15%

■ Design failures

Source: BCG Henderson Institute
Note: N=110 ecosystems

Figure 4.1: Seven Fundamental Failure Modes of Business Ecosystems.

bad execution. Occasionally, the design failures were strategic blunders in the initial design of the business ecosystem. But more frequently, they were due to insufficient adaptation of ecosystem design as technological or market conditions changed. The failure mode strongly depends on the context of the given business ecosystem – such as its industry, ecosystem type, or stage in the life cycle.

Failure Mode 1: Insufficient Problem to Solve

Among the ecosystems in our database, 10% failed because they did not address a problem that was substantial enough to justify the high upfront investment and to convince partners and customers to join the ecosystem. An ecosystem's value proposition is a function of the size of the market friction it addresses, the share of the friction that can be eliminated by the ecosystem solution, and the willingness of customers to pay for it.

Many ecosystems that were shipwrecked by this failure mode were B2B platforms that failed in the early 2000s. Encouraged by the success of B2C marketplaces like eBay and Amazon, many companies tried to transfer this model to the B2B space, building marketplaces for automotive parts, paper, chemicals, and other supplies. However, most failed because they did not realize that the underlying problem of high transaction costs in B2C was not as pronounced in B2B transactions. Most industrial buyers knew their more limited range of potential suppliers very well and had optimized their relationships with them.

The new B2B marketplaces did not add much value to the transaction, but only shifted value from suppliers to buyers because of increased transparency and competition, reducing the incentive of suppliers to join the platforms and leading to their demise.

We currently observe a resurgence of B2B marketplace models, such as XOM Materials, CheMondis, and Convictional, that focus on more-substantial problems in B2B transactions: supply chain coordination, data analytics, and other advanced value-added services.

Failure Mode 2: Wrong Ecosystem Configuration

Assuming that an ecosystem has found a substantial problem to solve, the next challenge is to configure the ecosystem to deliver the targeted value proposition. This involves defining the required activities and partners, their responsibilities and the links among them, and assigning roles to various partners – in particular, the role of orchestrator, which coordinates members, defines standards and rules, and arbitrates conflict. The initial configuration should focus on the core value proposition and incorporate the minimum number of partner types required for its delivery.

Among the ecosystems in our database, 18% stumbled at this stage. Most were solution ecosystems that involved multiple suppliers and complementors that needed to work together to develop and provide complex products or services. They failed mainly because they could not align all required innovations or because they could not convince all required contributors to join the ecosystem.

An example is the Sony e-reader, which came to market earlier than Amazon's Kindle but never managed to establish a successful ecosystem. Sony built a complex blueprint that required customers to purchase e-books online and manually upload them to the e-reader. Because of the open upload mechanism, publishers worried about copyright infringement and hesitated to join the ecosystem. By contrast, Kindle established an integrated ecosystem configuration that allowed users to automatically load content from Amazon and precluded the transfer of books to any other device or to a printer. Sony left the e-reader market in 2014, while Amazon became the market leader.

Failure Mode 3: Wrong Governance Choices

The most prevalent failure mode in our database – responsible for more than a third of the ecosystem failures we studied – was wrong governance choices.

The governance model is a critical design choice for an ecosystem because it replaces the hierarchical forms of control in traditional vertical supply chains with indirect forms of control appropriate to the complexity and dynamism of an ecosystem (see Chapter 6). Governance establishes the standards, rules, and processes that define an ecosystem's formal or informal constitution. Specifically, it needs to regulate access (who can become a member of the ecosystem and under what conditions), participation (how decision rights are distributed among ecosystem partners), and commitment (the level of ecosystem-specific investments and cospecialization required).

According to our analysis, the biggest challenge in ecosystem governance is finding the right level of openness. More-open ecosystems can benefit from faster growth, particularly around launch. They enable a greater diversity of participants and variety of offerings and encourage decentralized innovation. However, they are difficult to control. In the case of high failure cost, and a corresponding need to limit the downside, more-closed ecosystem governance may be the better choice because it allows for a more deliberate design of the ecosystem and for closer control of partners and of the quality of the offering.

We found that social networks were particularly prone to missing the right level of openness. Most of them failed because they opted for a high degree of openness in an attempt to quickly increase the number of users. They tended to underestimate the wisdom of a more closed approach, which can increase the quality of interactions and the perceived value of the network. Facebook got this right by starting with a very strict governance model that allowed users to view only people who went to the same school. Only after the network had established itself as a valuable ecosystem did it gradually increase its openness.

We also found an especially high rate of governance failure among ecosystems that tried to emulate successful models or transfer them to other domains or locations. Competitive pressure frequently forced these copycat ecosystems to differentiate from existing solutions. For example, Google made several attempts to establish a social network, as a latecomer to this market. Google+ used an asymmetric following model similar to Twitter's, in which one party can unilaterally establish a relationship to another. Initially, this led to strong growth, but user interactions were not considered very valuable, and users left the platform. Similarly, Orkut was designed very openly, with features that let you know when other people visited your profile. Users did not appreciate this lack of privacy, and the network went offline in 2014.

Failure Mode 4: Inadequate Monetization

Ecosystem monetization strategy defines what to charge and whom to charge. The orchestrator must balance the three competing objectives of increasing the overall size of the pie, enabling all important groups of ecosystem partners to earn a decent profit to ensure their ongoing contribution, and capturing its own fair share of the value. Effective monetization encourages and incentivizes participation by, for example, subsidizing the side of the market that is less willing to participate, charging for transactions rather than access, or offering rebates for increased usage.

Although inadequate monetization strategies were the primary reason for failure in only 5% of the investigated cases, this failure mode was particularly prevalent among B2C marketplaces. For example, eBay closed its operations in China in 2006 after realizing that charging for transactions, a model that served the company well in the US and Europe, was not accepted by Chinese consumers, who could benefit from cost-free transactions on the competing Taobao platform, which was financed by advertisements. Similarly, Table8, a platform for last-minute reservations in sold-out restaurants, failed because it charged customers, while competitors like OpenTable, Quandoo, and Bookatable succeeded by charging only restaurants for their reservation service.

Failure Mode 5: Weak Launch Strategy

A strategic challenge for many business ecosystems during launch is to solve the chicken-or-egg problem of securing enough participation from both buyers and suppliers. The goal is to achieve a critical mass for network and data flywheel effects to kick in (see also Chapter 9), whereby scale begets further scale. Success factors include focusing first on the core value proposition and building a minimum viable ecosystem around it that can be expanded over time; emphasizing building a dense network rather than a large network in order to improve the quality of interactions; and focusing investments on the side of the market that is more difficult to convince to join the ecosystem (most ecosystems we observed were initially supply-constrained).

More than two-thirds of the failed ecosystems we investigated struggled with solving the chicken-or-egg problem. However, as previously discussed, there can be many reasons for this, such as the wrong configuration or governance or monetization model. In 8% of the cases, a weak launch strategy was the primary reason for failure. This failure mode is particularly prevalent among solution ecosystems that require large investments from members, and among transaction ecosystems with only limited barriers to entry or high numbers of existing competitors.

An example of a failed solution ecosystem is the HD-DVD platform (an ecosystem led by Toshiba, Microsoft, and others), which lost the standards war of high-definition DVD players to the Blu-ray platform (backed by Sony, Apple, and others). Neither standard was technically superior to the other, and the HD-DVD ecosystem won the battle to sell more DVD players to consumers. However, Blu-ray ultimately prevailed because it secured the exclusive support of large film studios such as Warner Brothers and Fox Searchlight Pictures.

Uber China is an example of a transaction ecosystem that failed because it could not solve the chicken-or-egg problem in the highly contested Chinese ride-hailing market. The company managed to lure drivers and riders to its platform, but only at the cost of permanently subsidizing both sides of the market, resulting in substantial losses. Uber was not embedded enough in the Chinese mobile app landscape to achieve critical mass and finally sold its Chinese business to its competitor Didi.

Failure Mode 6: Weak Defensibility

Ecosystems that solve the chicken-or-egg problem frequently enjoy winner-take-all effects. Once they have achieved a dominant market position, strong barriers to entry can result from network effects and scale advantages on costs and data. However, we still identified 10% of ecosystems in our database that went down because they did not build effective defenses into their design.

The failed ecosystems suffered from one or several of the following five basic mechanisms of attack: (1) multihoming (suppliers or customers participate in multiple competing ecosystems at the same time or easily switch between ecosystems), (2) disintermediation (partners from two sides of a transaction ecosystem bypass the matching platform and connect directly), (3) differentiation (a subset of users has distinctive needs or tastes that can support a separate ecosystem that takes away market share from the dominant player), (4) ecosystem carryover (a successful business ecosystem expands into a neighboring domain), and (5) backlash (incumbents, consumers, suppliers, or regulators challenge the business model or practices of the ecosystem). Successful ecosystems respond to these threats by designing user lock-in into their models, incentivizing customer and supplier loyalty, increasing switching costs, and designing their ecosystems not only for legal compliance but also for long-term social acceptance.

We found weak defensibility as a primary failure mode to be particularly prevalent within highly regulated industries and among ecosystems with a high incentive to multihome. For example, from 1974 to 2006, Bankcard was the leading credit card ecosystem in Australia and New Zealand, managed by a joint venture of Australia's leading banks. However, once MasterCard and Visa entered the Australian market, Bankcard was not able to defend its leading position because of its purely local footprint. Similarly, StudiVZ was the leading social network in German-speaking countries, with more than 15 million members in 2009, but did not manage to defend its position when Facebook entered the European market with a superior value proposition and a global footprint.

Failure Mode 7: Bad Execution

We were surprised to find that only 15% of ecosystems failed because of execution issues. In some cases, the problems were operational, as in the case of Canvas Networks, a social network that allowed users to share and play with images and had to close because members of the community lost access to their artwork after a hacker attack. In other instances, failure could be attributed to management action, as in the case of Wikimart, a heavily funded marketplace that aspired to become the Russian version of eBay but went down after a series of questionable acquisitions of unprofitable retailers. Sometimes outright fraud contributed to demise, as in the case of Auctionata, a popular online auction platform that was among the first to develop the concept of livestream auctions but had to shut down after allegations that the company supported shill bidding on selected items.

A final source of bad execution that we uncovered was complacency. An example is Microsoft's Internet Explorer, widely considered to have won the browser war after capturing close to 95% market share in 2004. With no serious competitor left, Microsoft underinvested in further development of the browser and its underlying ecosystem, which allowed Firefox and Chrome to enter and eventually dominate the market.

When Do Ecosystems Fail?

The nature of many ecosystems – with their highly attractive winner-take-all characteristics based on strong network effects that justify persistent investments and loss-making to achieve a dominant position – implies that failure may become apparent only late in the ecosystem's life cycle and can thus be very costly.

The typical life cycle of an ecosystem can be divided into four phases with specific jobs to be done and corresponding success factors:

1. The *launch* phase, with a focus on developing a strong value proposition for all participants and on finding the right initial ecosystem design.
2. The *scale* phase, with a focus on increasing the number and intensity of interactions in order to grow toward a dominant market position.
3. The *maturity* phase, with a focus on increasing the loyalty of customers and suppliers, and on erecting barriers to entry for competitors.
4. The *evolution* phase, with a focus on expanding the offering and on continuous innovation to thrive and survive in the long term.

Our analyses confirm the assumption that ecosystems tend to fail late: seven out of ten failed ecosystems in our database made it into the scale phase before flaws in their design materialized and led to their demise (Figure 4.2). And even those 30% of ecosystems that failed during launch achieved a median survival time of 3.5 years while burning through $16 million of investors' money. Most of them failed because they could not address a large enough problem or establish an effective configuration (failure modes 1 and 2).

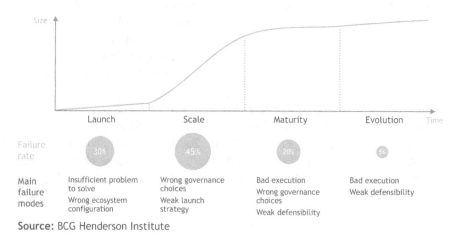

Source: BCG Henderson Institute

Figure 4.2: When Do Business Ecosystems Fail?

Of the ecosystems in our study, 45% failed during the scale phase, most of them because they could not solve the chicken-or-egg problem of bringing a critical mass of all required sides of the market to their platform. Detailed analyses revealed that this was mainly due to the wrong level of openness in their governance or a weak launch strategy (failure modes 3 and 5).

The maturity phase was the point of downfall for 20% of the ecosystems in our database. At the point of failure, they had received a median amount of $79 million in funding and survived for five years. The most prevalent root cause of failure was execution issues (failure mode 7), but design flaws in governance and defense also explain half of the downfalls (failure modes 3 and 6).

Finally, only 5% of ecosystems failed in the evolution phase, after successfully establishing and defending their leading position for an extended period, with a median survival time of 25 years. However, they neglected to continuously adapt, advance, and reinvent the ecosystem and failed because of execution issues or because they did not adjust their defense mechanisms to the changing environment (failure modes 6 and 7).

What Can Be Done About Ecosystem Failure?

Business ecosystems, in particular those built on digital platforms, are a relatively new phenomenon. Traditional management concepts of industry analysis and value chains are insufficient if we want to master the ecosystem model. Many founders, managers, and investors had to learn this the hard way. Their experience should humble us and make us realize the limits of our understanding. However, we should also learn from their failures.

If you are a founder, manager, or investor and are considering building or joining a business ecosystem, you can learn from these insights and increase the odds of success. Our checklist can help you assess the vulnerability of your ecosystem design (Figure 4.3).

Of course, business ecosystems cannot be entirely planned and designed in advance. The only way to succeed in the long run is to be adaptable and modify the design in anticipation of shifts in markets, technologies, regulations, and public sentiment. Nevertheless, our list of questions can help you regularly challenge the viability of your model. If not all answers are positive, you may need to adapt the design of your ecosystem – or accept that it is time to pull the plug rather than burn more money.

		High risk for …
Insufficient problem to solve	☐ Does your ecosystem have a clearly defined value proposition? ☐ Do you remove a substantial existing market friction? ☐ Do you address a substantial unmet or new customer need?	B2B marketplaces
Wrong ecosystem configuration	☐ Do you have a clear blueprint of all required activities, actors, roles and links? ☐ Can you convince all required partners to join and stay on board? ☐ Are all technologies that are needed to build the solution available and aligned?	Solution ecosystems with multiple partners
Wrong governance choices	☐ Is your ecosystem open enough to encourage growth and diversity? ☐ Is your ecosystem closed enough to ensure quality and control? ☐ Is your governance flexible enough to adapt to shifts in market and technology?	Social networks Copycat ecosystems
Inadequate monetization	☐ Does your monetization strategy allow all relevant partners to earn a profit? ☐ Does your monetization strategy encourage increasing use of the ecosystem? ☐ Do you subsidize the right side of the market?	B2C marketplaces
Weak launch strategy	☐ Can you achieve the required critical mass of both suppliers and buyers? ☐ Do you focus investments on the side of the market that is less willing to join? ☐ Can you create positive network effects that support self-reinforcing growth?	Ecosystems with strong competition or high investment needs
Weak defensibility	☐ Do you incentivize customer and supplier loyalty and increase switching cost? ☐ Do you actively build barriers to entry for new competitors? ☐ Do you encourage legal compliance and long-term social acceptance?	Ecosystems prone to multihoming

Source: BCG Henderson Institute

Figure 4.3: Ecosystem Design Vulnerability Checklist.

Ulrich Pidun, Martin Reeves, and Edzard Wesselink
Chapter 5
How Healthy Is Your Business Ecosystem?

Companies that start or join successful business ecosystems can reap tremendous benefits. In the startup phase, ecosystems can provide fast access to external capabilities that may be too expensive or time-consuming to build within a single company. Once launched, ecosystems can scale quickly because their modular structure makes it easy to add partners. Moreover, ecosystems are very flexible and resilient – the model enables high variety, as well as a high capacity to evolve. There is, however, a hidden and inconvenient truth about business ecosystems: Our past research found that less than 15% are sustainable in the long run (see Chapter 3).[1]

The seeds of ecosystem failure are planted early. Our new analysis of more than 100 failed ecosystems found that strategic blunders in their design accounted for 6 out of 7 failures. But we also found that it can take years before these design failures become apparent – with all the cumulative investment losses in time, effort, and money that failure implies (see Chapter 4).[2]

Witness Google, which made several unsuccessful attempts to establish social networks. It invested eight years in Google+ before shutting down the service in 2019. One reason for the Google+ failure was its asymmetric follow model, similar to Twitter's, in which users can unilaterally follow others. This created strong initial growth but did not build relationships, which might have fostered greater engagement on the platform. The downfall of another Google social network, Orkut, was built into its unusually open design, which let users know when their profiles were accessed by others. It turned out that users were uncomfortable with this lack of privacy, and the network went offline in 2014, 10 years after its launch.

Typically, ecosystems are assessed using two kinds of metrics: conventional financial metrics, such as revenue, cash burn rate, profitability, and return on investment; and vanity metrics, such as market size and ecosystem activity (number

---

1 M. Reeves, H. Lotan, J. Legrand et al., "How Business Ecosystems Rise (and Often Fall)," *MIT Sloan Management Review*, July 30, 2019.
2 U. Pidun, M. Reeves, and M. Schüssler, "Why Do Most Business Ecosystems Fail?" *Boston Consulting Group*, June 22, 2020.

Note: Republished with permission by *MIT Sloan Management Review*.

https://doi.org/10.1515/9783110775167-005

of subscribers, clicks, or social media mentions). The former are not very useful for assessing the prospects of ecosystems because they are backward-looking. The latter can be misleading because they are not necessarily linked to value creation or extraction. They indicate the current interest in the ecosystem, and presumably its potential, but may also reflect an ecosystem's ability to spend investors' money on marketing and other growth tactics more than its ability to generate value.

To improve the odds of success and mitigate the high costs of failure, leaders must be able to assess the health of a business ecosystem throughout its life cycle. They need metrics that indicate performance and potential at the system level and at the level of the individual companies or partners participating in the ecosystem, as well as the ecosystem leader or orchestrator. They need to be able to gauge growth in terms of scale not only in ecosystem participation but also in the underlying operating model. And most critically, they need metrics that reflect the success factors unique to each of the distinct phases of ecosystem development.

This chapter lays out a set of metrics and early warning indicators that can help you determine whether your ecosystem is on track for success and worthy of continued investment in each development phase. They can also help you identify emerging issues and decide if and when you may need to cut your losses in an ecosystem and/or reorient it.

The chapter is based on a research database of more than 100 failed ecosystems, including B2C, C2C, and B2B platforms; social networks; marketplaces; software solutions; and payment, mobility, entertainment, and health care services. The failed ecosystems were compared with their successful counterparts by industry using systematic qualitative and quantitative analysis. The development of all the ecosystems was studied and key success metrics and red flags were identified that are early indicators of emerging challenges in each of the four life cycle phases.

Four Phases in the Business Ecosystem Life Cycle

Our research revealed that the growth of business ecosystems typically occurs in four phases. Each encompasses unique jobs to be done with corresponding success factors and thus also requires specific indicators and metrics for assessing ecosystem health (Figure 5.1).

In the *launch* phase, the focus should be on developing a strong value proposition for all ecosystem participants (the orchestrator, partners, and customers)

Life cycle phases	Key success metrics	Red flags
Launch: Establish the ecosystem in the market, introduce it to users, and prove the viability of the concept	• Number and engagement level of marquee partners • Number and engagement level of high-value customers • Customer feedback	! Critical partners do not join the ecosystem ! The wrong users subvert the value proposition of the ecosystem ! Opinion leaders start to leave the ecosystem ! You frequently have to change your offering
Scale: Increase the amount of platform activity, expand the operating model, and grow toward profitability	• Number of new active customers • Number of new active partners • Number of successful transactions • Unit cost per transaction	! A persistent imbalance between participants on both sides of the market develops ! Ecosystem growth reduces value for one side of the market ! Increasing numbers of users misuse the ecosystem ! Quality indicators begin to decline ! The operating model complexity begins to rise
Mature: Consolidate and defend the ecosystem's position	• Churn rates of customers/partners • Revenue per customer • Contribution margin per transaction • Retention costs for customers/partners • Acquisition costs for customers/partners	! The engagement level of customers or suppliers declines ! Early ecosystem adopters start to leave ! Aggressive copycats and/or niche competitors emerge ! Partners begin to create competing platforms of their own ! Successful ecosystems from other sectors expand into your field
Evolve: Continuously adapt, advance, and reinvent the ecosystem	• Share of revenue from new products or services • Customer satisfaction • Partner satisfaction	! The orchestrator's take rate from partners rises ! Partners increasingly complain about predatory behavior ! Negative coverage in (social) media begins to accumulate ! Legal actions against the ecosystem accelerate

Source: BCG Henderson Institute

Figure 5.1: The Four Phases of Business Ecosystem Growth.

and on finding the right initial design. After the ecosystem is established, it enters the *scale* phase, in which the key focus is on increasing the number and intensity of interactions in the ecosystem and to decrease the unit cost of each interaction. An ecosystem that has successfully scaled enters the *maturity* phase, in which growth slows and focus turns to bolstering customer and partner loyalty, and on erecting barriers to entry by competitors. Once a defensible position is attained, the ecosystem enters the *evolution* phase, in which the focus shifts to expanding the offering and continuous innovating.

To assess ecosystem health in each of these phases, leaders need to ask and answer the following questions:

- **What is the definition of success?** What are the primary milestones that you need to achieve to master the current life cycle phase and enter into the next phase?
- **What do you need to get right?** What are the key factors that make the difference between success and failure in this phase?
- **What are key success metrics?** Which numbers should you track to assess the performance of your ecosystem in this phase?
- **What are red flags?** What are early warning indicators that signal your ecosystem may not be on the path to success, you may have to change your initial design, or you should shut it down?

Phase 1: Launch

The goal in the launch phase is to establish the ecosystem in the market by introducing it to users and proving the viability of the concept. To this end, the orchestrator needs to formulate the value proposition and delineate the initial structure of the ecosystem. This work includes defining the activities and partners needed to deliver the value proposition, the links among them, the roles and responsibilities of the different participants, and the design of the governance and operating models. We identified four key factors that make the difference between success and failure during the launch phase.

1. The profit potential of the ecosystem must be large enough to justify the investment required to establish it and attract the partners needed to operate it. This ultimately depends on the value that the ecosystem can create for its customers and their willingness to pay for it. To achieve this, the ecosystem must, for example, remove a substantial source of friction for customers or fulfill a sizable unmet or new customer need.
2. The orchestrator must motivate the required participants to commit and contribute to the ecosystem. This is about not just the sheer number of

participants but also the right participants (such as popular developers on a gaming platform) in the right proportions (a balanced number of drivers and riders on a ride-hailing platform, for example).

3. The orchestrator must determine the proper level of openness for the ecosystem and create the standards, rules, and processes to regulate access and decision rights. Open ecosystems usually experience faster growth, particularly during the launch phase. They enable greater diversity and encourage decentralized innovation. Closed ecosystems allow for a more deliberate design of the ecosystem and for greater control over business partners and the quality of offerings.

4. The orchestrator must decide how to charge for the ecosystem's products and services, and determine how to share the value created in ways that motivate participants to foster ecosystem growth.

Metrics

Many metrics can be tracked during the launch phase of your ecosystem, including marketing expenses, technology costs, revenues, funding, burn rate, total number of users, and media attention. But to assess ecosystem health during this phase and evaluate the odds of success, we suggest focusing on the following three key metrics:

1. **Number and engagement level of marquee suppliers.** For example, a restaurant booking platform would want to track the number of subscriptions and reservations among the leading restaurants in key cities.

2. **Number and engagement level of high-value customers.** For a gaming platform, this might be heavy users who buy add-ons to enhance play; for a B2B marketplace, it might be the largest companies in target sectors; and for a social media platform, it might be prominent opinion leaders.

3. **Customer feedback.** This is measured based on quality ratings of the ecosystem's products and services in comparison to competing offerings, or Net Promoter Scores in customer surveys. In this case, aggregated metrics should be augmented with qualitative feedback from individual customers to understand the root causes of customer satisfaction or dissatisfaction.

Red Flags

If your scores on these three metrics are strong and trending higher, it is likely that your ecosystem is performing well in the launch phase. If, however, any of the following red flags appear, your ecosystem may be veering off the path to success, and you may have to change your initial design or shut down altogether:

1. **Critical partners do not join the ecosystem.** Better Place was founded in 2007 to provide an infrastructure for the efficient charging or exchange of electric car batteries. In this model, a buyer purchased a vehicle without a battery and paid a mileage-based monthly fee for leasing, charging, and exchanging it. Better Place failed in 2013, after receiving more than $900 million in funding, because it was unable to secure the participation of automakers, an essential group of partners in the ecosystem.[3]

2. **The wrong users subvert the value proposition of the ecosystem.** YouTube was set up as a platform for people to share personal videos, but in its early years many people used the platform to post illegally copied content. As a result, YouTube was sued by several record labels for billions of dollars, and it had to install a strong copyright identification system and monetization options for copyright holders.[4]

3. **Opinion leaders begin to leave the ecosystem.** In the DVD player war that started in 2005, the HD DVD platform, developed by Toshiba, Microsoft, and others, initially sold more players than the Blu-ray platform, championed by Sony and Apple. However, the HD DVD camp had to concede defeat after large film studios, including Warner Brothers and Fox Searchlight Pictures, defected to Blu-ray.[5]

4. **The ecosystem's value proposition is changed frequently.** Frequent changes to the value proposition suggest that it is not sufficiently compelling or that it appeals to too few customers. Club Nexus, created at Stanford in 2001, was the first college-specific social network. It reached 1,500 members within six weeks of its launch, but growth leveled off just as quickly. The network responded by adding new features, such as chat, email, classified ads, articles, and events. However, the added complexity only made the platform more difficult to use, and the network soon closed down.[6]

---

3 R. Adner, "The Wide Lens: A New Strategy for Innovation" (New York: Penguin/Portfolio), 2012.

4 B. Popper, "YouTube to the Music Industry: Here's the Money," *The Verge*, July 13, 2016.

5 Y. Kageyama, "Toshiba Quits HD DVD Business," *Los Angeles Times*, Feb. 19, 2008.

6 D. Kirkpatrick, "The Facebook Effect: The Inside Story of the Company That Is Connecting the World" (New York: Simon & Schuster), 2010.

Phase 2: Scale

When ecosystems survive the launch phase, the focus of orchestrators shifts toward increasing the amount of platform activity, scaling the operating model, and growing toward profitability. Two key factors determine the difference between success and failure during this phase.

1. The ability to establish and harness strong positive network effects that provide demand-side economies of scale. Direct network effects occur when the value derived by users on one side of an ecosystem grows as their numbers increase (such as social network users). Indirect network effects manifest when the value derived by participants on one side of an ecosystem grows with the number of participants on another side (for example, drivers on a ride-hailing platform prosper as the number of riders increases).

2. The ability of the ecosystem's operating model to keep up with growing demand and realize economies of scale. Successful digital ecosystems benefit from asset-light business models, low-to-zero marginal costs, and increasing returns. However, the economies afforded by supply-side scale can be limited by rising marketing, recruiting, and technology expenses. As networks grow, increased complexity and quality control can drive up costs and diminish economies of scale, too.

Metrics

To assess the extent to which your ecosystem is fulfilling these success factors during the scale phase, we suggest that you focus on the following four key metrics:

1. **Number of new active customers.** Rapidly attracting new active customers to the ecosystem is the key to achieving scale on the demand side.

2. **Number of new active partners.** Increasing the scope, diversity, and scale of the offering is an important precondition for appealing to new customer segments.

3. **Number of successful transactions.** Increasing the number of transactions is crucial because ecosystems create value for customers, partners, and orchestrators through transactions, not through media attention, number of registered users, or click rates.

4. **Unit cost.** Unit cost – that is, the average total ecosystem cost per transaction – must decrease during the scale phase in order for ecosystem growth to provide value for all participants.

Red Flags

In addition to these metrics, a number of early warning signs may indicate that your ecosystem is not on track during the scale phase and that you need to adjust its design or governance model:

1. **A persistent imbalance develops between the number of participants on different sides of the market.** US fleet-card companies, such as Comdata (now owned by FleetCor Technologies) and Wex, sought to orchestrate ecosystems that cut maintenance and administrative costs for the owners of truck fleets and drove business to truck stops. But they found it hard to scale initially because they could not convince enough fleet operators to pay for the service. To resolve the imbalance and attain profitable scale, the orchestrators changed their pricing structure from one in which truck fleets paid and truck stops were subsidized to one in which truck stops contributed considerably more to revenues than fleets.[7]

2. **Ecosystem growth reduces value for one side of the market.** Covisint, an auction marketplace in which automotive suppliers bid for contracts from car manufacturers, quickly attracted $500 million in funding from five major automakers. But as the ecosystem reached the scale phase, it became increasingly unattractive for suppliers: As more of them joined the ecosystem, the competition for contracts led to lower and lower winning bids. Suppliers abandoned the platform, and in 2004 it was sold for just $7 million.[8]

3. **Increasing numbers of users misuse the ecosystem.** As OpenTable, the restaurant booking platform, scaled, the incidence of no-show reservations grew along with it, alienating its restaurant partners. To mollify them, the platform introduced a policy that banned users who failed to show up or canceled reservations less than 30 minutes in advance four times within a 12-month period.[9]

4. **Quality indicators begin to decline.** If the quality of an ecosystem's offerings deteriorates during the scale phase, a downward spiral in both supply and demand can develop. For example, social media platform MySpace did not require users to provide their real identity. As a result, the platform became littered with spam and attracted inappropriate content, which, in

---

7 D.S. Evans and R. Schmalensee, "Matchmakers: The New Economics of Multisided Platforms" (Boston: Harvard Business Review Press), 2016.

8 "Covisint Price Tag: $7 Million," *aftermarketNews*, June 10, 2004.

9 J. Phillips, "OpenTable Launches New Campaign to Combat Reservation No-Shows," *San Francisco Chronicle*, March 21, 2017.

turn, made it less attractive for major brands to be associated with the ecosystem and ultimately contributed to its demise.[10]

5. **Operating model complexity begins to rise.** In the early days of the internet,
Yahoo became a leading internet portal and search engine by manually curating and categorizing websites into topic areas. This operating model worked
well until the internet started to grow exponentially and the number of websites exploded. It quickly became apparent that Yahoo's model was not scalable, and it was overtaken by Google and its automatic page-rank algorithm.[11]

Phase 3: Maturity

In the maturity phase, the growth of the ecosystem begins to slow because its
market is increasingly saturated and it has captured a substantial share. Management's primary objective shifts to consolidating and defending the ecosystem's position. This can be challenging because competitive attacks can target
either the demand or the supply side of the ecosystem. Moreover, mature ecosystems must avoid complacency and continue being the technology and innovation leaders in their industries. Two key factors make the difference between
success and failure during the maturity phase.

1. The orchestrator needs to find ways to enhance the loyalty of ecosystem participants, because competitors will increasingly try to poach them. This is a particularly dangerous threat when ecosystem participants can simultaneously join
multiple competing ecosystems and/or easily switch between ecosystems.
For example, restaurants and consumers often use more than one food-
delivery platform. To reduce this risk, orchestrators can offer additional services to participants and add user incentives, such as loyalty programs.

2. Orchestrators of mature ecosystems must erect barriers to entry to defend
their positions against incursions by competitors and imitators. Digital ecosystems require lower initial investments, and their network effects are weaker and
can be more easily reversed than the physical network effects of, say, a railroad
or telephone network. To build barriers to entry, orchestrators can harness network, scale, and learning effects (such as using customer data and advanced
analytics to continuously improve and personalize offerings) that are difficult
for new entrants to match.

---

10 F. Gillette, "The Rise and Inglorious Fall of MySpace," *Bloomberg Businessweek*, June 22,
2011.
11 G. Press, "Why Yahoo Lost and Google Won," *Forbes*, July 26, 2016.

Metrics

To assess ecosystem health during the maturity phase, orchestrators and partners should focus on the following five metrics:

1. **Churn rates of customers and partners.** Churn rates, the annual percentage rates at which customers stop using an offering or partners stop contributing to the ecosystem, are the most direct measures of loyalty and performance vis-à-vis competing ecosystems.

2. **Revenue per customer.** This metric quantifies users' engagement levels and loyalty. Increasing revenue per customer is an important growth lever after a high level of market penetration is achieved.

3. **Contribution margin per transaction.** This metric reflects the value that consumers assign to the transactions within the ecosystem. Declining contribution margins per transaction indicate increasing price pressure and competitive intensity.

4. **Retention costs for customers and suppliers.** Frequently, retention costs are treated as a fixed cost or not explicitly measured at all, but they can undermine the economics of the ecosystem if they continuously escalate.

5. **Acquisition costs for customers and partners.** Similar to retention costs, acquisition costs are frequently not broken out separately, but they are also potentially detrimental to ecosystem economics.

Red Flags

A number of early warning signs can help you recognize if your ecosystem is not on track during the maturity phase and when you need to take action:

1. **The engagement level of customers or partners declines.** Declining levels of engagement among ecosystem participants often presage revenue declines. The demise of MySpace was foretold when the frequency of use began falling (with only 3% of users checking the app multiple times daily), while more than 30% of users of emerging competitor Facebook checked that app multiple times per day. This was at least partially caused by design choices: MySpace was profile-based, and most profiles were static; Facebook was feed-based and constantly delivered new content to users.[12]

---

12 Kirkpatrick, "The Facebook Effect."

2. **Early ecosystem adopters begin to leave.** Early adopters are always in search of the most exciting and advanced offering in a given domain. If they are leaving your ecosystem, there is a good chance that a serious competitor has emerged. At the time of this writing, Twitch is the dominant platform for livestreaming online video games; it had a 73% market share at the end of 2019.[13] However, some of its key early adopters are switching to competing platform YouTube. For instance, Activision Blizzard announced a multiyear exclusivity deal with YouTube in January 2020, which means that Twitch has lost what was at one time its second-most-watched gaming channel, Overwatch League. In addition, a few high-profile gamers with millions of followers have switched from Twitch to YouTube.[14]

3. **Aggressive copycats and/or niche competitors emerge.** Successful business models attract competition from me-too players that offer a similar value proposition at a lower price and from niche competitors that bring specialized offerings to specific segments of the market. For example, Upwork, the leading marketplace for freelance labor, faces competition from hundreds of niche platforms that focus on specific industries, job types, and locations.

4. **Ecosystem partners begin to create competing platforms of their own.** Sometimes partners in successful ecosystems decide to become orchestrators of their own ecosystems. Handset maker Samsung, for example, is a partner in Google's Android ecosystem but has developed its own app store, the Samsung Galaxy Store, which is in direct competition with the Google Play Store.

5. **Successful ecosystems from other sectors launch competitive thrusts.** Ecosystem carryover – the expansion of a successful business ecosystem into a neighboring domain – is an important route for ecosystem growth and expansion, but it is also a substantial threat for incumbent ecosystems. For example, the credit card ecosystems orchestrated by Visa and Mastercard are under pressure from retail marketplaces that are moving into payment services.

---

13 A. Yosilewitz, "State of the Stream 2019: Platform Wars, the New King of Streaming, Most Watched Game and More!" *StreamElements* Blog, Dec. 19, 2019.
14 A. Khalid, "YouTube Is Now the Biggest Threat to Twitch," *Quartz*, Jan. 28, 2020.

Phase 4: Evolution

When ecosystems master the maturity phase, they shift their focus to continuously adapting, advancing, and reinventing themselves before their competitors do. According to our research, three key factors explain most of the difference between success and failure during the evolution phase.

1. The ability to both learn and innovate faster than competitors. The exact evolution of a business ecosystem cannot and should not be planned in advance. Instead, a key strength of the model is its responsiveness to customer needs and technological changes. To support this, orchestrators must be open to the creativity of ecosystem participants and build flexibility and adaptability into their platforms.

2. Sustainable ecosystems find ways to expand their value propositions. This expansion can stem from the addition of new products or services to an existing ecosystem (such as LinkedIn's addition of online recruiting and content publishing services), expanding into adjacent markets (such as the expansion of ride-hailing platforms into food delivery), or full ecosystem carryovers (such as Apple leveraging its strong position in the music player ecosystem to conquer the smartphone ecosystem).

3. Risk management strategies become increasingly important as the ecosystem expands. Dominant ecosystems may have significant negative impacts on internal and external stakeholders, who will naturally push back. Such pushback can come from incumbents (local taxi companies that fight Uber), partners (who complain about unfair pricing on the Amazon marketplace), users (who criticize Facebook's data privacy policies), or regulators (the European Union, which fined Google for anticompetitive behavior in the Android ecosystem). Ecosystems that succeed over the long term avoid predatory behavior, ensure fair value distribution among all relevant stakeholders, and proactively manage stakeholder perceptions.

Metrics

In addition to the health metrics for the maturity phase, which continue to be highly relevant, ecosystems should focus on three additional key metrics during the evolution phase:

1. **Share of revenue from new products or services.** The revenue derived from new additions to an ecosystem are a direct measure of ability to innovate and of progress in expanding the offering.

2. **Customer satisfaction.** This is a defensive measure that not only alerts orchestrators if their ecosystem is losing its edge but also reflects the quality of the expanded offering. As in the launch phase, aggregated measures of customer satisfaction should be complemented by one-on-one conversations and qualitative feedback.

3. **Partner satisfaction.** This measures the extent to which partners feel they are treated fairly and are loyal to the ecosystem, and it reflects the new business opportunities provided by the expanding ecosystem. Again, it is important to listen carefully to qualitative feedback from partners and to act on what you hear.

Red Flags

A number of early warning signs may indicate that your ecosystem is not on track during the evolution phase and that you need to adjust your development path or behavior:

1. **The orchestrator's take rate from partners rises substantially.** Rising take rates can significantly alter partner economics and may encourage partners to leave the ecosystem. They can also indicate that the orchestrator is more focused on extracting value from the ecosystem than on growing it and creating attractive new opportunities. For example, Etsy, which offers a marketplace for craftspeople and artists, recently raised its take rate from 3.5% to 5%, forced its partners to use its internal payment platform, and required participation in a program that charges an additional 12% to 15% on sales resulting from Etsy ad click-throughs. While Etsy continues to do well, this alienated many partners, leading some of them to protest and leave the platform.[15]

2. **Partners increasingly complain about predatory behavior.** Successful orchestrators can be tempted to exploit their dominant position and impose unfair terms and conditions on the ecosystem. Take, for example, EU regulators' investigation into Amazon's marketplace practices and its dual position as both retailer and platform. That scrutiny was spurred by critics' accusations that Amazon used sales data from its third-party merchants to launch its own competing product lines and unfairly promoted its own

---

15 L. Debter, "Etsy's Push to Compete With Amazon Leaves Sellers Squeezed by Rising Costs," *Forbes*, Feb. 27, 2020.

brands.[16] Perceptions of predatory behavior create opportunities for competing ecosystems to attract important partners.

3. **Negative coverage in (social) media begins to accumulate.** Network effects cut both ways. When negative comments accumulate, they can become amplified and lead to a downward spiral that threatens the viability of an ecosystem. This is what happened to MonkeyParking, a platform that enabled drivers to auction vacated public parking spaces to other drivers. After being broadly criticized for privatizing and monetizing a public good, MonkeyParking pivoted into a platform that helps owners of parking spaces rent them.[17]

4. **Legal actions against the ecosystem accelerate.** Napster, a peer-to-peer file-sharing website, didn't check the copyright status of files that were shared on its platform, leading many people to use it for illegal music sharing. At its peak, Napster had 80 million registered users, but too many of them illegally shared copyrighted content. As a result, Napster was sued by several record labels and popular musicians, such as Metallica and Dr. Dre. In 2001, it was forced to shut down after losing a major lawsuit. The company tried, but failed, to relaunch with appropriate copyright filters, and eventually its name was sold and used to rebrand an online music store.[18]

Conducting an Ecosystem Health Assessment

The odds are against ecosystem success, but if you are an orchestrator or a partner, you can improve your odds by using the metrics and red flags described above. To be successful, you should recognize that different phases of ecosystem development require very different managerial focal points and explicitly adopt new metrics as needed. Incorporate the metrics into your management information system and discuss them and the red flags in your strategy reviews. If you find that your ecosystem is performing weakly on one or more metrics or experiencing the red flags, seek to identify the underlying drivers so that you can address them and prevent future damage.

---

16 K. Cox, "Antitrust 101: Why Everyone Is Probing Amazon, Apple, Facebook, and Google," *Ars Technica*, Nov. 5, 2019.

17 T.S. Perry, "Drawing the Line Between 'Peer-to-Peer' and 'Jerk' Technology," *IEEE Spectrum*, July 18, 2014.

18 M. Harris, "The History of Napster: How the Brand Has Changed Over the Years," *Lifewire*, Nov. 18, 2019.

Be open to failure and have a clear pivot or exit plan. Given the hard reality that 85% of ecosystems fail to achieve long-term sustainability, the ecosystem you initially aim to set up or join will most likely not succeed. This means that it is critical to have clear targets and plans for when and how to change course.

The metrics and red flags described above aren't the only metrics needed to assess a business, but they can help you track the key drivers of ecosystem health and ensure that your company beats the odds and succeeds.

Ulrich Pidun, Martin Reeves, and Niklas Knust
Chapter 6
How Do You Manage a Business Ecosystem?

It is widely acknowledged that business ecosystems offer great potential. Compared to more traditionally organized businesses, such as vertically integrated companies or hierarchical supply chains, business ecosystems are praised for their ability to foster innovation, scale quickly, and adapt to changing environments.

However, many companies that try to build their own ecosystems struggle to realize this potential. Our research has shown that less than 15% of business ecosystems are sustainable in the long run (see Chapter 3) and that the most prevalent reason for failure is weakness in the governance model – the way the ecosystem is managed (see Chapter 4).

Governance Failures

Business ecosystems are prone to different types of governance failures. Many ecosystems struggle because they choose a governance model that is too open. For example, Shuddle launched in 2014 with the ambition to become the Uber for kids. The company offered relatively open access to its platform and did not subject its drivers to fingerprint background checks, in contrast to its more successful competitor HopSkipDrive, which was convinced that such checks are necessary if children are involved. As a result of its open governance model, Shuddle not only faced security concerns but also found it difficult to ensure the required service quality. It had to shut down in 2016.

Other ecosystems fail because of a governance model that is too closed. For example, when the iPhone launched in 2007, the BlackBerry was still widely considered a superior smartphone for corporate users – in terms of its data security, keypad, and battery life. RIM, the company behind the BlackBerry, understood that it needed to follow an ecosystem approach to the development of applications for its device. However, with the aim to maintain its high data security standards, the company chose a rather closed governance model, limiting the incentive for app developers to join the platform. As a consequence, the BlackBerry lost ground to the smartphone ecosystems based on iOS or Android and became a niche product.

https://doi.org/10.1515/9783110775167-006

Some business ecosystems struggle because they cannot control bad behavior on their platforms. For example, many restaurant booking platforms suffer from large numbers of "no show" reservations that alienate their restaurant partners. OpenTable addressed this challenge by requiring diners to cancel reservations they make through the platform at least thirty minutes in advance, banning users who fail to follow this policy four times within a twelve-month period.

Another type of governance failure involves conflicts among ecosystem partners – in particular, conflicts between the orchestrator and its complementors. Early warning signs include complaints from complementors about the orchestrator exploiting its dominant position and imposing unfair terms and conditions on the ecosystem. For example, Amazon was accused of using sales data from third-party merchants on its marketplace to identify attractive market segments and enter them with its own brands. Similarly, Epic Games, the developer of the popular online video game Fortnite, recently filed antitrust lawsuits against Apple and Google, accusing both companies of misusing their dominant positions in mobile operating systems by requiring that payments for in-app digital content be processed via their app stores' respective internal billing systems.

Some business ecosystems experience backlash from consumers or regulators, indicating weaknesses in their existing governance that may threaten their license to operate. For example, social networks are harshly criticized for their data privacy policies and for disseminating false or misleading information on their platforms. Ride-hailing and lodging marketplaces are accused of circumventing regulation in the transportation and hospitality sector in order to avoid costly requirements for safety, insurance, hygiene, and workers' rights.

Finally, an extreme case of governance failure can result in legal actions against the platform or its ecosystem. For example, Backpage.com, a classified ad website, did not restrict the types of ads it would accept, leading to many solicitations for illegal activities. This led to at least eight lawsuits between 2011 and 2016. Backpage won each of these lawsuits, but the website was eventually seized as part of an investigation by federal law enforcement agencies.

Objectives and Challenges

Getting the governance of your ecosystem right is thus a major factor for success as well as a big challenge. Orchestrators must establish an effective governance model, which we define as the set of explicit or implicit structures, rules, and practices that frame and govern the behavior and interplay of participants in a business ecosystem.

Many orchestrators struggle with this challenge because managing an ecosystem is very different than managing an integrated company or a vertical supply chain. Ecosystems are built on voluntary collaboration between independent entities, rather than on clearly defined customer-supplier relationships and transactional contracts. Instead of exerting hierarchical control, the orchestrator must convince partners to join and collaborate in the ecosystem. This challenge is magnified by the dynamic nature of the ecosystem model. Most business ecosystems develop very quickly. They continually add new products and services, connect new members, and change roles and interactions; this poses very high requirements for flexibility and adaptability in the governance model.

In some ways, the governance of an ecosystem can be compared to the governance of a market economy. The role of the orchestrator is not to manage but to enable the other players and to act as the steward of the ecosystem. The governance model is needed to avoid market failures, and it must pursue three objectives:

1. **Support value creation of the ecosystem.** The governance model must facilitate recruiting, motivating, and retaining partners; align partners' interests, strategies, and actions; and optimize resource allocation across partners.
2. **Manage risk in the ecosystem.** The governance model must ensure that all partners comply with laws and norms; protect the reputation of the ecosystem; ensure its social acceptance to avoid backlash from consumers, incumbents, or regulators; and minimize all other kinds of negative externalities.
3. **Optimize value distribution among ecosystem partners.** The governance model needs to establish a fair way to share the value that is created by the ecosystem and ensure that all partners can earn a decent profit and are compensated in accordance with the value they add to the system.

A Framework for Ecosystem Governance

How can the orchestrator and partners of an ecosystem develop a governance model that best achieves the above objectives? Based on our analysis of the governance of more than 80 business ecosystems from various domains, we have developed a comprehensive framework of ecosystem governance (Figure 6.1).

Elements	Dimensions	Key questions
Mission	Purpose	What is the common purpose that aligns the stakeholders of the ecosystem?
	Culture	What is the common set of values that guides the stakeholders of the ecosystem?
Access	Entry	Who can participate in the ecosystem and under which conditions?
	Commitment	What level of exclusiveness or specific co-investments are required?
Participation	Decision rights	How are decision rights distributed among ecosystem stakeholders?
	Transparency	How transparent are the governance model and the strategic roadmap?
	Conflict management	How are conflicts between ecosystem stakeholders resolved?
Conduct	Input control	Which requirements regulate the contributions of stakeholders?
	Process control	How are the behavior and interactions of stakeholders regulated?
	Output control	How are the products/services generated by the ecosystem regulated?
Sharing	Data rights	What are the rules that regulate data ownership, access, and use?
	Property rights	Who owns the tangible and intangible assets created by the ecosystem?
	Value distribution	How is the value created by the ecosystem shared among stakeholders?

Source: BCG Henderson Institute

Figure 6.1: Five Building Blocks of the Ecosystem Governance Framework.

The framework covers the five main building blocks that must be used in managing a business ecosystem:

1. **Mission:** What are the common purpose and culture that guide and align the stakeholders of the ecosystem?
2. **Access:** Who is allowed to enter the ecosystem, and what level of commitment in terms of exclusiveness and/or specific co-investment is required?
3. **Participation:** How are decision rights distributed among ecosystem stakeholders, how transparent are the governance model and strategic roadmap, and how are conflicts resolved?
4. **Conduct:** How is the behavior of ecosystem stakeholders regulated by controlling the input they provide, the process they need to follow, and the output they generate?
5. **Sharing:** What are the rules that regulate data rights and other property rights, and how is the value created by the ecosystem distributed among stakeholders?

To elucidate how the governance model of a business ecosystem can be systematically designed, we discuss the five building blocks of ecosystem governance in more detail, explain the choices for each dimension, and illustrate them with examples.

Mission

Partners in a business ecosystem can be aligned by a common mission that is expressed as a connecting sense of purpose or a joint set of values and culture.

Purpose can be a strong motivation for joining and contributing to an ecosystem. It typically relates to a major problem that can be solved through the ecosystem, a big goal that is to be achieved, or an important contribution to society. For example, Kiva, a nonprofit crowdfunding platform operating across 76 countries, aligns partners behind its purpose to "expand financial access to help underserved communities thrive." The ecosystem wants to create a "financially inclusive world where all people hold the power to improve their lives" and contribute to society because "through Kiva's work, students can pay for tuition, women can start businesses, farmers are able to invest in equipment, and families can afford needed emergency care."

A strong culture can also help align partners in an ecosystem. Sometimes the culture is codified in a defining set of values, as in Wikipedia's five fundamental principles, which state that Wikipedia (1) is an encyclopedia (not an advertising platform), (2) is written from a neutral point of view, (3) is free content that anyone can use, edit, and distribute, (4) has editors who treat each other with respect and civility, and (5) has no firm rules.

In other ecosystems, culture is tacit but nonetheless strong, as in the case of Topcoder, a global talent network and crowdsourcing platform that connects more than a million designers, developers, data scientists, and testers with corporate clients. Topcoder rests on the coder communities' values of, for example, "intrinsic motivations for doing the work or learning from the work, career concerns, status and recognition in the community, or simple affiliation with the community."[1]

Admittedly, some commercial business ecosystems lack a strong culture and are driven mainly by financial objectives. But if you can identify a compelling purpose for your ecosystem and establish a positive culture early in its development, you have a very potent instrument for attracting and retaining the right partners and encouraging the right behavior in your ecosystem without having to regulate every detail with complex rules and written standards.

Access

Controlling access can be an effective way to manage an ecosystem because it establishes not only who can participate in the ecosystem, and under what conditions, but also the level of commitment required in the form of exclusivity agreements and ecosystem-specific co-investments. Such access rules must be defined for the ecosystem's partners and suppliers as well as its customers and users.

On the supply side, many ecosystems are very open and have no participation restrictions. Most online marketplaces are open to all sellers. Some platforms restrict entry by segmentation. The restaurant booking platform OpenTable, for example, recruited mainly restaurants from specific areas in selected cities as part of its launch strategy.[2] Others restrict participation based on qualification. Many gig economy ecosystems (Belay Solutions, for example) allow only qualified suppliers on their platforms. Some orchestrators follow more closed approaches and establish a staged entry model like the one at Amazon Web Services (AWS), which segments its partner network into consulting partners and technology partners. Other orchestrators go so far as to handpick ecosystem

---

1 K.J. Boudreau and A. Hagiu, "Platform Rules: Multi-Sided Platforms as Regulators" in *Platforms, Markets and Innovation*, edited by Annabelle Gawer (Edward Elgar Publishing), 2009.
2 D. Evans and R. Schmalensee, "Matchmakers: The New Economics of Multisided Platforms," *Harvard Business Review Press*, 2016.

partners on a case-by-case basis, as does Climate Corporation for its FieldView smart-farming platform.

On the demand side, most ecosystems don't limit participation. If restrictions exist, they are driven mainly by the scope of the product and service offering. For example, the B2B marketplace Covisint deliberately focused on the automotive industry. Similarly, car sharing platforms such as Getaround address only car drivers and require confirmation of a driver license for participation. Staged entry and freemium models are also common on the demand side, such as on the Amazon marketplace, where entry is free for all customers but premium services and offerings are available only for subscribers to Amazon Prime.

Another way to control access is to ask for a certain level of ecosystem-specific co-investment to enhance commitment to the ecosystem. As expected, this governance instrument is more common on the supply side. Some platforms simply try to achieve this commitment by demanding an access fee. For example, Google and Apple both charge app developers a one-time or annual fee to access their application programming interfaces (APIs). Some orchestrators require partners to invest in ecosystem-specific assets. For example, Apple initially demanded that its smart-home partners purchase Apple's MFi (Made for iPod/iPhone/iPad) chips and include them in their hardware. And other platforms encourage the development of ecosystem-specific capabilities. For example, SAP offers four partner levels. To move up, partners earn "value points" for contributions and investments. On the demand side, such co-investment requirements are less common and typically take the form of an access fee or the need to buy platform-specific equipment (for instance, a console for a video gaming platform).

Finally, orchestrators can link access to the ecosystem with incentives or requirements for exclusiveness, demanding that their partners not offer their products or services on competing platforms. While exclusiveness may be desirable, for most ecosystems it is not feasible. For example, most transaction ecosystems, such as marketplaces or booking and rental platforms, don't demand exclusivity from either their suppliers or their users. Some platforms establish incentives for exclusive use, in the form of monetary rewards, additional services, or privileged information. For example, Amazon Fulfillment Services charges suppliers higher fees for orders not placed via the Amazon marketplace.[3] Lyft operates driver centers with discounted services to incentivize exclusiveness, and drivers can rent a vehicle for a weekly fee via Lyft's Express Drive program if they agree to facilitate

---

3 F. Zhu and M. Iansiti, "Why Some Platforms Thrive and Others Don't," *Harvard Business Review*, January 2019.

20 Lyft rides per week (Express Drive rentals cannot be used for any other for-hire services). Finally, some platforms even negotiate exclusivity contracts with specific suppliers, such as the Blu-ray Disc Consortium did with leading film studios to beat the competing HD DVD format and as Spotify does with individual podcast providers.

Participation

Once partners are admitted to an ecosystem, the next governance question relates to the degree of their participation in the system's development. Participation is reflected in the distribution of decision rights, transparency, and conflict management.

A small number of ecosystems opt for joint decision making and establish institutions and processes to share responsibility for governance and the strategic roadmap of the ecosystem. For example, the open-source operating system Linux is managed by a committee comprising members of the Linux community, including corporate members, individual open-source leaders, vendors, users, and distributors. Similarly, Wikipedia is governed by a structure of committees whose members are elected by the community and whose decisions are made by consensus.

At the other end of the spectrum, the orchestrators of most transaction ecosystems claim a central authority for deciding about the governance and strategic roadmap of the platform. For example, Uber and Airbnb both decide centrally which offerings to include on the platform, while ecosystem partners (drivers and lessors) are restricted to providing the service. Most solution ecosystems select an intermediate option with largely decentralized decision making that is guided by the orchestrator. For example, in many smart-home ecosystems, complementors decide independently about their offering and strategic roadmap, while the orchestrator defines the overall governance.

Participation requires transparency, and we observe a wide range of practices. Some ecosystems are largely transparent, even to nonmembers. For example, Dassault Systèmes (DS) shares a clear innovation roadmap for its product life cycle management (PLM) ecosystem, laying out the target industries and planned solutions as well as the role DS wants to play.[4] Other ecosystems are largely transparent, but only to members. For example, complementors on Apple's

---

4 A. De Meyer and P.J. Williamson, *Ecosystem Edge: Sustaining Competitiveness in the Face of Disruption* (Stanford Business Books), 2020.

smart-home platform HomeKit need to sign a nondisclosure agreement when joining and before receiving detailed information about governance-related questions such as Apple's royalties.

The majority of ecosystems we investigated, however, are mostly not transparent. Such systems may follow a "rainforest" model, as do Google and Apple, which cannot provide much transparency about the future development of their mobile platforms owing to the independent, decentralized development of apps and the (deliberate) lack of a coordinated strategic roadmap. Or they may follow a "walled-garden" model, as do Uber and Airbnb, who don't want to disclose how they will develop their platforms, which verticals they are going to join, or which additional services partners are invited to offer in the future.

The final governance question related to participation is how conflicts between ecosystem stakeholders are resolved. Some ecosystems have no meaningful internal regulations for conflict management and rely on outside jurisdiction. Many emerging platforms have no defined processes and use the orchestrator as arbiter. For example, most social media platforms start with only limited guidelines for conflict resolution and must decide on a case-by-case basis which content to take down.

When clear resolution processes are in place, we observe two models. In some ecosystems, conflicts are centrally managed by the orchestrator, as is the case at Uber, where riders and drivers can complain about each other via the Uber app and the conflict is resolved by a dedicated, central team. In other ecosystems, stakeholders are more strongly involved in conflict resolution. For example, community platforms such as Craigslist and Reddit use volunteers and professional moderators to solve conflicts. Alibaba even established a "market judgment committee" for its Taobao platform to regulate product classification; members are selected from qualified buyers and sellers, and decisions are made by voting.[5]

Conduct

Most orchestrators don't want to manage their ecosystems by relying only on a strong mission, access rules, and regulations for participation; they want to directly influence stakeholder behavior. They can choose from three approaches: input, process, and output control.

---

5 Ibid.

Input control specifies the requirements for the partners' contributions to the ecosystem. Some ecosystems, such as most social platforms, have no input standards or only limited standards. For example, Twitter's restriction of posts to a length of 280 characters is only a weak form of input control. Most digital solution ecosystems go one step further and control input through prescribed interfaces that specify input formats and technical interactions through APIs (application programming interfaces), SDKs (software development kits), and IDEs (integrated development environments).

Other ecosystems have established standards and instruments for quality control of new contributions. For example, Apple deploys extensive quality checks on newly developed apps before approving them for the platform. Taking yet another step, some orchestrators claim the right to handpick and curate input on their platform. New applications on John Deere's smart-farming platform, for instance, must be individually approved and separately licensed. Initially, the online gaming platform Steam curated new games in its ecosystem, first by handpicking them centrally and then by letting users vote on which games to include (the "Steam Greenlight" process), but later it restricted itself to quality control by only reviewing game configurations and checking for malicious content (the "Steam Direct" process).

In process control, the orchestrator tries to regulate the behavior of partners as they interact with each other and with the platform. Again, many social platforms are examples of ecosystems with no process control or only limited control. For example, Craigslist provides only an open interface for communication and matching, while the process for the resulting transactions and their fulfillment is not regulated. At the other end of the spectrum, some ecosystems stipulate end-to-end process regulation. For example, Kiva centrally defines every step on its microfinance platform, from loan application to underwriting, approval, posting, fundraising, disbursal, and repayment. Uber even prescribes the routes that drivers should take.

Other ecosystems establish partial regulation of the process. Apple, for instance, uses the AppStore as a control point for the distribution and purchase of apps. And some orchestrators try to softly govern behavior on their platform by offering process support with central services. Software ecosystems such as SAP and AWS provide forums, services, and training to help partners develop new applications and improve the scope and quality of the offering.

Finally, the output control approach directly regulates the quality of products and services created by the ecosystem. Very few platforms deliberately apply no output control or only limited control. For example, Doctolib, an online booking platform that matches doctors with patients, explicitly refrains from evaluating doctors because objective measures are difficult to apply in health care. The most frequent mechanism for output control in transaction ecosystems is customer feedback. It can be used just for transparency, as with most app store ratings or customer reviews on marketplaces or booking platforms, but it can also be used to exclude partners with evaluations below a certain threshold, as in the cases of Airbnb and Uber.

A more active instrument for regulating output is editorial control. It can be accomplished by the orchestrator, as it is at Facebook and Twitter, which have substantial internal units for content curation, but it can also be performed by qualified users. For example, the online gaming platform Steam appoints users as curators, who review games and connect with developers on Curator Connect, and explorers, who look for fake games. Lastly, some platforms use AI-based algorithmic control to curate output. On the Topcoder platform, for instance, code submitted in competitive programming matches is automatically assessed by algorithms, and the results are used for rating and ranking developers.

Sharing

The final building block of ecosystem governance regulates data rights, property rights, and how the value that is created by the ecosystem is shared among partners.

The regulation of data rights needs to address the ownership, access, and use of data in the ecosystem. We observe four basic models:

1. **Data is owned and shared by the creator.** The owner of the data shares it case by case, only with the orchestrator (as do complementors of the Apple HomeKit), or more broadly with other partners in the ecosystem (in Germany, for example, patients decide on an individual basis which parties they grant access to their electronic health records).

2. **Data is owned and used by all partners.** Tracr, an end-to-end blockchain-based diamond tracing platform, uses this model. Although this model is still rare today, we expect it to become more popular with further advancement and spread of blockchain technology.

3. **Data is owned and shared by the orchestrator.** Alibaba, for example, owns transaction data on its marketplaces but voluntarily shares information on demand patterns with its merchants, encouraging them to invest in advanced data analytics.

4. **Data is owned and used by the orchestrator.** Some platform orchestrators, such as Uber and Lyft, own all of the transaction data generated on their platforms and do not share it with their partners.

The regulation of property rights over the intangible assets that are created by the ecosystem faces similar challenges. In rare cases, there are explicitly no intellectual property rights derived from ecosystem activity. For example, contributors to Wikipedia agree to waive all property rights and release their contribution under the Creative Commons Attribution-ShareAlike license. In most solution ecosystems, however, intellectual property is owned and used by the creator. For instance, developers and complementors in the Linux ecosystem own the intellectual property of their Linux versions (for example, RedHat) or solutions built with Linux. Occasionally, property rights are partially limited by the orchestrator, as is the case with SAP, which offers "timed" property rights for partner applications and provides an ecosystem roadmap for the next two years, laying out which existing products will be integrated into SAP's core platform.[6] Lastly, in some ecosystems, such as ride-hailing and food delivery platforms, intellectual property is developed, owned, and used mainly by the orchestrator.

When it comes to value distribution, many ecosystems follow a strict market-based approach and encourage independent pricing by ecosystem members. For example, on the Apple and Android mobile platforms, the orchestrator sets a take rate and developers are free to set prices for their applications. Topcoder has established an inverse market mechanism in which corporate clients set the price they are ready to pay and developers compete for the project. Some solution ecosystems try to optimize value capture for their platform by coordinating pricing and negotiating value distribution. Many video game console platforms, for instance, subsidize hardware with game sales. Climate FieldView sets package prices for its smart-farming offering and individually negotiates value distribution with its partners and suppliers. Finally, some ecosystems apply central pricing and value distribution, letting partners decide to accept or to leave. For example, Uber and Lyft use central algorithmic pricing schemes, and content providers on media and entertainment platforms such as YouTube, Medium, and Spotify receive a share of value based on the engagement level of users.

How to Select the Right Governance Model

Given the many essential elements of ecosystem governance and the many options for each element (Figure 6.2), how can you select the best governance model for your ecosystem?

---

6 G. Parker and M. Van Alstyne, "Innovation, Openness and Platform Control," *Management Science*, August 11, 2017.

Purpose	What major problem do we solve?		What do we want to achieve?		How do we contribute to society?
Culture	Codified culture			Tacit culture	
Entry	No restrictions	Segmentation	Qualification	Staged entry	Handpicking
Co-investment	No co-investment	Access fee	Ecosystem-specific assets	Ecosystem-specific capabilities	
Exclusiveness	No exclusiveness demanded	Incentives for exclusive use	Exclusivity contracts		
Decision rights	Joint decision making	Decentralized, guided by orchestrator	Central authority		
Transparency	Transparent (non-members)	Transparent (members)	Not transparent (rainforest)	Not transparent (walled garden)	
Conflict management	Outside jurisdiction	Orchestrator as arbiter	Process involving stakeholders	Centrally managed process	
Input control	No input standards	Quality control	Prescribed interfaces	Curated input	
Process control	No process control	Support with central services	Partial regulation	End-to-end regulation	
Output control	No output control	Customer feedback	Editorial control	Algorithmic control	
Data rights	Owned & shared by creator	Owned & used by all partners	Owned & shared by orchestrator	Owned & used by orchestrator	
Property rights	No intellectual property rights	Owned & used by creator	Partially limited by orchestrator	Owned & used by orchestrator	
Value distribution	Independent pricing	Coordinated pricing and value distribution	Central pricing and value distribution		

Source: BCG Henderson Institute

Figure 6.2: The Option Space of Ecosystem Governance Models.

For starters, there are some general characteristics of good ecosystem governance (Figure 6.3):

- **Consistency.** Governance models should be clear and simple, no more complex than necessary, and easy to understand for all stakeholders. At the same time, they should comprehensively address all relevant governance questions. In addition, the individual elements of governance should be self-consistent, free of contradictions, and consistent over time to provide a predictable framework for all partners.
- **Fairness.** Good ecosystem governance ensures fair and trusted dealings with all stakeholders. In particular, it should be compliant with local laws and norms and avoid inappropriate biases in, for example, data algorithms and access. Overall, the governance model should create trust among partners and, in particular, inhibit the misuse of orchestrator power.
- **Effectiveness.** In order to be effective, the governance model should foster collaboration and alignment between participants, secure the quality of the ecosystem's products and services, and encourage participation and growth of the ecosystem. In this way, effective governance can become a source of differentiation and competitive advantage for the ecosystem.
- **Flexibility.** Finally, ecosystem governance must be regularly monitored. Instruments and early-warning indicators for emerging governance issues should be in place, and the governance model should be flexible enough to adapt to changing circumstances and new challenges.

		Yes	Partly	No
Consistent	Clear and simple, easy to understand, no more complex than necessary	☐	☐	☐
	Comprehensive, leaving no relevant governance questions open	☐	☐	☐
	Self-consistent, no contradictions between elements of governance	☐	☐	☐
	Consistent over time, predictable and projectable for partners	☐	☐	☐
Fair	Complies with (local) laws and norms	☐	☐	☐
	Avoids biases (for example, in data algorithms and access)	☐	☐	☐
	Creates trust among participants (no misuse of orchestrator power)	☐	☐	☐
Effective	Fosters collaboration and alignment between participants	☐	☐	☐
	Secures quality of ecosystem products and services	☐	☐	☐
	Encourages participation and growth of the ecosystem	☐	☐	☐
	Serves as a source of differentiation and competitive advantage	☐	☐	☐
Flexible	Regularly monitored for governance issues	☐	☐	☐
	Easy to adapt to changing circumstances	☐	☐	☐

Source: BCG Henderson Institute

Figure 6.3: General Characteristics of Good Ecosystem Governance.

Besides these general characteristics of good ecosystem governance, ecosystem-specific criteria play a role in selecting the right governance model. For example, we find that many successful transaction ecosystems opt for a rather open access model with only limited requirements regarding the commitment of partners. Decision rights are owned mainly by the platform orchestrator, and data sharing is limited. Behavior on the platform is tightly regulated on the basis of standard terms and conditions and sophisticated instruments for input, process, and output control. In contrast, many successful solution ecosystems that we investigated are more selective in granting access to the ecosystem. They are more frequently aligned by a common purpose and set of values and require a higher level of commitment in the form of ecosystem-specific investments or capabilities. In exchange, solution ecosystems give partners more decision rights, share data more broadly, and curtail the behavior in the ecosystem less strictly.

More generally, the right governance model also depends on the strategic priorities of the ecosystem. If the focus is on fast growth, flexibility, decentralized innovation, exploration, and value creation, the governance model should be rather open and follow the rainforest paradigm of diversity, autonomous creativity, and adaptability – as exemplified by Alibaba's Taobao marketplace and the Android mobile operating system. If, on the other hand, the focus is on quality, commitment, coordinated innovation, exploitation, and value capture, the governance model should be rather closed and follow the walled-garden paradigm of consistency, alignment, and control – as exemplified by the B2B platforms for smart farming and smart mining.

Finally, it is important to acknowledge that ecosystem governance is not static; it must be actively developed over time. The initial governance model can be tailored to the early set of ecosystem partners, but the orchestrator must make sure that the model is scalable and doesn't become too complex as the ecosystem grows. The development of an ecosystem is strongly path dependent, and many successful platforms start with a rather closed approach to establish the right quality and behavior but then scale up and open up as the ecosystem grows.

As digital platforms and business ecosystems become more widespread, they will increasingly compete on the basis of their governance (see Chapter 7). Companies that build their own platform and ecosystem can use the frameworks presented in this chapter to systematically think through the building blocks and options for ecosystem governance and find the right model for their ecosystem. Companies that consider joining an ecosystem as a complementor or supplier can use the frameworks to analyze an ecosystem's governance model and assess its consistency, fairness, effectiveness, flexibility, and ability to meet the company's specific requirements.

Ulrich Pidun, Martin Reeves, and Niklas Knust
Chapter 7
Setting the Rules of the Road

Business ecosystems are prone to different types of governance failures. One reason why the BlackBerry OS lost its competition with Apple's iOS and Google's Android was because Research In Motion failed to open its app ecosystem widely to developers until it was too late.[1] Conversely, the video game industry fell into recession during the so-called Atari Shock in the 1980s in part because of overly open access to its ecosystem, which resulted in a flood of inferior games. Badly behaved platform participants, conflicts among ecosystem partners, and backlash from consumers or regulators are other indicators of governance flaws that can bring down an ecosystem.[2]

Many orchestrators struggle to find an effective governance model because managing an ecosystem is very different from managing an integrated company or a linear supply chain. Ecosystems rely on voluntary collaboration among independent partners rather than clearly defined customer-supplier relationships and transactional contracts. The orchestrator cannot exert hierarchical control but must convince partners to join and collaborate in the ecosystem. These challenges are exacerbated by the dynamic nature of many ecosystems, which develop and evolve quickly and continually add new products, services, and members.

Ecosystem leaders who understand the components of a comprehensive governance model (see Chapter 6) and glean insights from ecosystem successes and failures can make more informed and explicit governance decisions. In doing so, they can improve the odds that their ecosystems will be among the lucky few that survive and prosper over the long term. To derive the success factors, we studied the governance models of more than 80 business ecosystems from different domains and tracked their evolution over time. We developed a profile to describe, measure, and compare ecosystem governance intensity and applied it to derive four recommendations for using ecosystem governance as a source of competitive advantage.

---

1 A. Moazed and N. Johnson, "Modern Monopolies: What It Takes to Dominate the 21st Century Economy" (New York: St. Martin's Press), 2016.
2 U. Pidun, M. Reeves, and N. Knust, "How Do You Manage a Business Ecosystem?" *Boston Consulting Group*, Jan. 20, 2021.

Note: Republished with permission by *MIT Sloan Management Review.*

https://doi.org/10.1515/9783110775167-007

Align Your Ecosystem's Governance Model With Its Strategic Priorities

The strategic priorities of business ecosystems vary by their competitive situation and developmental maturity. No matter what the strategic priorities of an orchestrator, the dimensions of governance can be manipulated to support their attainment.

Ecosystem growth, for example, can be fostered by lowering entry barriers, easing the controls on conduct, and/or offering a more generous distribution of value. The Android ecosystem used all of these governance levers to gain scale in the early days of its competition with iOS. Google maximized access by opening it to all developers. It used open-source coding that offered partners the freedom to introduce variations and to integrate their own applications. To attract and support the developer community and spark innovation, Google initially awarded cash prizes to developers for superior applications.[3]

The governance model can help orchestrators maintain the quality of an ecosystem's offerings. Belay does this by controlling access: It allows only qualified suppliers of virtual support services, such as administrative assistants and bookkeepers, on its gig economy platform. Kiva, the nonprofit crowdfunding platform that created a field partner network spanning 76 countries to make loans to low-income entrepreneurs, uses the conduct element to ensure loan quality. It has a strict process control system that defines every step on its platform, from applying for loans to underwriting, approving, and posting them; raising and disbursing funds; and receiving loan payments. The online publishing platform Medium uses the dimension of value distribution to incentivize the creation of high-quality content: It pays the writers in its partner program based on the level of reader engagement their articles generate.

If the strategic focus is on improving alignment among the partners of an ecosystem, again the different dimensions of governance can help. The smart-farming platform FieldView uses the dimension of entry to create alignment. It hand-picks its partners to ensure that each offers unique services that complement its overall offering, and it uses individual partner contracts to specify the products and services that partners are allowed to offer.[4] The Linux open-source operating system creates alignment among its developer community by leveraging several governance dimensions: a common mission, strict technical

---

3 "Google Announces $10 Million Android Developer Challenge," *Google*, Nov. 12, 2007.
4 E. Cosgrove, "Checking in With Climate Corp's Open Platform Strategy and the Future of Ag Data," *AgFunder News*, Jan. 30, 2018.

guidelines and processes for conduct, and administrative decision rights that are assigned to specific users.

Generally speaking, very open governance models support a rainforest paradigm, in which a diverse set of autonomous players bolster systemic creativity and adaptability. Such models are well suited for ecosystems that must react quickly to changing technologies and customer preferences and whose strategic focus is rapid growth, exploration, and decentralized innovation. In contrast, very closed governance models support a walled garden paradigm by enabling consistency, alignment, and control. They are preferred when an ecosystem's strategic priorities are focused on ensuring quality, improving efficiency, and coordinating innovation that requires committed partners.

But the strategic priorities of ecosystem orchestrators are rarely this clear-cut. Often they have competing priorities, such as the need to promote a diverse set of participants while also ensuring the quality of their offerings. Finding the right balance between the two paradigms can mean the difference between success and failure.

Nuanced choices regarding the dimensions of governance can help orchestrators simultaneously achieve conflicting objectives. Apple's iPhone ecosystem, for instance, achieved rapid growth by offering low-barrier access to app developers while at the same time ensuring a high level of quality and consistency by centralizing decision rights and using extensive quality checks before approving newly developed apps for the platform.

Use Your Governance Model to Stand Apart From Competitors

Just as countries and companies compete and prosper depending on the quality of their governance, ecosystem governance can serve as a source of competitive differentiation.[5] This is particularly noticeable when the orchestrators of competing ecosystems come from different industries. In smart mining, equipment manufacturers Caterpillar and Komatsu have built closed ecosystems focused on their own products, whereas technology companies like Dassault Systèmes

---

5 "Doing Business 2020," PDF file (Washington, DC: The World Bank), 2020; and P. Gompers, J. Ishii, and A. Metrick, "Corporate Governance and Equity Prices," *The Quarterly Journal of Economics* 118, no. 1 (February 2003): 107–156.

and Cisco are building universal internet-of-things platforms that are more open to third parties.

When orchestrators are in the same sector, they can develop different governance profiles to differentiate their competing ecosystems. In the smart-home arena, Apple established a rather closed governance model for its iHome ecosystem compared with competitors Amazon, Google, and Samsung. The key differences in the governance of Apple's ecosystem include stricter access rules, extensive quality control for new applications, and more restrictive data-sharing policies.[6] The company is trying to differentiate itself with a more coherent user experience, even though this could limit its growth rate.

The orchestrators of new ecosystems can adopt an open governance model to counter the network effects enjoyed by incumbents.[7] By 2004, Microsoft's Internet Explorer had won the browser war after capturing nearly 95% of the market. With no serious competitors, however, Microsoft underinvested in the browser's development and took a relatively closed approach to third-party innovation. Google countered with an open governance model for the Chrome browser and opened a web store for third-party Chrome applications in 2011. Its browser became the market leader soon after.[8]

Of course, no competitive strategy is risk-free. Orkut, Google's first attempt at a social network, was launched in 2004, the same year as Facebook. Facebook initially followed a closed governance model, limiting access to users with university email accounts and allowing them to interact only with users at their schools.[9] It later opened up access but kept relatively strict privacy controls in place. In contrast, Orkut decided to compete on the basis of an open governance model. The platform applied fewer restrictions on user behavior and less-strict privacy controls than Facebook. This resulted in fast initial growth, but also in many fake profiles and lower-quality interactions, which contributed to Orkut's demise in 2014.[10]

Moreover, while competing ecosystems initially experiment with diverse governance models and use them for competitive differentiation, over time the more successful models eradicate the weaker ones. As orchestrators learn what

6 D. Nield, "The Best Smart Home Systems 2021: Top Ecosystems Explained," *The Ambient*, June 30, 2021.
7 G.G. Parker and M.W. Van Alstyne, "Two-Sided Network Effects: A Theory of Information Product Design," *Management Science* 51, no. 10 (October 2005): 1494–1504.
8 M.A. Cusumano, A. Gawer, and D.B. Yoffie, *The Business of Platforms: Strategy in the Age of Digital Competition, Innovation, and Power* (New York: Harper Business), 2019.
9 S. Phillips, "A Brief History of Facebook," *The Guardian*, July 25, 2007.
10 S. Raju, "Main Reasons for the Failure of Orkut," *StartupTalky*, Aug. 4, 2021.

works and as competition becomes more oligopolistic, governance models tend to converge. In December 2019, a group of large players that included Amazon, Apple, and Google launched the Connected Home over IP alliance to increase the compatibility of smart-home products for consumers, a move that will lead to greater harmonization of their governance models.

If one ecosystem gains a competitive advantage by adapting its governance model, others may be forced to do the same to keep up. For example, most of today's social media networks have similar governance models and tend to move in lockstep on emerging issues, such as establishing independent oversight boards for content curation.

Use Governance to Ensure Social Acceptance

Societal and regulatory scrutiny of ecosystems is on the rise. Sharing-economy and gig-economy platforms are coming under fire for avoiding costly requirements related to safety, insurance, hygiene, and workers' rights. Social networks are criticized for lax data privacy policies and the dissemination of false and misleading information. E-commerce marketplaces are accused of undue price pressure and unfairly giving their own products an advantage. There are mounting concerns about the alleged concentration and misuse of power by dominant digital platforms.

Despite and perhaps due to their great success, an increasing number of orchestrators see their ecosystems being challenged by regulators, and they run the risk of being broken up or losing their licenses to operate. Beyond regulation, the mutual trust that is foundational to the success of an ecosystem is threatened: In previous research, we found that a lack of trust critically contributed to over half of the 110 ecosystem failures we studied (see Chapter 10).[11]

Thus, good governance is rapidly becoming a prerequisite for building social capital and securing the social legitimacy required by business ecosystems. To meet this dictate, orchestrators must understand that it is not sufficient to optimize the value proposition and experience of customers; they must also enhance the value and experience of other ecosystem contributors and external stakeholders. Moreover, the governance model must be designed to engender and maintain social acceptance, as well as legal compliance, over the long term

---

11 M. Aguiar, U. Pidun, S. Lacanna et al., "Building Trust in Business Ecosystems," *Boston Consulting Group*, Feb. 10, 2021.

and in the face of changing demands. Superior governance, understood in this way, must be consistent and fair.

Consistency means that the mechanisms of governance are transparent and easy to understand, comprehensive, internally consistent, and stable over time. HopSkipDrive uses consistent governance to establish trust for its particularly sensitive offering: ride-sharing services for children. The platform accepts only drivers who adhere to multiple ecosystem guidelines and have at least five years of caregiving experience; a clean multiagency, fingerprint-based background check; and a good driving record for at least the past three years. It employs strict process control, tracking each ride in real time to detect unsafe driving behavior and proactively address any issues. Moreover, the platform regularly reports on the frequency of safety-related issues such as traffic incidents, collisions, and distracted driving.[12]

Fairness means that governance complies with local laws and norms, avoids bias (for example, in data algorithms and access), and creates trust among participants (for example, by forbidding the misuse of orchestrator power). The importance of fair governance is illustrated by the recent rise of platform cooperatives. These platforms, which include hospitality platform Fairbnb.coop, ridehailing service The Drivers Cooperative, and stock photography platform Stocksy United, are owned and governed by their contributors.[13] Many of them have emerged in reaction to exploitation by ecosystem orchestrators.

Adapt Your Governance Model Over Time

Adaptability is a key strength of a successful ecosystem. Typically, this adaptability stems from a modular setup that features a stable core (or platform) and interfaces, with highly variable components that can be easily added or subtracted. This enables ecosystems to evolve along with changes in the competitive environment, the needs of orchestrators and participants, social mores, and technology. This same kind of adaptability must also be reflected in the governance model of an ecosystem.

Consider Steam, the video game distribution platform. Originally launched in 2003 as an online platform for the distribution and patching of Valve games,

---

12 M. Aguiar, F. Candelon, U. Pidun et al., "Designing for Trust: Business Lessons From an Underdog Ride-Share Startup," *Fortune*, May 4, 2021.

13 C. Cennamo, "Competing in Digital Markets: A Platform-Based Perspective," *Academy of Management Perspectives* 35, no. 2 (May 2021): 265–291.

its initial governance model was rather closed. In 2004, some 50 titles were available on the platform. Then Steam started to open up by lowering the barriers to entry, reducing input controls, and negotiating its first partnerships with game publishers. The number of available games quickly doubled.

Between 2007 and 2010, Steam further opened to external developers with the launch of the Steamworks software development kit and a number of APIs that facilitated data sharing with partners. Major publishers joined the platform, driving the total games available to more than 1,000.

Over time, Steam increasingly relied on user-based mechanisms for governance of the ecosystem. For example, in 2012 it introduced Greenlight, which allowed users to vote on which new games would be added to the platform. User feedback and reviews became increasingly important for the output control needed to secure the quality of the platform's games.

Another major shift in governance took place in 2017, when Valve recognized that, with the growing size of the Steam ecosystem, Greenlight had become a major bottleneck for onboarding new developers and games. Accordingly, it replaced Greenlight with the Steam Direct submissions portal for developers to further reduce entry restrictions and input control while relying on more effective user feedback mechanisms to ensure quality. By 2020, Steam had evolved into a very liberal and open ecosystem, with more than 10,000 games and 120 million monthly active players.

Steam illustrates a phenomenon that we see in many successful ecosystems: They tend to start with rather closed governance and become more open over time. One reason for this: The development of an ecosystem is strongly path-dependent, with early decisions having a significant impact on the trajectory and future scope of the ecosystem. Hence, many ecosystem orchestrators prefer a closed governance model at the beginning to control quality and behavior and to get the ecosystem on the path to success.

There is one caveat: While most business ecosystems tend to become more open as they grow, some ecosystems begin to tighten governance once they reach a certain size and market position. This can be a reaction to misuse of the platform, such as ride-hailing services reinforcing background checks for drivers after passengers are attacked, or to public or regulatory pressure, such as social networks strengthening input control to prevent the spread of misinformation during the pandemic.

The orchestrators of successful ecosystems also tighten governance to increase their own value capture, particularly if they have achieved a leading market position and partners are increasingly dependent on the platform. Reinforcing the rules for participation, conduct, and sharing are the most effective levers for achieving this. Google tightened its grip on Android after handset manufacturers and other partners began developing variations of the operating system that were incompatible with some applications and made it difficult for Google to profit from the platform by selling advertising and software.[14] By moving the APIs for app development from the operating system layer to the Google Play app store, the company regained control of large parts of the Android ecosystem and could adapt its governance largely independently of the underlying operating system.[15]

As ecosystems become more widespread and established, the quality of their governance is an increasingly important success factor. But there is no single best way to design your governance model: It will be contingent on the strategic priorities, competitive dynamics, societal demands, and life-cycle stage of the ecosystem.

If you are – or want to become – an orchestrator, you should not treat governance as an afterthought but should instead think through and actively design the governance model. You need to understand the benefits and risks of being open or closed, align governance and strategy, and resolve strategic trade-offs by balancing the different dimensions of governance. You ought to put yourself into the shoes of ecosystem partners and users to understand the impact of your governance decisions on their incentives to participate and contribute. You should also analyze the governance models of competing ecosystems and use your governance choices to gain competitive advantage. And you will have to adapt your governance model over time to react to changes in user preferences, technology, competition, and strategy.

If you are joining an ecosystem as a partner, you need to understand how its governance model works and evolves over time. An ecosystem's governance will strongly influence how attractive it is for you. You should consider governance as an important criterion for deciding in which ecosystem to participate by asking yourself several questions: How well does the purpose and culture of the ecosystem resonate with your values and preferences? What kinds of commitments and ecosystem-specific investments are required that may limit your future flexibility? Are the transparency and decision rights that you need to understand and influence the development of the ecosystem in place? To what extent do regulations for input, process, and output limit your customer access

14 R. O'Donoghue, "Android Forks: Why Google Can Rest Easy, for Now," *mobiForge*, Oct. 9, 2014.
15 R. Amadeo, "Google's Iron Grip on Android: Controlling Open Source by Any Means Necessary," *Ars Technica*, July 21, 2018.

and freedom to operate? And are regulations in place that ensure that you benefit in a fair way from the data, intellectual property, and value that you contribute to the ecosystem?

Good governance is an essential key to the success of both ecosystem orchestrators and their partners.

Ulrich Pidun, Martin Reeves, and Balázs Zoletnik

Chapter 8
How Do You Succeed as a Business Ecosystem Contributor?

Business ecosystems are on the rise. In 2000, just three among the S&P top 100 global companies relied predominantly on ecosystem business models. In 2020 this number had grown to 22 companies, which together accounted for 40% of total market capitalization. Among the 772 startup firms that achieved unicorn status (a valuation of more than $1 billion) between 2015 and 2021, 179 (23%) were built on ecosystem business models.[1]

It is no wonder that many leaders of established companies are afraid of missing out on this trend and feel compelled to come up with their own business ecosystems. Among the 2020 S&P top 100 global companies, more than 50% have already built or bought into at least one business ecosystem, most of them within the past five years. In a recent BCG global survey, 90% of multinational companies indicated that they were planning to expand their activities in business ecosystems.[2]

Most of these incumbent firms seem to assume that they need to become orchestrators of their own ecosystems. However, not every company is in a position to play the role of orchestrator. Fortunately, being a contributor to an ecosystem can be just as attractive. Remember that the biggest winners of the California gold rush in the 19th century were the suppliers of pots, pans, and jeans. Acting as contributors to existing or emerging ecosystems presents huge and neglected business potential for many companies, and their leaders should be more strategic in exploiting these opportunities.

The Growing Role of Ecosystem Contributors

Admittedly, most of the largest and best-known ecosystem players, such as Alibaba, Amazon, Apple, Facebook, Gojek, Grab, Tencent, and Yandex, have built their success on owning the platforms and being orchestrators of their

---

1 CBInsights, as of March 31, 2021.
2 Unpublished survey of 206 heads of strategy of companies from 56 industries and 18 countries, with average revenues of more than $20 billion (spring 2021).

https://doi.org/10.1515/9783110775167-008

ecosystems, which we define as a dynamic group of largely independent economic players that create products or services that together constitute a coherent solution. As orchestrators, they build the ecosystem, encourage others to join, define standards and rules, and act as arbiters in cases of conflict. However, a successful ecosystem needs not only orchestrators but also contributors. Actually, for every orchestrator there can be hundreds to thousands of contributors (as in smart-home ecosystems), or even up to several million (as in large marketplaces or mobile operating systems).

Not every company has the capabilities to be an orchestrator. You cannot unilaterally choose to be the orchestrator; you need to be accepted by the other players in the ecosystem. There are four requirements to qualify as ecosystem orchestrator: (1) the orchestrator needs to be considered an essential member of the ecosystem, and it must control critical resources, such as a strong brand, customer access, or key skills; (2) the orchestrator should occupy a central position in the ecosystem network, with strong interdependencies with many other players and the ability to coordinate effectively; (3) the orchestrator should be perceived as a fair partner by the other members, not as a competitive threat; and (4) the best candidate is likely to be the player with the greatest net benefit from the ecosystem and a correspondingly high ability to shoulder the large upfront investments and risk.

Besides orchestrators, there are two types of contributors to an ecosystem: complementors and suppliers (Figure 8.1). *Complementors* contribute to the ecosystem solution by directly providing customers with products or services that enhance the value of other ecosystem components. In this way, complementors grow the offering of the ecosystem, contribute to its variety, and drive innovation. Customers can freely decide which complementors to engage with. Examples are vendors on a digital marketplace, weather data providers in a smart-farming ecosystem, and app developers for mobile operating systems. In contrast, ecosystem *suppliers* are upstream providers of products or services to other partners in the ecosystem. Suppliers may enable the entire ecosystem (for example, by providing the cloud or payment infrastructure) or serve individual players (for example, by offering cleaning services to Airbnb hosts). With their more generic offering, suppliers can serve ecosystems from different domains, but they typically do not have direct access to the ecosystem's customers.

In the past, most startups and incumbents that considered engaging in ecosystems were attracted by the orchestrator role and its position of power as the rulemaker, gatekeeper, allocator of profits, and judge and jury of the ecosystem. The contributor role seemed much less appealing because contributors depend on an ecosystem that they can hardly influence. They are exposed to a high level of uncertainty regarding the development of the scope, composition,

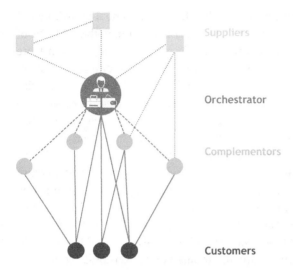

Suppliers

Orchestrator

Complementors

Customers

Source: BCG Henderson Institute

Figure 8.1: Orchestrators, Complementors, and Suppliers Comprise Business Ecosystems.

and governance of the ecosystem. Moreover, many potential contributors are afraid of being commoditized by the orchestrator – of being forced to share critical data and relinquish their direct access to customers, thus losing their differentiation.

However, there are also substantial benefits from being a contributor to an ecosystem. For starters, contributors do not face the high upfront investment risk for building the ecosystem. The broad scope of the orchestrator role comes with the bulk of responsibility for ecosystem success and for the sustained level of investment that is required to get the ecosystem going. In contrast, contributors can typically choose among multiple competing ecosystems and join the most attractive one. What's more, they can limit their exposure, hedge their bets, and increase their strategic flexibility by participating in more than one ecosystem at the same time. In this way, contributors may have a strong bargaining position vis-à-vis the orchestrator. In particular, if they provide essential or bottleneck components to an ecosystem, contributors can secure a substantial share of the overall profits.

Indeed, the contributor role can be as financially attractive as the orchestrator role, or even more attractive. For example, the mobility platform orchestrator Uber achieved an impressive annual revenue growth rate of 24% between 2016 and 2020, but it was clearly outperformed by one of its less well-known suppliers, the payment services provider Adyen, which achieved an annual growth rate of 43% over the same period. Moreover, Adyen earned a cumulative EBITDA of $1.1 billion over the five-year period, whereas Uber accumulated losses of more than $20 billion. Adyen recently surpassed Uber even in terms of market capitalization, reaching $82.8 billion (versus Uber's $81.3 billion).[3] We observe similar trends in many industries and contributor domains. Several companies with significant strategic focus on ecosystem contributor plays are in the S&P top 100 global companies as well. Among them are smartphone manufacturer Samsung, streaming service pioneer Netflix, and software specialist Adobe.

Not surprisingly, ecosystem contributors increasingly attract the attention of investors, as reflected in the list of startup firms that achieved unicorn status (Figure 8.2). For many years, the share of ecosystem contributors among new unicorns has been on the rise, and in 2019 they surpassed the number of ecosystem orchestrators for the first time. Two parallel trends explain this situation. On the one hand, given the recent growth and proliferation of business ecosystems, the opportunity space for new ecosystem business models is shrinking. On the other hand, the emerging large platforms and their ecosystems, such as mobile operating systems, cloud platforms, and digital marketplaces, open up new opportunities with considerable scale for contributors.

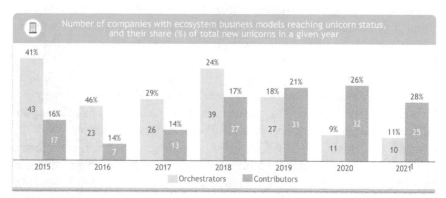

1. 2021 data is for Q1 only
Sources: CBInsights; BCG Henderson Institute

Figure 8.2: Ecosystem Contributors Increasingly Achieving Unicorn Status.

Even many of the large tech ecosystem orchestrators have started to pivot and take on the role of contributors to their own or other ecosystems. Consider

---

3 Based on S&P Global Market Intelligence as of July 30, 2021; EUR-USD exchange rate 1.1869.

Facebook moving into virtual reality headsets with its acquisition of Oculus, Amazon offering fulfillment services for its marketplace and moving into film production, and Google providing cloud infrastructure for an increasing number of newly emerging ecosystems.

Company leaders who reflect on how to expand their activities in business ecosystems should thus carefully consider the contributor role. However, this poses a number of new strategic challenges that companies may not be used to. As an ecosystem contributor, you need to build and develop robust relationships with the platform orchestrator and with other contributors. You need to find a good balance between cooperating to grow the pie and competing when dividing the pie. You need to solve potential conflicts regarding mutual commitment, customer access, and data sharing. And the resulting complexity is amplified by the dynamic evolution of the ecosystem and changes in scope, composition, and governance.

Many companies are unsure how to deal with these new challenges. In our research and work with clients, we have identified several key strategic imperatives that can address the challenges and lead to success for contributors, but with which most companies struggle:

- Select the right ecosystem to join.
- Define the right level of engagement.
- Stand out against other contributors.
- Avoid being commoditized by the orchestrator.
- Know when it is time to leave the ecosystem.

To help leaders determine how to accomplish these strategic imperatives, we conducted two systematic historical analyses to enable a comprehensive overview of ecosystem contributor plays and to observe their development over time. First, we analyzed the global top 100 most valuable private companies based on S&P Capital IQ from 2000 through 2020, in five-year intervals. We observed their strategic moves building or entering business ecosystems as a contributor or as an orchestrator. We analyzed in detail the 72 players with relevant contributor plays. Second, we analyzed the 772 startup companies that reached unicorn status (valuation of more than $1 billion) between January 2015 and March 2021 based on CBInsights' unicorn database. We looked into their business models to identify those that rely mainly on ecosystem business models. Among this group, we identified 152 ecosystem contributor companies. The systematic data set from these two sources was complemented by insights from 74 additional contributor plays by both established and startup companies. The resulting total number of nearly 300 analyzed ecosystem contributors was well balanced in terms of geography, industry, maturity, company size, and ownership. We further validated our findings with more than 20 interviews with founders and managers.

Select the Right Ecosystem to Join

The first step in a good contributor strategy is to select the right ecosystem to join. We identified three important considerations: pick a winning ecosystem, scrutinize its governance model, and ensure a good strategic fit.

Competition between ecosystems is frequently characterized by winner-take-all-or-most dynamics because direct or indirect network effects increase the advantage of the leading players and make it difficult for laggards to catch up. Contributors should thus carefully assess the competitive positions of the ecosystems they consider joining and pick those with a high likelihood of being among the winners in their respective domains. To this end, they should scrutinize the value proposition of potential candidates, their overall design and scalability, the strength of other contributors, their ability to defend their position against existing and new competitors, and their social legitimacy.

As we have shown in previous research, the specific metrics to assess the health of an ecosystem depend on its stage in the life cycle (see Chapter 5). For example, during the launch phase of an ecosystem, the red flags that contributors should look for include frequent changes in the core value proposition, essential partners not joining the ecosystem, and the wrong users subverting its value proposition. During the scale phase, the red flags could be persistent imbalances between participants on both sides of the market, declining quality indicators, or increasing complexity of the operating model. And during the mature phase, declining engagement levels of customers, decamping early adopters, or aggressive competition from copycats or niche competitors could be signs that contributors should stay away.

The second important consideration is the governance model of a candidate ecosystem because it will largely determine how attractive the ecosystem is for the contributor (see Chapter 6). Ecosystem governance should be transparent, consistent, fair, and predictable. Due diligence should include the following questions:

- How well do the purpose and culture of the ecosystem resonate with your own values and preferences?
- Are commitments required (exclusivity, for example, or ecosystem-specific investments) that could limit your future flexibility?
- Do you have the transparency and decision rights to understand and influence the development of the ecosystem?
- To what extent do regulations for input, process, and output control limit your access to customers and your freedom to operate?
- Are regulations in place that ensure that you benefit in a fair way from the data, intellectual property, and value that you contribute to the ecosystem?

Moreover, contributors should assess the risk that the orchestrator will misuse its position of power. We will return to this question when we discuss how to avoid being commoditized.

As a final consideration for selecting the right ecosystem to join, contributors should make sure that the ecosystem serves their strategic priorities. To this end, contributors need to be clear about what they want to achieve by entering an ecosystem. For example, they may pursue an ecosystem model to react to a new competitive threat, to gain access to new market segments, to enhance an existing offering, or to create new business opportunities. Depending on the specific strategic objective, certain ecosystems may be better partners than others.

In this context, contributors should also consider their own potential position in the targeted ecosystem. An ecosystem may be more attractive to join if the contributor faces only limited competition in the segment that it wants to serve, if it can establish a unique selling proposition in the ecosystem, or if it has a competitive advantage due to the specific design of the ecosystem. For example, the insurance group Axa achieved an exclusive agreement with the ridesharing platform BlaBlaCar to develop an insurance offer for members of the BlaBlaCar ecosystem.

Most likely, no single ecosystem will meet all criteria, so it is also a question of tradeoffs and priorities. The tradeoffs may be resolved by joining more than one ecosystem and multihoming.

Define the Right Level of Engagement

To determine the right level of engagement in an ecosystem, contributors need to consider two questions: Should they exclusively commit to one ecosystem or multihome in multiple ecosystems at the same time? And should they bring the full breadth of their offering to the ecosystem or only certain products and services, reserving others for alternative sales channels? For example, a restaurant owner may decide to participate in one or multiple online food delivery platforms, and she may offer her full menu or only selected dishes on the platform.

Exclusive commitment to one ecosystem brings some clear benefits. It allows a contributor to strategically focus its efforts, limit the complexity of its operating model, and realize economies of scale. This may be particularly relevant in solution ecosystems that have a high need for co-specialization and co-innovation. For example, in the early days of the microcomputer, Intel and Microsoft deliberately focused their research and development efforts on the IBM PC ecosystem, rather than attempting to also contribute to competing platforms such as Apple's.

Temporary exclusive commitment can also be a good way to test, learn, and refine an ecosystem play. For example, McDonald's opted to introduce food delivery service through exclusive platform agreements so it could pilot the right approach through close cooperation. Once the model was proved and tested, the fast-food giant started to also join competing delivery ecosystems.

Many orchestrators incentivize their complementors for exclusive commitment and offer rewards or privileges in exchange, such as lower fees, additional services, access to privileged information, prominent positioning on the website, or even the right of exclusive offering in a certain category.

The toy retailer Toys "R" Us highlighted the risk of such an exclusive commitment when it entered the Amazon ecosystem. In 2000, the company gave up its efforts to establish its own online presence and announced a partnership with Amazon in which Amazon would create a Toys "R" Us site on Amazon.com and handle all e-commerce activities for the company, including order fulfillment. Toys "R" Us executives believed they would be the exclusive toy seller on Amazon. When they noticed that competitors were also selling toys on Amazon, they terminated the partnership. However, the resulting delay in development of a robust e-commerce strategy contributed to the company's bankruptcy in 2017.

The alternative to exclusive commitment is to multihome and participate in more than one ecosystem at the same time. In this way, contributors can not only hedge their bets by limiting their exposure to any individual ecosystem but also reach a wider customer base and improve their strategic flexibility to react to changes in competition, customer demand, or technology. Moreover, by limiting their dependency on any single platform, they may be able to negotiate better deals with the ecosystem orchestrator and capture more of the value they contribute. For example, the video games company Electronic Arts (EA) develops games for all major consoles, including PlayStation, Xbox, and Nintendo Switch, which increases its bargaining power with the platforms and allows it to achieve profitability levels comparable to those of successful console providers.[4]

For most ecosystem suppliers, multihoming is a strategic imperative. Suppliers of generic products or services frequently serve not only multiple competing ecosystems but also different verticals – such as sensor manufacturers that supply all kinds of IoT ecosystems, or logistics providers that are active on all kinds of marketplaces. The insurance startup Zego provides special on-demand insurance for a range of ride-hailing and delivery ecosystems (among them

---

4 Comparing EA's average operating margins with the weighted average operating margins of Sony Game & Network Services and Nintendo, based on official annual reports over the 2016–2020 period. No profitability figures are publicly available for Microsoft's gaming division.

Uber, Deliveroo, and Stuart). We could find no examples of successful suppliers that restricted themselves to only one ecosystem. The payment services provider Billpoint failed after it was acquired by eBay, taken offline, and integrated into eBay's auction platform. eBay learned from this failure – after the acquisition of PayPal, it kept PayPal operating as a generic payment service for all kinds of online transactions, targeting all marketplaces.

For the second question, about the scope of the offering that is contributed to an ecosystem, similar considerations apply. Offering the full portfolio can improve focus and economies of scale and reduce operational complexity. On the other hand, restricting the ecosystem offering to certain products or services may limit exposure and dependency while improving strategic flexibility and bargaining position. For example, an effective strategy for sellers on a digital marketplace can be to use the platform as a showroom to test products and get access to new customers to direct them to their own website or other sales channels.[5] A recent study found that book publishers that participated in the Kindle ecosystem included only about half of their printed book portfolios in their e-book portfolios. They used the ecosystem mainly to offer their high-demand products as e-books and to benefit from logistics savings. Larger publishers withheld their most profitable books to safeguard them from appropriation by the platform.[6]

Stand Out Against Other Contributors

Competition within an ecosystem is different from competition in an open market because the rules of ecosystem competition are defined largely by the orchestrator, and they can change over time. For example, the orchestrator may initially restrict competition for certain complementors by limiting access to the ecosystem, but then at a later stage decide to open up the governance model. Moreover, the dynamics of coopetition in an ecosystem – partners collaborating to create value but competing to divide the value – establish new sources of competitive advantage, such as strong relationships with the orchestrator and other contributors and the ability to capitalize on the functionality of the ecosystem and adapt to changing ecosystem governance.

---

5 A. Hagiu and J. Wright, "Don't let platforms commoditize your business," *Harvard Business Review*, May 2021.
6 R.D. Wang and C.D. Miller, "Complementors' engagement in an ecosystem: a study of publishers' e-book offerings on Amazon Kindle," *Strategic Management Journal*, 2020 (41), 3–26.

Some of the structural positions in an ecosystem are more attractive than others because they can serve as control points. For starters, it helps to contribute a component to the ecosystem that is not optional (such as travel insurance on a booking platform) but essential for the ecosystem to function or to deliver its full value proposition (such as payment services on a digital marketplace). Contributors that offer such components can benefit from their central position in the network because other contributors depend on their cooperation.

Contributors that provide physical access to an ecosystem occupy an even stronger control point. They profit from directly interacting with the customer and frequently influence the functionality of the overall solution. For example, handset manufacturers in smartphone ecosystems specify near-field-communication (NFC) standards for payment functions and decide whether to provide fingerprint screeners for identity verification.

Finally, contributors should look for bottlenecks, those components that limit the performance, growth, or innovation of the ecosystem. Bottlenecks can shift over time and require a dynamic strategy. For example, IoT ecosystems were initially limited by the number of devices and sensors providing data; later, data aggregation and processing became the bottleneck; today, connectivity seems to be the limiting factor.

Occupying such control points can be very attractive for ecosystem contributors because it increases their value added to the ecosystem and, at the same time, improves their bargaining position to capture this value. However, contributors must be aware that they will likely compete with the ecosystem orchestrator for these control points. The large tech players and platform providers themselves are increasingly offering the complements that are essential for the ecosystem (payment services, cloud infrastructure), controlling access (devices, app stores), and representing bottlenecks (fulfillment services, connectivity).

Beyond occupying control points, what strategies can ecosystem contributors use to stand out against competitors? We analyzed all 152 startup firms with an ecosystem contributor strategy that reached unicorn status over the past five years and identified five successful strategies:

1. **Become a category leader.** Roughly one quarter (26%) of contributors beat their ecosystem rivals by focusing on one category and offering a product or service that outperformed those of their rivals in terms of quality or price. In this way, the French game developer Voodoo came to dominate the category of "hypercasual games" for iOS and Android, achieving 5 billion downloads and 300 million monthly active users.
2. **Dominate a niche.** Among contributor unicorns, 18% succeeded by differentiating their offering and catering to a specific, narrow customer segment. The California-based software company Calm reached a $2 billion

valuation by focusing on sleep issues within the crowded segment of meditation apps.

3. **Create a new category.** Identifying an unmet customer need and establishing an entirely new subcategory is a more challenging but potentially very rewarding strategy. Only 16% of contributor unicorns accomplished this. The financial services company Robinhood was the first to offer commission-free trades of stocks and exchange-traded funds via a mobile app, and it achieved a pre-IPO valuation of a whopping $40 billion.

4. **Collaborate within a subset.** More than a third (35%) of contributor unicorns harnessed the network structure of an ecosystem by connecting a subset of complementors and tightly cooperating with them. Zapier, for example, provides workflows to automatically coordinate the operation of more than 3,000 web applications, allowing consumers to integrate the apps they use. This strategy is widely used among contributors to cloud platforms.

5. **Exploit the ecosystem mechanics.** A small group (5%) of contributor unicorns based their success on deeply understanding the functionality of an ecosystem and tailoring their operating model to exploit it. For example, Thrasio became one of the fastest growing unicorns in our sample by acquiring successful Amazon third-party private-label businesses from small owners and integrating them into its proprietary operating platform to optimize and scale them for performance on the Amazon marketplace.

Avoid Being Commoditized by the Orchestrator

One of the biggest fears of ecosystem contributors is that of being commoditized by the orchestrator. Indeed, orchestrators of successful ecosystems may be tempted to increase their own value capture at the expense of their partners, particularly if their platform has achieved a leading market position and partners increasingly depend on it.

For example, orchestrators sometimes alter the rules of the ecosystem in their favor by changing fees or prices, adapting ranking or matching algorithms, and restricting access to resources or information. They interfere with free competition by restricting competitive differentiation or by privileging certain players. Some orchestrators even directly compete with their contributors and integrate complementor offerings into the core platform or imitate their lucrative products or services, often exploiting the privileged information they possess as platform operators.

What can ecosystem contributors do to protect themselves against such threats? As a start, they need to set the right strategic course, as discussed above, select the proper ecosystem to join, limit their dependency, and offer a superior product or service.

Second, innovation is a key to ongoing differentiation. It can even bring seemingly invincible platform orchestrators to their knees, as Google Chrome did in winning the browser war in the Windows ecosystem against the incumbent Internet Explorer. Some successful contributors prevent commoditization by linking their R&D agenda to the orchestrator's innovation roadmap, as did many software partners in the SAP ecosystem.

Shazam, the sound recognition app, illustrates the importance of developing and protecting intellectual property. Its algorithm was already developed at the turn of the century and launched as a service in 2002. After the advent of the smartphone, Shazam became one of the most downloaded apps of all time. In 2014, Apple integrated Shazam into its virtual assistant Siri, but Shazam managed to protect its technological edge against all competitive attacks until it was finally acquired by Apple in 2018 for a reported $400 million.

A third success factor in avoiding commoditization is to secure ongoing direct access to customers and their granular data. This is the only way to deepen customer relationships, understand their changing needs, and improve the contributor's own offering. For example, having direct customer access and protecting the contributor brand is particularly important in the luxury segment. That is why large marketplaces like Amazon and Alibaba have struggled for many years to attract luxury fashion brands, despite serious attempts to crack down on counterfeit products. In contrast, Farfetch, a retail platform specializing in luxury fashion, offers white-label solutions to luxury brands and retailers to build their own stores and seamlessly interact with their customers.

Many contributors on digital marketplaces – restaurants, hotels, service providers, retailers, and others – are using practices like special discounts and targeted marketing to pull customers to their direct channels. As the underlying technology solutions are increasingly commoditized and offered by external vendors such as Shopify, contributors are given the chance to run their own webshops while still maintaining their presence on the leading platforms.

As a last resort, contributors that think that they are being taken advantage of by their orchestrator must be ready to fight back, which can even include lobbying the regulator, mobilizing public support, or initiating legal action. For example, Spotify, Epic Games, and others have established the Coalition for App Fairness to fight what they perceive as unfair practices by the large app stores. As a result, both Apple and Google rethought some of their policies and, for example, halved the fees for the first $1 million in revenue from sales of apps and in-app purchases each year.

Know When It Is Time to Leave the Ecosystem

Joining a business ecosystem need not be a decision that holds for life. Contributors should regularly review the decision and be open to reversing it. Several indicators suggest that leaving an ecosystem should be seriously considered.

– **Risk of brand damage.** If the contributor's brand is at risk, the long-term costs of being part of an ecosystem can be much higher than the short-term benefits. For example, Nike never managed to curb the sale of counterfeit or gray market products on the Amazon marketplace. Because of this, in November 2019, Nike decided to leave the platform and focus instead on a small number of retail partners to keep full control of its brand. Brand risks can also emerge if the negative image of an ecosystem impinges on its contributors. For instance, in 2017, following a Wall Street Journal report on how YouTube had failed to act against ads appearing next to hateful and offensive content, several advertisers, among them Walmart, PepsiCo, and Starbucks, decided to boycott the platform. Only after serious steps made by Google to better monitor content did the companies return.

– **Competitive discrimination.** If the orchestrator is not able to ensure fair competition within the ecosystem, or even if it systematically favors some contributors over others, the alarm bells should ring. Early on, Microsoft appeared to alienate both HTC and Samsung as partners in its mobile operating ecosystem by seemingly favoring Nokia through a strategic partnership in 2011. Following the acquisition of the former mobile-phone giant in 2014, neither HTC nor Samsung released any new phones supporting Windows Mobile. Samsung even entered a legal battle with Microsoft, claiming that their previous agreement was void because of this deal.

– **Erosion of trust.** Business ecosystems are built on mutual trust, and lack of trust and erosion of trust are major causes of ecosystem failure. A perceived breach of trust can make contributors leave an ecosystem, as in the exclusivity conflict between Toys "R" Us and Amazon described above. A gradual erosion of trust should also serve as a warning sign. In particular, if the orchestrator misuses its power and claims a disproportionate share of the value that is created by the ecosystem, relationships and culture may become toxic, and contributors should consider leaving.

– **Better alternatives.** Finally, canny contributors always look out for better alternatives to the existing ecosystem. New winners – ecosystems with a better strategy, better governance, or better strategic fit – may emerge. Even building your own ecosystem can be an attractive option. The task is becoming much easier as more and more companies offer supporting services. For example, Mirakl, a cloud-based software company that recently joined the unicorn club, has helped hundreds of players in a variety of industries set up their own marketplaces.

However, leaving an ecosystem should not be an unmindful decision. Being partners in a business ecosystem means supporting each other, fighting together, and winning together. Even if a contributor eventually does not leave the ecosystem, having signaled its willingness to do so may strengthen its position and resolve or improve some of the issues identified. In the end, when an ecosystem is in true decline, a company in the contributor role can exercise one of that role's benefits and easily jump ship.

Business ecosystems will continue to be on the rise in many sectors and geographies. Companies that want to benefit from this trend must understand that they do not necessarily need to be orchestrators of their own ecosystems. Being a complementor or supplier to an ecosystem can be just as attractive – and it brings some additional benefits. To succeed in such a contributor role, as Figure 8.3 summarizes, companies need to select the right ecosystem to join, define the right level of engagement, stand out against other contributors, avoid being commoditized by the orchestrator, and recognize when it is time to leave the ecosystem.

Select the right ecosystem to join	Define the right level of engagement	Stand out against other contributors	Avoid being commoditized by the orchestrator	Know when it is time to leave the ecosystem
Pick a winning ecosystem	Benefits of exclusivity and full commitment · Strategic focus	Occupy control points · Essentials · Access · Bottlenecks	Set the right strategic course	Risk of brand damage
Scrutinize the governance model	· Limited complexity · Economies of scale · Privileges	Beat the competition · Become a category leader	Ensure ongoing innovation	Competitive discrimination
Ensure a good strategic fit	Benefits of limited commitment and multihoming · Hedging of risk · Wider reach · Strategic flexibility · Bargaining power	· Dominate a niche · Create a new category · Collaborate within a subset · Exploit ecosystem mechanics	Secure direct access to customers	Erosion of trust
			Be ready to fight back	Better alternatives

Source: BCG Henderson Institute

Figure 8.3: Imperatives to Succeed in Being an Ecosystem Complementor or Supplier.

Ulrich Pidun, Martin Reeves, and Balázs Zoletnik

Chapter 9
What Is Your Business Ecosystem Strategy?

From media and technology to energy and mining – no major industry is untouched by the rise of business ecosystems. These dynamic groups of largely independent economic players working together to deliver solutions that they couldn't muster on their own come in two flavors: *transaction ecosystems* in which a central platform links two sides of a market, such as buyers and sellers on a digital marketplace; and *solution ecosystems* in which a core firm orchestrates the offerings of several complementors, such as product manufacturers in a smart-home ecosystem. Both types can quickly generate eye-popping valuations: since 2015, more than 300 ecosystem startups have reached unicorn status.

Given the success of this cohort of startups, as well as the Big Tech ecosystem players now numbered among the world's most valuable companies, it's no surprise that ecosystems are high on the strategic agendas of incumbent companies. More than half of the S&P Global 100 companies are already engaged in one or more ecosystems, and in a recent BCG survey of 206 executives in multinational companies, 90% indicated that their companies planned to expand their activities in this field. Yet many leaders of incumbent companies are still unsure how to define their ecosystem strategies. This chapter aims to help them in that pursuit. It is informed by the insights we've gleaned from three years of ecosystem research and engagements with large enterprises across industries and geographies. Organized in eight fundamental questions, it offers a step-by-step framework for developing a company's ecosystem strategy (Figure 9.1).

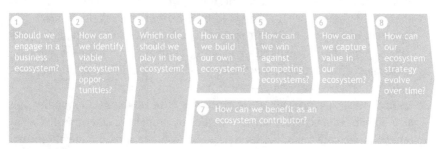

Source: BCG Henderson Institute

Figure 9.1: Step-by-Step Framework to Develop a Company's Ecosystem Strategy.

https://doi.org/10.1515/9783110775167-009

1 Should We Engage in a Business Ecosystem?

Startups and tech companies are not the only kinds of companies that can benefit from ecosystems. Incumbent firms also use ecosystem-based business models
to create value. In financial services, for instance, DBS in Singapore, Sberbank in
Russia, and PingAn in China developed successful ecosystems and were re-
warded with outsized shareholder returns, outperforming their local peers by
more than a factor of two between 2015 and 2020.

Ecosystems are not a slam dunk, however. They are expensive and risky to
launch, and most of them fail. We found that fewer than 15% of ecosystems are
sustainable over the long run. Moreover, when we investigated value creation at
more than 50 of the largest banks between 2015 and 2020, we found no significant correlation between ecosystem engagement and total shareholder return.

The motivational impetus behind an ecosystem is a foundational element
in a successful strategy (see Chapter 2). Before you embark on an ecosystem ad-
venture, you must be very clear why you want to take the risk and what specifically you want to achieve. We've identified five sound motivations for creating
or joining an ecosystem:

1. **Expand market access for existing offerings.** Ecosystems can open new
   sales channels for existing products or services. This is why many appli-
   ance manufacturers, for example, joined smart-home ecosystems.
2. **Strengthen the core business through complements.** Ecosystem partners can provide products and services that add value to a company's core
   offering. This is why video game console manufacturers established ecosystems of game developers.
3. **Protect the core business from other ecosystems.** Engaging in an ecosystem can be an effective defense against threats from adjacent ecosystems. Several agrochemical companies have engaged in smart-farming
   ecosystems to defend their seed, fertilizer, and crop protection businesses
   against the competitive threats posed by precision-farming platforms.
4. **Tap revenue pools adjacent to the core business.** Ecosystem partners
   can help a company expand its existing business into adjacent markets.
   Some banks, for example, build ecosystems to expand their mortgage business into broader real estate services.
5. **Launch new ventures separate from the core business.** Companies can
   also benefit from ecosystem opportunities by launching new ventures separate from the core business, for the purposes of learning, financial returns,
   or diversification. Allianz X, the German insurance giant's investment arm,
   has built up a portfolio of companies, over two-thirds of which rely on ecosystem business models.

If one of these motivations resonates with the priorities of your company, and if you are ready to invest for the long run, experiment, fail, and learn, you should seriously investigate the ecosystem opportunity. If multiple motivations apply, choose the one that is associated with your highest priorities, because your primary objective will shape your answers to subsequent strategic questions and decisions.

2 How Can We Identify Viable Ecosystem Opportunities?

Every successful ecosystem is based on a compelling value proposition – it solves a concrete business problem. Thus, the proper starting point in the search for ecosystem opportunities is an outside-in market perspective, not an inside-out view dictated by a company's existing assets and capabilities.

The most effective way to identify a viable ecosystem opportunity is to examine the customer journey and identify market frictions – frustrations, unmet needs, and unfulfilled desires – that are too big or complex to be solved by one company alone. It is important to focus on frictions that represent substantial problems for customers or suppliers and correspondingly large opportunities to justify the investment and effort required to build a successful ecosystem. Frictions that are indicative of such opportunities include:

- **Fragmented Demand.** Ecosystem platforms are well suited to aggregate the demand of many small customers and make them accessible to suppliers in an economically viable way. For example, online food delivery platforms provide restaurants with easy access to a highly fragmented base of potential customers.
- **Fragmented Supply.** Platforms can aggregate the offerings of a large number of small-scale suppliers to facilitate the search and transaction process for potential buyers. Alibaba's initial success came from providing large companies with access to small and medium-size Chinese suppliers that had previously been difficult to identify and contact.
- **Matching Problem.** Platforms can enable real-time matching of the two sides of a market and ensure a deal. Ride-hailing platforms address this friction by identifying the driver best positioned to serve a given rider and facilitating the transaction.
- **Lack of Trust.** Business ecosystems can establish the transactional trust required when partners don't know each other and are vulnerable to fraud or misbehavior. By vetting guests and securing payments, Airbnb creates the trust necessary for owners to invite perfect strangers into their homes.

- **Lack of Supplier Coordination.** Ecosystems can enable the delivery of coherent customer solutions that require the intricate coordination of various independent suppliers of products or services. John Deere's smart farming platform coordinates suppliers of seeds, fertilizers, crop protection, equipment, and agronomic and weather data to help farmers become more productive.
- **Lack of Co-Innovation.** Sometimes the resolution of a friction requires multiple innovations by companies from different domains that must be closely aligned to achieve their full impact. For example, Intel removed performance bottlenecks in the personal computer industry by orchestrating an ecosystem of PC component developers and their innovations through the Intel Architecture Lab.

Once you identify an attractive market opportunity and value proposition, ask yourself whether an ecosystem is the best way to deliver the solution. Typically, ecosystems work best when solutions feature high levels of modularity with easily and flexibly combined components and require high levels of coordination to identify and match partners, align innovation activities, or manage interfaces. Otherwise, other business models, such as vertically integrated organizations, hierarchical supply chains, or open-market models, may be better choices.

If the opportunity is attractive and suitable for an ecosystem solution, consider if your company has a right to play and to win. What can you contribute to the solution? Do you have essential assets and capabilities that can serve as a jump-off point for building an ecosystem? Do you own underutilized assets (such as data) that could be of value in someone else's ecosystem? But don't let your existing capabilities fully dictate your strategic choices. If the opportunity is right, it may justify building or acquiring the required capabilities, or finding partners to close the gaps. As Hannah and Eisenhardt observed, "Perhaps in complex strategic settings like ecosystems, strategy is more consequential than initial capabilities."[1]

3 Which Role Should We Play in the Ecosystem?

Too often, when large incumbent players see an ecosystem opportunity, they automatically assume that they should lead the ecosystem as its orchestrator. When unexamined, this assumption can blind companies to two realities: (1) there are

---

[1] D.P. Hannah and K.M. Eisenhardt, "How firms navigate cooperation and competition in nascent ecosystems," *Strategic Management Journal*, 2018.

other ecosystem roles that may be more desirable and profitable than orchestrator, and (2) a company can play different roles in different ecosystems.

Besides orchestrators, there are two types of ecosystem contributors: complementors and suppliers. Complementors directly provide customers with products or services that enhance the value of other components of an ecosystem. Suppliers operate upstream (and at arm's length from customers) by providing products or services to orchestrators and complementors.

If strong and attractive existing ecosystems are already present in the domain you've identified, consider whether you can achieve your strategic objectives by joining one or more of them as a contributor. But don't stop there. Also consider the tradeoffs among ecosystem roles.

Orchestrators are in a position of power as the rule maker, gatekeeper, allocator of profits, and judge and jury of the ecosystem, but they also must shoulder the high upfront investment and the risk entailed in launching it. Contributors are exposed to risks, too. There are the uncertainties associated with a lack of control over the orchestrator related to the scope, composition, operations, and governance of the ecosystem, as well as risks related to sharing critical data and access to customers. But contributors typically have lower upfront costs than orchestrators and can choose among competing ecosystems, or even limit their exposure and increase their strategic flexibility by participating in more than one ecosystem at the same time. Our research shows that the contributor role can be as financially rewarding as the orchestrator role, or even more so. Startup companies and their investors seem to have realized this already. For many years, the share of ecosystem contributors among new unicorns has been on the rise, and in 2019 they surpassed the number of ecosystem orchestrators for the first time.

If you decide to go for the orchestrator role, confirm that you are properly positioned and have the capabilities needed to succeed. There are four qualification requirements for ecosystem orchestrators. First, the orchestrator needs to be an essential member of the ecosystem and have control over critical resources, such as a strong brand, customer access, or key skills. Second, the orchestrator should occupy a central position in the ecosystem network and have linkages to many players and the ability to coordinate them effectively. Third, the orchestrator must be able to shoulder the generally large upfront investments and risk required to realize high net financial benefits from the ecosystem. Finally, the orchestrator should be perceived by the system contributors as a fair partner, not a competitive threat. You cannot unilaterally choose to be the orchestrator; you must be accepted by the other players in the ecosystem.

If your analysis suggests that your company is not fully qualified for the orchestrator role, you can consider co-orchestrating the ecosystem with other companies, including direct competitors. The Here geolocation platform is owned by a consortium of major German auto manufacturers, among other investors. Alternatively, you can orchestrate an ecosystem as a cooperative with other contributors, such as the artist-owned stock photography and video platform Stocksy United. (But don't underestimate the challenges of managing the additional layer of governance in a consortium, which can be a material burden when fast decisions and flexible adaptation are needed.)

4 How Can We Build Our Own Ecosystem?

If building a traditional business is like constructing a single-family home, building an ecosystem is akin to constructing a mixed-use development, with all the additional complexity, coordination, interaction, and emergent outcomes that implies. Our research revealed six critical success factors that you need to get right in the design of your ecosystem to increase your odds of being among the 15% of ecosystems that survive in the long run (see Chapter 4).

1. Ensure that essential partners join. You cannot force partners to join your ecosystem. Instead, you must convince them to join by offering them a compelling set of benefits and incentives. In addition to a clear customer value proposition, this demands an appealing value proposition for contributors to the ecosystem. Better Place, which launched an innovative ecosystem solution to battery rental and replacement for electric vehicles, learned this lesson the hard way. It shut down after six years and $900 million of funding because it was unable to convince leading car manufacturers to join.[2]

2. Establish the right governance model. Our analysis of 110 failed ecosystems found that weaknesses in governance are the single most common cause of failure, accounting for more than a third of the cases. The governance model must establish the proper level of openness by balancing open elements (which attract partners, stimulate growth, and enable innovation) and closed elements (which ensure consistent quality and alignment) (see Chapter 7). Publishers refused to join Sony's e-reader platform because they believed that its openness did not sufficiently protect their copyrights. Instead, they opted for Amazon's Kindle and its very closed platform that loaded content only from Amazon and precluded users from transferring books to other devices, printers, and readers. On the other hand, overly closed governance may choke an ecosystem's growth, as experienced by the BlackBerry in its competition with the iPhone.

---

2 R. Adner, *The Wide Len* (New York: Penguin Group), 2012.

3. Focus on scale before scope. In the traditional approach to innovation, a new product or service is developed to its full scope, tested in a pilot market, and subsequently rolled out to full scale. Successful business ecosystems follow a different path. They start with a clear value proposition of limited scope and focus on building scale before expanding the scope of the offering. LinkedIn started as a pure-play social network aimed at connecting professionals through simple profiles. It didn't add online recruiting, advanced messaging features, and a publishing platform until it had established a broad network of active users. In contrast, General Electric struggled to establish Predix as a leading IoT platform partly because it lacked focus and tried to be everything to everyone at once.

4. Solve the chicken-or-egg problem. One of the biggest conundrums that companies face when launching ecosystems is the chicken-or-egg problem of securing sufficient participation of both customers and contributors. The key to solving it is to identify and subsidize whichever side of the market must be developed in order to achieve critical mass. Several early restaurant reservation platforms failed because they tried to attract restaurants by charging them little or no fees and, instead, charged diners for the service. Diners balked, and when the platforms couldn't fill seats, so did the restaurants. OpenTable succeeded by attracting a critical mass of diners with no fee and charging restaurants for filling seats.

5. Create three flywheels. The secret sauce in the design of many successful business ecosystems is three mutually reinforcing flywheels (Figure 9.2). The *growth flywheel* is based on indirect network effects and bolsters the value of

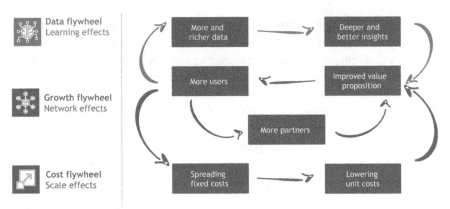

Source: BCG Henderson Institute

Figure 9.2: The Three Flywheels of Successful Business Ecosystem Design.

the ecosystem to orchestrators and contributors as the number of customers grows, and vice versa. The *data flywheel* is based on learning effects and taps user growth to generate more and richer data, which in turn is used to improve the value proposition and attract more users. The *cost flywheel* is based on economies of scale and uses ecosystem growth to spread fixed costs and lower unit costs to generate more growth. All three flywheels are essential; consider the many ride-hailing platforms that created effective growth and data flywheels but struggled to activate the cost flywheel and thus accumulated losses.

6. Ensure social acceptance. A number of successful ecosystem players have recently experienced substantial backlash from consumers, partners, competitors, and regulators. In order to build social capital and secure social legitimacy, orchestrators must establish an ecosystem governance model that is consistent and fair. Consistency means that the mechanisms of governance are transparent and easy to understand, comprehensive, internally consistent, and stable over time. Fairness means that governance complies with local laws and norms, avoids biases (for example, in data algorithms and access), and engenders trust among participants. An ecosystem can only prosper in the long run if it creates tangible value and distributes it in a fair manner among its participants.

5 How Can We Win Against Competing Ecosystems?

Ecosystem competition differs from conventional market competition in three ways. First, boundaries are fuzzier with ecosystems. Market borders become fluid as expanding ecosystems follow customer needs. Automakers find themselves competing with tech players for mobility solutions, and banks find themselves competing with e-commerce retailers for payment services. Corporate borders become less relevant as the competitive context shifts from products and companies to the broader context of ecosystems. As CEO Stephen Elop rightly observed in a 2011 speech to Nokia's employees: "Our competitors aren't taking our market share with devices; they are taking our market share with an entire ecosystem!"[3]

---

3 C. Arthur, "Nokia's chief executive to staff: 'we are standing on a burning platform,'" *The Guardian*, February 9, 2011.

Second, ecosystems must compete for contributors as well as customers. In addition to a compelling customer value proposition, they need a powerful contributor value proposition, as well as the ability to strike a nuanced balance between collaboration (to grow the pie) and competition (to divide the pie). Also required is the willingness to give up full strategic control and accept that ecosystem strategies, even more than traditional competitive strategies, are to some extent emergent and may pivot from time to time.

Third, ecosystem competition is frequently winner-take-all or winner-take-most. Network, learning, and scale effects bolster the competitive advantage of the leading ecosystems and make it ever more difficult for other ecosystems to catch up. This suggests that there is a first-mover advantage that is less about being the first in the market and more about being the first with a complete solution. Apple's iPod was not the first digital music player, but it was the first to offer a comprehensive solution by combining the hardware product with the iTunes music management software.

While some aspects of competition are different in an ecosystem context, others are the same. Ecosystems still need to differentiate themselves from their competitors. Orchestrators can use the architecture and technology of their platforms, data analytics frameworks and algorithms, and their governance model to differentiate along three dimensions: the scope of the ecosystem, its customer value proposition, and its contributor value proposition.

The *scope of the ecosystem* answers the timeless strategic question of where to play. Which market segments and geographies will you target? Niche plays can succeed when some customers have divergent needs that are not fully served by mass solutions or when they develop a yen for more sophisticated solutions. Thus, we see Uber and Lyft competing head-on in the mass market for ride-hailing, while their competitors Wingz, HopSkipDrive, and Veyo focus on airport transfers, small children, and non-emergency medical transports, respectively. Geographically focused models can succeed when local network effects or network density is more important than network size, as it is for platforms that focus on well-defined neighborhoods.

The *customer value proposition* is part of the answer to the strategic question of how to play. In ecosystems, one of the major tradeoffs in the customer value proposition is between an emphasis on the scale and breadth of the offering and an emphasis on the quality of the customer experience. The used-fashion platform Poshmark focuses on expanding its offering by setting very few boundaries for sellers and driving engagement and social interaction among platform participants. By contrast, its competitor ThredUp focuses on customer experience and quality by actively curating and positioning products on the platform.

A strong focus on customer experience typically requires a higher investment in areas such as enhanced platform functionality, curation processes, and additional services. Ecosystems that pursue this strategy can compete in ways that can be difficult for competitors to match without jeopardizing their core business model. When Google launched Google Maps on Android, TomTom, the leading location technology provider at that time, managed to avoid head-to-head competition by refocusing its customer value proposition, emphasizing transparency of data usage, which enhanced its appeal to major car manufacturers, ride-hailing service providers, and mobile operating systems. Google could not follow without jeopardizing its core business model of data monetization.[4]

The *contributor value proposition*, which defines the ecosystem's desired contributors and what they will receive in return for their participation, provides the second part of the answer to the question of how to play. The governance model of the ecosystem is an important source of competitive advantage here (see Chapter 7). An open model makes it easy for contributors to join and offers them greater freedom, while a closed model limits internal competition and enables strong alignment among contributors. Both approaches can be successful, as seen in the video game industry where Nintendo adopted rather strict quality controls and quantity limitations for externally developed games and Microsoft Xbox offered external game developers a good deal more freedom.

We've seen that the development of an ecosystem is strongly path dependent and that early governance decisions can significantly change its trajectory and future position. Thus, many successful ecosystems started with rather closed governance (to control quality and behavior and avoid a vacuum that contributors could fill) and became more open over time. However, new entrants to ecosystem competition are frequently forced to start with a more open governance model to quickly gain scale and catch up with their more established competitors.

Of course, positioning an ecosystem on the three dimensions of competitive differentiation does not represent dichotomous choices – the dimensions are more like spectrums that contain many potential positions. Moreover, the combination of the dimensions and the way they reinforce each other offer additional opportunities for differentiation. HopSkipDrive focuses its ride-hailing platform on the narrow customer segment of small children. Correspondingly, it emphasizes trust, transparency, and safety in the customer experience (for instance, by publishing regular safety reports and offering real-time tracking of rides). This positioning is further reinforced by a very strict governance model

---

4 R. Adner, *Winning the Right Game* (Boston: The MIT Press), 2021.

that requires drivers to prove their qualifications and pass a detailed background check.

6 How Can We Capture Value in Our Ecosystem?

Numerous platform-based businesses – many of them fueled by cheap venture capital – have achieved impressive revenue growth, market positions, and valuations but are still far from earning profits. And they may be right not to focus too much on profit because in an ecosystem world, the question of value appropriation should not come first. The best way to benefit from an ecosystem is to focus on creating value for the customer. This will increase the total size of the pie and thus the size of your slice. An ecosystem where all participants focus on their own advantage will find it hard to establish the level of cooperation that is required to create some value to distribute in the first place.

Nevertheless, at some point, boards and investors will want to know how the platform owner is going to capture a fair share of the value that is created by and for the ecosystem. For this, it is important to understand the peculiar economics of the ecosystem business model. Most traditional businesses experience diminishing returns; as the number of customers grows, the value per customer declines, naturally limiting the economically viable size of the business. In contrast, most business ecosystems enjoy increasing returns – driven by network and learning effects, the value per customer increases as additional customers join the ecosystem. This enables many ecosystems to benefit from exponential growth and winner-take-all or winner-take-most dynamics.

There is a dark side to the story, however. An exponential growth profile also implies that it may take a long time before the ecosystem reaches the tipping point and really takes off. Accordingly, platform owners tend to wait and hope that they will eventually reach the tipping point, so if they fail, they fail late, after spending substantial amounts of money. This makes ecosystems an investment with potentially high returns, but also with high risks. Many venture capitalists are attracted by this profile, but it is much harder for most incumbent firms.

For orchestrators, this economic profile is even more pronounced than it is for contributors. The orchestrator is the residual-claim holder of the ecosystem. While it has a big influence on the distribution of the value created, it must also make sure that all players earn enough to keep them on board. In return, the orchestrator can retain the residual profit, which may eventually be very high but is negative for an extended period. By comparison, a contributor role offers lower upside potential at a lower risk.

Orchestrators must consider two levels of value capture. They must monetize the benefits that the ecosystem creates for its participants (ecosystem monetization), and they must distribute the value among its participants (value distribution).

In terms of *ecosystem monetization*, the orchestrator must balance three competing objectives: (1) maximizing the size of the pie; (2) enabling essential contributors to earn enough profit to ensure their ongoing participation; and (3) capturing its own fair share of the value. To achieve this, the orchestrator must decide whom to charge and what to charge for from a wide range of options. For example, it could charge all participants or charge only one side of the market while subsidizing the other side, or it could offer reduced charges for particularly price-sensitive customers. Similarly, the orchestrator could demand an access fee, licensing fee, transaction fee, or revenue share, or it could monetize the ecosystem through the sale of supplementary products or services, or through advertising revenues.

In general, ecosystem monetization should not stifle the growth of the ecosystem; it should encourage and incentivize participation. This can be achieved, for example, by charging for transactions versus access, subsidizing the side of the market that is less willing to participate, and/or offering rebates for increased usage and rewards for recruiting new participants. Moreover, monetization efforts should be directed at overcoming bottlenecks in the ecosystem and encouraging innovation by, for example, subsidizing bottleneck players and/or lowering prices on new products.

Value distribution, which is regulated by the ecosystem's governance model, can include access to customers, data, and intellectual property, as well as money. The orchestrator can secure its share of the value by harnessing its role as a gatekeeper and occupying critical control points, such as access to customers, essential products or services, and bottlenecks in the system.

Orchestrators can use a variety of strategies to increase their value share. Some improve and extend their offering by integrating their own versions of successful applications developed by complementors, a strategy called "coring."[5] Apple, for instance, launched the screen extension and mirroring feature Sidecar for macOS 13, an application similar to popular apps like Luna and Duet Display. Other orchestrators exploit their knowledge of what is selling well in their marketplaces to offer such products themselves, in direct competition with contributors. Still others attempt to build their share of value by commoditizing

---

5 A. Gawer and M.A. Cusumano, "How companies become platform leaders," *MIT Sloan Management Review*, 2008.

contributors' offerings (creating rules that stimulate more intense competition among them, restricting opportunities for differentiation, controlling pricing, or fostering the entry of new competitors).

Orchestrators should take care not to reach beyond their grasp in the quest for value appropriation or to misuse their power. They must manage the risks of losing the support of their contributors as expressed by increased multihoming (when contributors participate in multiple competing ecosystems), disintermediation (when participants bypass the platform and connect directly), or forking (when contributors exploit the resources of the ecosystem to become direct competitors). Toward this end, orchestrators should continuously monitor the health of their ecosystems (see Chapter 5) and look for red flags, such as declining engagement levels, complaints about predatory behavior, negative coverage in social media, or increases in the number of legal actions filed against the platform.

7 How Can We Benefit as an Ecosystem Contributor?

Not every company is ready, willing, and able to be an ecosystem orchestrator. Indeed, given the vastly greater demand for contributors, it is far more likely that your company will fill that role.

Fortunately, being a contributor can offer as many opportunities as being the orchestrator. Many incumbent firms have successfully followed this path and shared in the success of large ecosystems. Axa launched a first-of-its-kind ridesharing insurance product on the BlaBlaCar platform, and Philips executed on its strategy of becoming the leading lighting expert in the smart-home market by first partnering with Apple and then joining most other smart-home ecosystems as a complementor.

There are five key success factors that contributors need to get right (see Chapter 8).

1. Join the right ecosystem. Contributors should identify ecosystems that are aligned with their strategic priorities. They should assess the competitive position of potential ecosystems to find the one with the highest likelihood of success. Then, they should scrutinize its governance model, paying particular attention to transparency and decision rights, rules that limit access to customers and the freedom to operate, required commitments and investments that may restrict future flexibility, and the design of the data and value sharing plan.

2. Define the right level of engagement. The right level of engagement can be determined by asking two questions:
- Should we commit to just one ecosystem or multihome in several ecosystems?
- Should we bring the full breadth of our offering to the ecosystem or limit it to specific products and services?

A high level of commitment to one ecosystem allows a contributor to strategically focus its efforts, limit the complexity of its operating model, and realize economies of scale. On the other hand, it can maximize exposure to and dependency on the ecosystem and reduce strategic flexibility and bargaining power.

3. Stand out from other contributors. Competition within an ecosystem is different from competition in an open market because the rules of ecosystem competition are largely defined by the orchestrator and can change over time. A contributor can stand out from its internal competitors and improve its bargaining position by occupying control points within an ecosystem – such as essential components, customer access points, and bottlenecks. It can also stand out by enhancing the value it adds to an ecosystem – becoming a category leader, dominating a niche, creating a new category, closely collaborating within a subset of contributors, or finding creative ways to exploit the mechanics of the ecosystem.

4. Avoid being commoditized by the orchestrator. Contributors can avoid commoditization using preventive and defensive measures. To mitigate the chances of such a threat materializing, contributors need to stay innovative and deliver value that orchestrators cannot. They also should secure direct access to customers and their granular data whenever possible. And, if the orchestrator begins to act in ways that commoditize contributors' offerings, the contributors should be ready to resist through lobbying, mobilizing public support, and, if necessary, legal action.

5. Know when it is time to leave. Contributors should regularly review their decision to participate in an ecosystem and be open to reversing it. Indicators that it may be time to seriously consider leaving an ecosystem include a rising risk of brand damage, competitive discrimination, erosion of trust, the decline of the ecosystem, and the emergence of better alternatives. Leaving an ecosystem should not be an unmindful decision – joining an ecosystem should entail a commitment to support and fight for it. But in the end, one of the benefits of being a contributor is not having to go down with the ship.

8 How Can Our Ecosystem Strategy Evolve over Time?

The evolutionary development of ecosystems cannot be predicted. It is an emergent process that is influenced by many factors, such as competition, regulation, the evolving needs of customers, and your resources, underutilized assets, and appetite for risk. Many of the successful ecosystems we studied have pivoted multiple times and in unexpected ways. Indeed, adaptability is one of the major strengths of ecosystems.

Would-be orchestrators should consider the evolutionary possibilities when planning ecosystems because those possibilities can inform the initial design and guide future strategic decision making. In addition, the orchestrators of existing ecosystems should consider their future possibilities as they seek to build and expand. We've identified eight vectors of ecosystem evolution in two categories. The vectors can be pursued individually or in various combinations (Figure 9.3).

The first set of vectors offers options for growing an existing ecosystem:

1. Geographic Expansion. An ecosystem with a global business model can grow by gradually increasing its geographic coverage, as did Airbnb, which, as of June 2021, was active in more than 220 countries and regions. Local business models can also be transferred to additional locations, as did Uber, which started in San Francisco and expanded into 100 new cities within three years.

2. Market Consolidation. Ecosystems can expand their offerings and gain market share through acquisitions. Roll-up strategies aimed at acquiring multiple smaller competitors and consolidating the market are an effective way to compete in a winner-take-all environment, as we've seen in the online food delivery sector.

3. Scope Expansion. The scope of an ecosystem can be expanded by adding new products or services (as LinkedIn did by offering publishing and recruiting services); by transitioning from a pure-play solution or transaction ecosystem to a hybrid (as Airbnb did by inviting providers of supplementary services, such as tour guides and cooking instructors, onto its platform); or by becoming an all-encompassing super-app (such as WeChat, which started as a messenger service and developed into the Chinese "app for everything" with more than 1 billion monthly active users).

4. Business Model Change. In some instances, the next stage of development can best be achieved by giving up the ecosystem model. For example, smart-home ecosystems may slowly develop into open-market models by establishing

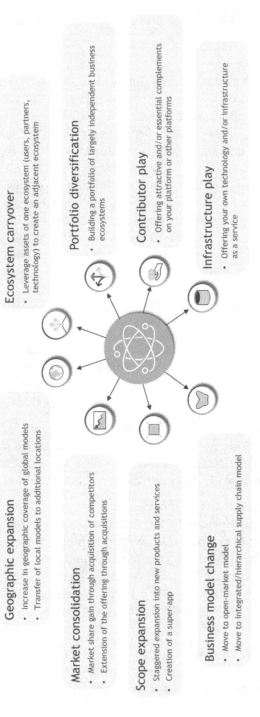

Growing an existing ecosystem

Geographic expansion
- Increase in geographic coverage of global models
- Transfer of local models to additional locations

Market consolidation
- Market share gain through acquisition of competitors
- Extension of the offering through acquisitions

Scope expansion
- Staggered expansion into new products and services
- Creation of a super-app

Business model change
- Move to open-market model
- Move to integrated/hierarchical supply chain model

Moving beyond an existing ecosystem

Ecosystem carryover
- Leverage assets of one ecosystem (users, partners, technology) to create an adjacent ecosystem

Portfolio diversification
- Building a portfolio of largely independent business ecosystems

Contributor play
- Offering attractive and/or essential complements on your platform or other platforms

Infrastructure play
- Offering your own technology and/or infrastructure as a service

Source: BCG Henderson Institute

Figure 9.3: Two Categories and Eight Vectors of Ecosystem Evolution.

Matter as an interoperable home automation connectivity standard, and ride-hailing companies could use self-driving cars to move their business model away from a gig-economy matching platform toward a more integrated organization with its own fleet.

The second set of vectors offers options for moving beyond an existing ecosystem:

5. Ecosystem Carryover. Leveraging the success of one ecosystem to construct a new one can be an effective pathway to growth. Apple used its strong position in the music player ecosystem to conquer the smartphone ecosystem by positioning the iPhone as the next-generation iPod, while Uber leveraged the large base of drivers and passengers on its ride-hailing platform to build the Uber Eats food delivery ecosystem.

6. Portfolio Diversification. A shift in emphasis from synergies to experimentation and diversification yields a portfolio approach to ecosystem growth. The Allianz Group exemplifies this vector with its digital investment unit Allianz X and its broad portfolio of ecosystem investments.

7. Contributor Play. Some ecosystem orchestrators grow by contributing products and services they offer in their own ecosystem to other ecosystems. For example, Alipay was initially launched on Alibaba's Taobao platform, but it has developed into a leading provider of mobile and online payment services and a contributor in many ecosystems worldwide.

8. Infrastructure Play. Finally, some successful ecosystem operators grow by offering their technology and infrastructure as a service to outside partners. AWS, which was developed to support Amazon's e-commerce ecosystem, now powers other major ecosystems, including Airbnb, Twitch, and Twitter, and has become the company's most profitable division.

Business ecosystems are not a panacea for every market opportunity, but neither are they a fleeting fad. Although they have gained an enormous boost from digital technologies, they have been around for centuries. Accordingly, every company, including industry incumbents, should master the ways and means of ecosystems.

Currently, many incumbent firms are playing catch-up in this arena, but they are fast learners. As the technology for building and running digital platforms becomes increasingly commoditized and the success factors for managing them become more clear, more and more incumbents will be well positioned to unlock the rich opportunities for innovation and value creation offered by ecosystem models. We hope this step-by-step framework for developing an ecosystem strategy will support them on the journey.

Part II: **Special Topics and Applications
of Business Ecosystems**

Section A: **Trust in Business Ecosystems**

Marcos Aguiar, Ulrich Pidun, Santino Lacanna, Niklas Knust, and François Candelon

Chapter 10
Building Trust in Business Ecosystems

Trust, we instinctively realize, is a precious quality that binds relationships, and nowhere more so than in business ecosystems. It's foundational, but also fragile because all the participants in an ecosystem must learn to work with, and rely on, each other, knowing that no external force compels them to do so. Mutual trust, as much as mutual interest, binds business ecosystems.

Yet few business leaders focus on fostering trust when they create and orchestrate ecosystems. Instead of systematically and specifically incorporating trust into the fabric of their ecosystems, most operate under the assumption that trust will automatically grow over time. However, trust is difficult to build and easy to erode. When it is neglected, trust withers and distrust blooms, dooming ecosystems to failure.

Data shows that trust-related issues are a major cause of ecosystem failure. The BCG Henderson Institute (BHI) recently conducted one of the first global research projects focused on the role of trust in business ecosystems. To evaluate the role that trust plays in ecosystems, BHI first studied 110 ecosystems that launched and died between 1974 and 2020. These B2C, C2C, and B2B ecosystems included social networking companies, online marketplaces, and software solutions firms, as well as payment, mobility, entertainment, and health care service companies. On average, the ecosystems existed for 6.8 years and raised $185 million in funding. We used quantitative and qualitative data – such as history, capital raised and deal sizes, industry classification, and geography, as well as a database of unstructured data that we created from public sources such as company reports, corporate databases, and global media – to study the role that trust-related factors played in these ecosystems. In a second step, to distinguish successful trust-building efforts from unsuccessful ones, we conducted paired comparisons between a successful ecosystem and an unsuccessful ecosystem in 45 industries.

Our analysis found that trust was a proximate factor – albeit not necessarily the root cause – in the failure of 57 of the 110 unsuccessful ecosystems that we studied. A third of those companies, we concluded, had attributed the failure of their ecosystems – we define "failure" as the dissolution, shrinking to insignificance, or acquisition of an ecosystem for a price below the investments made in

https://doi.org/10.1515/9783110775167-010

it – to making the wrong choices about ecosystem governance standards, rules, and processes. When we analyzed those cases, we found that most of them (94%) had arrived at that conclusion because of trust-related issues. Thus, our research spotlights the critical, and often neglected, role that trust plays in the failure of business ecosystems.

Of course, trust plays just as significant a role in ensuring the success of ecosystems. That became evident from the second step of our study, in which we conducted paired comparisons between 45 of the ecosystems that had failed and one purposely chosen peer ecosystem from each of the industries to which the former belonged. We found that trust mattered a great deal in the success of 73% of the ecosystems that succeeded. Like blood in biological systems, trust is critical to keeping ecosystems alive and working.

Based on our research, this chapter offers a systematic process that business leaders can use to design and manage trust in ecosystems, thereby setting themselves up for sustained success.

How Trust-Related Issues Fuel Ecosystem Failure – and Success

In our digital era, more and more companies are setting up business ecosystems, but few are likely to succeed. That's why, we believe, CEOs must anticipate and be prepared to tackle the fallout from trust-related issues in ecosystems.

When there's no trust, or if the level of trust falls in an ecosystem, participants are less likely to cooperate, and their interactions become transactional. They become increasingly reluctant to do anything for the ecosystem as a whole, and each participant's focus shifts from growing the ecosystem's value to capturing value for only itself. As a result, the scope of joint activities shrinks, costs increase, and the growth of network effects slows. Eventually, the ecosystem is unable to grow as fast as rival ecosystems, and it implodes because of the lack of trust.

Trust can be a crippling factor even for global market leaders, and several ecosystems have been stillborn because of trust-related issues. Consider Sony's electronic book (e-book) reader, the PRS-500, which the company launched in 2006 – a full year before Amazon launched the Kindle. Light as a feather, the reader incorporated electronic ink technology that didn't hurt readers' eyes. Many experts hailed it as the book industry's equivalent of the iPod. The PRS-500 offered sharp screen resolution (800 x 600 dpi) and processors that got faster over time. And although the first model could store just 10 MB, Sony soon upgraded it to 256 MB, which ensured that a consumer could store 500 books at a time on the device.

Nothing stood between Sony and success, it seemed, except for the trust of book publishers. Gaining that proved to be impossible. Sony had equipped the PRS-500 with a relatively open download mechanism, so users could connect the device to a PC, via the USB port, to access books. The notion that the device would allow copyrighted content to be downloaded openly over the internet – and possibly be hacked – scared book publishers, particularly because Sony's broadband e-book format was untested. Most decided to stay away from the platform despite sensing that the future of reading was going to be digital.

Twelve months later, Amazon entered the fray with the Kindle, which critics then described as "industrially ugly." It was larger than the Sony PRS-500, weighed more, and had an inferior screen. However, it was a proprietary device with a closed system that could download content only from Amazon. com. The Kindle prevented buyers from transferring e-books to or from any other device, sharing them, or even connecting to a printer. It enabled Amazon to gain the trust of book publishers, and, by 2014, Sony was forced to announce that it would not make another e-book reader for the consumer market.

Trust is especially relevant in the launch, scale, and maturity stages of an ecosystem's life cycle – although it is most critical during the scaling phase. At launch, the orchestrator must convince potential participants to join before the ecosystem has proven itself. That requires fostering trust in the orchestrator and the ecosystem's business model. When the ecosystem is scaling, partners must focus on growing the pie rather than on maximizing their individual slices. Every participant must trust the commitment of the orchestrator and the other players to keep the ecosystem going until it attains critical mass. When the ecosystem is mature, its partners will be dependent on it, so they must trust the orchestrator not to misuse its position of power.

Only 25% of the unsuccessful ecosystems failed *after* scaling, according to our study, while 30% did so at the launch stage. By far the largest portion (45%) collapsed *during* the scale phase, with two-thirds of them exhibiting trust-related issues at that stage (Figure 10.1).

Without trust, it's impossible for ecosystems to mature. Beepi, an automobile buying and selling platform launched in the US in 2014, exemplifies the dilemma in an ecosystem that is scaling. The startup allowed people to buy and sell used cars at the touch of a button by sending a Beepi inspector to conduct a 240-point, two-hour evaluation of every seller's vehicle. If the vehicle passed

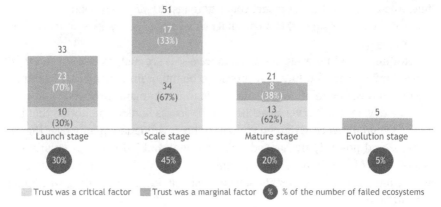

Note: The size of our sample of failed ecosystems was 110; the number of cases with trust as a critical factor was 57
Source: BCG Henderson Institute

Figure 10.1: Failed Ecosystems and Business Stage Where Trust Was a Factor in the Failure.

the test, Beepi would list it. If someone bought the vehicle, Beepi would transfer the money to the seller, and one of its employees would pick up and deliver the car to the buyer. If the automobile didn't sell within 30 days, Beepi would buy the vehicle and continue to list it until it sold. By 2015, Beepi was on Forbes' list of the hottest e-commerce startups in the US and was valued at roughly $550 million.

Despite the convenience of the process, Beepi could not grow beyond a certain point because of a key issue. Even though Beepi offered a ten-day return window and a warranty, buyers could not inspect or test-drive vehicles before they purchased them. Buying a car entails a large financial outlay, and most buyers weren't comfortable making the investment sight unseen. They didn't trust sellers – or Beepi – and wanted the tactile experience of kicking the tires, sitting in the driver's seat, and driving a car to determine if it met their needs. Beepi didn't realize it had to earn buyers' trust by other means, and it folded in 2017.

A Trust-Building Framework

Building trust into an ecosystem and fostering it is critical for success, but it's a complex process. All the participants in an ecosystem must be involved, but groups of them play distinctive roles, creating and capturing value in different ways. Besides, ecosystem relationships extend from many to many – not from one to many, as in a supply chain. Companies must use a multi-faceted approach to building trust. To help, we've developed a trust-building framework that comprises five elements. Like the lenses in a microscope, the elements work as a cohesive system to bring into sharp focus the dynamics of trust in any ecosystem (Figure 10.2).

Business leaders can use the framework to detect trust-related issues and to take the right combination of steps to develop trust. In the rest of this chapter we discuss the five elements of the framework as a sequence of action steps:

1. Surface trust-related frictions.
2. Identify the drivers of trust.
3. Reshape the games ecosystem participants play.
4. Embed trust into platforms.
5. Deploy combinations of trust-building instruments.

Surface Trust-Related Frictions

When the participants in an ecosystem run into trust-related issues, the first telltale sign is friction. Trust-related friction manifests itself in two tangible ways: an increase in costs and a loss of opportunity.

Friction leads to an increase in costs because it usually results in churn, which was evident in 62% of the failed ecosystems we studied. Costs rise because of both higher customer churn, as buyers stop engaging with the troubled ecosystem, and greater participant churn, as established participants leave the ecosystem. In order to tackle the fall in demand and to maintain supply, the orchestrator must woo new customers and fresh participants. That leads to restitution or reinstatement costs, shown in 69% of our sample.

Consider, for instance, ride-hailing companies, such as Uber and Lyft, which are struggling to become profitable, despite their popularity, because of the high costs they incur to recruit and retain riders and drivers. On the one hand, because local taxi and ride-sharing companies are trying to create monopolies in their markets, Uber and Lyft have spent millions fighting smaller rivals, attempting to drive their revenues down and their costs up. On the other hand, a high driver-churn rate has forced Uber and Lyft to incur hefty sales, marketing, and promotion costs to keep people driving for them. In an otherwise normal 2019, Uber lost $8.5 billion and Lyft lost $2.6 billion.

Friction also shows up as the loss of opportunity, or opportunity costs. Participants may not be able to chase, or fully capitalize on, new opportunities because of trust-related issues, and this is bound to affect the ecosystem's

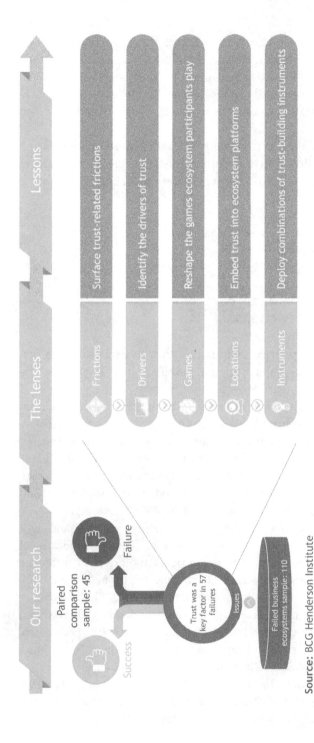

Source: BCG Henderson Institute

Figure 10.2: Elements of a Trust-Building Framework.

performance. For instance, although RIM's BlackBerry tried to become a platform company, it failed to recruit app developers to its cause. For years it ignored developers' demands for a less clunky software platform and a more flexible app approval process. One developer found RIM's bureaucracy so frustrating that he gave up, and wrote a blogpost, "You Win, RIM!" The post went viral, getting over 30,000 hits on the first day. Losing faith in the ability to generate revenues from RIM, app developers simply shifted to developing apps for Apple's iOS and Google's Android platforms. By 2013, RIM was on the auction block.

Ecosystem leaders must watch out for signs of friction before a cycle of destruction begins. Rising friction, if it isn't nipped in the bud, will curb an ecosystem's pursuit of economies of scale and limit network effects. That will increase friction and undermine trust even further, derailing the ecosystem's ability to retain partners.

Trust Takeaway #1: Orchestrators must keep both eyes open for early signs and weak signals of ecosystem trust erosion. They must quickly take countermeasures to foster trust and eliminate distrust before a vicious cycle is triggered.

Identify the Drivers of Trust

Orchestrators must develop an in-depth understanding of the factors that drive trust-based relationships in an ecosystem. Participants usually decide to engage with an ecosystem after evaluating three key criteria: competence, fairness, and transparency.

1. **Competence.** Has the ecosystem delivered on its promise to partners and customers? Does it use metrics to constantly evaluate if it has? Competence is, by far, the most prevalent trust driver in the ecosystems we studied, so orchestrators would do well to focus on it. For example, Handy, the US marketplace for residential cleaning, installation, and other home services, realizes that it's critical that customers perceive the competence of its workers. It rigorously applies several criteria before choosing professionals for tasks, and it makes customer satisfaction ratings public. Initially, Handy even docked the pay of workers who didn't deliver quality, charging them a fee if they showed up late or left jobs incomplete.

2. **Fairness.** Do partners believe that the orchestrator is fair? Does the orchestrator display empathy toward its partners and sometimes place partner interests above its own? If orchestrators don't do that, a backlash is inevitable – as Apple found. The giant has faced a storm of protest from developers over the fees it charges for listing apps on the App

Store. Companies such as Spotify, Basecamp, Blix, Tile, Match, and, recently, Epic Games have all protested, some filing lawsuits. They coordinated their protests, forming the Coalition for App Fairness. Eventually (in January 2021), Apple cut fees from 30% to 15% for small app developers that earn less than $1 million a year from the App Store. That will help 98% of app developers, while reducing Apple's App Store revenues by less than 5%.

3. **Transparency.** Are the orchestrator's decisions and actions open and unambiguous, so participants believe they are competent and fair? For instance, in order to win the trust of potential partners and encourage them to join its ecosystem, Amazon's AWS announced a detailed plan in 2014. It covered the future of digital technologies, the cloud, and use cases; the roles other firms could play; and a training and certification program for partners. The high level of transparency helped AWS build an ecosystem that has grown rapidly and incorporates many thousands of partners.

Trust Takeaway #2: An ecosystem that delivers on its value proposition is likely to be trusted, so ensuring value delivery must be the orchestrator's priority. It must check if every participant in the ecosystem is delivering on, and living up to, its promise every day.

Reshape the Games Ecosystem Participants Play

Game theory suggests that the interactions among ecosystem participants create incentives that shape their behavior. Participants will decide whether or not to cooperate with one another depending on the nature of the incentives. Our study found evidence of games with non-cooperative equilibriums in 71% of failed ecosystems, and games with cooperative equilibriums were evident in 62% of the successful ones.

Orchestrators must incentivize participants to ensure cooperation and discourage uncooperative behavior. If they don't, mistrust and defection are more than likely. Orchestrators are central to the process because of their relationships with customers, which, our research shows, were key in about 95% of the cases we studied.

Successful orchestrators shape participants' behavior toward cooperative equilibriums by shifting from a reliance on trust between participants to actively fostering trust in the ecosystem. Airbnb, for instance, doesn't focus on winning the trust of its hosts and guests. That matters at one level, but what's more important is that hosts and guests trust *each other*. Airbnb has designed its platform to ensure that happens – guest ratings and reviews determine hosts' reputations. Also, by providing host protection insurance, Airbnb has ensured that the workings of its platform build trust in the ecosystem.

Trust Takeaway #3: Orchestrators must reshape the games that ecosystem participants play, so that they become the rationale for cooperation. They can also foster cooperation by ensuring that there is clarity about roles. When participants live up to the expectations set by the orchestrator, it fuels systemic trust.

Embed Trust into Ecosystem Platforms

Trust affects the behavior of all participants in an ecosystem, which plays out in the decline in trust levels in failed ecosystems and the increase in trust in successful ones. In our study, the ecosystems that didn't work exhibited high levels of trust erosion (44%), poor trust building (29%), or both (27%). Conversely, 76% of the successful ecosystems demonstrated a high level of trust by participants in their ecosystems, while 24% showed a rise in trust between the participants, either alone (11%) or in tandem with measures that embedded trust into the ecosystems (13%).

Trust must never be an after-the-fact consideration; it should be a deliberate consequence of ecosystem design. Leaders should build trust into their ecosystem platforms and governance systems by ridding themselves of the naive belief that trust will arise spontaneously. For instance, when eBay entered China, it assumed that buyers on the platform could trust sellers to deliver products and services. That didn't happen naturally in many cases, so buyers on eBay mistrusted sellers. They defected to rival platforms such as Alibaba Group's Taobao, which didn't make the mistake of assuming that sellers would live up to their promises. Instead, Taobao ensured that they would by embedding trust-building measures into the platform. Typically, it holds the money due to the seller until the buyer confirms that the delivery matches expectations. The measure may appear draconian, but it has ensured cooperation among Taobao's buyers and sellers, fueling the ecosystem's success in China.

Trust Takeaway #4: Orchestrators must create ecosystems in which the interactions and relationships between participants generate and sustain trust; they should never leave it to chance. Embedding trust into the workings of platforms ensures that it becomes part and parcel of day-to-day operations.

Deploy Combinations of Trust-Building Instruments

Ecosystem orchestrators can use many kinds of instruments to build trust. Their options include monetary incentives, standards, rules, and, in recent times, digital solutions, such as ratings and blockchain, which have expanded the trust toolkit.

However, the rise of digital platforms has led to the facile conclusion that technology is sufficient to ensure trust in an ecosystem. That's far from true; there's no single instrument or technology that can create trust in an ecosystem. In our study, combinations of instruments were essential for success in 90% of ecosystems.

Many kinds of instruments can be combined to ensure cooperation among ecosystem participants. Consider, for instance, HopSkipDrive (HSD), a ridesharing company for children ages 1 through 12 who must use hired vehicles when traveling without their parents. Parents can access the service through a mobile app and schedule rides up until the night before. HSD offers single-family rides as well as flat-rate pool rides that one family can set up and invite others to join.

Set up by three working mothers, HSD uses a combination of several instruments to ensure that parents can trust HSD's drivers to ferry their children around safely:

- **Checks.** HSD's drivers are mostly women who have at least five years of experience in childcare. CareDrivers, as they're called, must go through a 15-step screening process. HSD conducts background checks against criminal and sex offender databases, checks driving records, and then interviews and fingerprints the drivers before hiring them.
- **Monitoring.** HSD uses Zendrive software to monitor driver behavior in real time. It can detect if a driver is talking on a cellphone or texting while driving. During the ride, parents can get updates and track the progress of their child's journey on a cellphone app.
- **Incentives.** By offering more rides and higher incomes to better-rated drivers, HSD creates incentives that reduce the possibility of misbehavior and increase the likelihood of driver cooperation.

There's a science and an art to using instruments to build participants' trust and ensure the right behavior in an ecosystem. The challenge is to find the combination of instruments that leads to cooperation by all participants, but that's the subject of the next chapter.

Trust Takeaway #5: Orchestrators would do well to acknowledge that there is no silver bullet that builds trust in ecosystems. They should use a combination of several trust-building instruments that leads to a conducive environment and culture in the ecosystem, fosters cooperation among participants, and ensures the ecosystem's success over time.

Companies that plan to create ecosystems must design trust into their platforms from the outset. Doing so will, on the one hand, enhance the ecosystem's operation, because trust catalyzes greater cooperation among participants. On the other hand, trust protects the ecosystem, because it generates the network effects that drive its growth. In this way, ecosystems generate competitive advantage via trust. Above all, ecosystems in which trust continues to rise over time require lower levels of orchestration; each participant influences and is affected by the others, creating an ever-evolving ecosystem that can sustain itself in the long run.

Marcos Aguiar, Ulrich Pidun, Santino Lacanna, Niklas Knust,
Matthew Williams, and François Candelon

Chapter 11
Discovering the Tools and Tactics of Trust in Business Ecosystems

As business grows ever more digital – as virtual relationships increasingly become the norm in the post-COVID reality – winning and maintaining stakeholder trust becomes as crucial to a company as ensuring product or service integrity. Nowhere is this truer than in business ecosystems, the dynamic alliances of largely independent economic entities that create products or services that constitute a coherent solution. Ecosystems depend on well-functioning networks of buyers, sellers, and various other parties in between to thrive and grow.

As business ecosystems become more commonplace, the importance of trust – between and among participants and between the end user and the platform itself – becomes a more salient issue. For example, buyers on an e-commerce marketplace need to know they will receive what they have paid for and that their data won't be abused. Participants on fundraising platforms need to be protected from fraud. Controls for bad behavior, protocols for resolving disputes, and quality assurances are essential for everything from gig economy platforms to smart, IoT-based ecosystems. For any and all kinds of ecosystems, incentives for members to cooperate are absolutely necessary in order for everyone to reap the benefits of their interactions.

Indeed, a lack of trust is one of the most important reasons why ecosystems fail. At the same time, trust is also a core success factor in business ecosystems, a direct contributor to a company's value proposition (see Chapter 10). Therefore, watching out for weak signals of potential failure due to mistrust is one of the most important tasks ecosystem leaders perform. It's important throughout the life cycle of an ecosystem, from launch to maturity. But it is most critical in the scaling-up phase, when network effects kick in and exponential growth can make or break market leadership.

While most ecosystem members recognize that trust is important, it is often treated as a feature that arises organically, on its own, over time. And although most ecosystems adopt some mix of instruments to engender trust among their members and customers, few consciously and proactively build it into their platform. Trust doesn't happen automatically, however; it must be designed into an ecosystem. It can be hard to build, but it is easy to erode.

https://doi.org/10.1515/9783110775167-011

Through our in-depth analysis of both successful and failed ecosystems – B2C, C2C, and even B2B – we identified key tools and processes (herein referred to as "instruments") and their combinations for major types of ecosystems. Instead of taking a hit-or-miss approach, ecosystems can use these findings to forge and maintain trust as they launch, scale, and sustain their businesses.

In this chapter, we aim to help ecosystem leaders design and ingrain trust by answering three questions:

1. What instruments can be used to build trust in business ecosystems?
2. How do successful ecosystems combine those instruments, and why?
3. What are some of the most critical considerations that ecosystem leaders should focus on when designing an ecosystem for trust?

The Difference Between Success and Failure

To understand the role trust plays in ecosystems, we analyzed failures and successes in a two-part study (as described in Chapter 10).

A stunning 85% of ecosystems – even the most promising ones – fail. By that, we mean they dissolve, shrink to insignificance, or are bought out for below investment cost. In analyzing the demise of more than 100 failed ecosystems over the past 46 years, we discovered that trust (or lack thereof) played a pivotal role in their failure. More than half of them (52%) struggled to build trust altogether. This caused friction among participants, drove up costs, and thwarted network effects, which are effectively the entire basis of ecosystems' benefits and a fundamental reason participants join them.

On the flip side, trust is a cornerstone of success for thriving ecosystems, according to our study of 45 successful ecosystems across 20 industries. Among the successful ones, 86% actively embedded trust in the platform and their governance practices, achieving what we call "systemic trust." These organizations understood that trust between strangers ("relational trust") doesn't arise spontaneously; it takes cultivation. The cooperation needed to fuel success was anchored chiefly in systemic trust, and this trust is what spelled the difference between success and failure (Figure 11.1). Some 88% of ecosystems used a combination of digital instruments (such as ratings and escrow models) and nondigital instruments (such as guarantees and access rules).

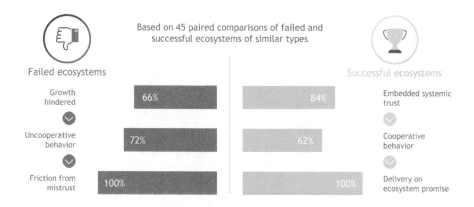

Source: BCG Henderson Institute

Figure 11.1: Trust Spells the Difference Between Ecosystem Success and Failure.

The Trust Instruments

We uncovered 22 trust instruments, which can be grouped into seven basic classes (Figure 11.2):

1. **Access** – which ensures that the right members join and remain engaged
2. **Contracts** – which guarantee mutually beneficial interactions through binding agreements
3. **Incentives** – which encourage participation and cooperation
4. **Controls** – which guide interactions and behavior
5. **Transparency** – which makes past and present behavior visible to all
6. **Intermediation** – which facilitates interaction by establishing a neutral middleman
7. **Mitigation** – which ensures a beneficial outcome even amid disputes or adverse situations

Access

Fostering high-quality, cooperative interactions is critical for ecosystem success, and that means screening players to ensure that the right ones join and stay. Access instruments serve this purpose. Just as important, they block bad actors – those that have already demonstrated they don't play by the rules and those that are likely to be noncompliant.

Access
Ensuring that the right members join and remain engaged

· Access restrictions
· Exclusion of noncompliant members
· Shared purpose and culture

Transparency
Making past and present behavior observable

· Reporting
· Reputation building
· Certification

Contracts
Ensuring mutually beneficial interactions via binding agreements

· Terms and conditions
· Transactional contracts
· Smart contracts
· Relational contracts

Intermediation
Fostering interaction by establishing an intermediary

· Platform as transaction partner
· Algorithmic/automated pricing and matching
· Blockchain

Incentives
Encouraging participation and beneficial interactions

· Compensation models
· Reputation premium
· Commitment

Mitigation
Ensuring a beneficial outcome even in adverse interactions

· Conflict management
· Insurance policies
· Guarantees

Controls
Steering and controlling provision and interaction

· Input controls
· Process controls
· Output controls

Source: BCG Henderson Institute

Figure 11.2: The Seven Classes of Trust Instruments.

Access regulation may start with a strong ecosystem culture with shared norms and a common purpose, both of which support trust by attracting and keeping desirable participants. The software platform Linux is built on the open-source community's values. Access restrictions help engender trust and prevent problems; a good example is HopSkipDrive, an "Uber for kids" that requires drivers to have certain qualifications and pass a detailed background check before they can join. Exclusion tactics include after-the-fact measures, such as Uber's policy of banning drivers whose customer ratings fall below a certain threshold, or actions such as Linux banning contributions from University of Minnesota participants after discovering that researchers knowingly submitted code with security flaws as a test. (Perceived inconsistencies in exclusion decisions and different interpretations of what constitutes bad behavior have drawn public and congressional criticism. Clearly, as a reflection of contemporary culture and attitudes, social media may, more than any other type of ecosystem, need a routine reassessment of trust instruments.)

Contracts

Building trust through contracts is more difficult in an ecosystem context than in bilateral or hierarchical relationships because the ecosystem operates on voluntary collaboration between largely independent economic players. Still, contracts can play a role in fostering trust. Various types of binding agreements formalize ecosystem participants' commitment to fulfill their obligations. One example is the Terms and Conditions agreement. Signed upon entry, Terms and Conditions agreements stipulate the various parties' rights, obligations, roles, and responsibilities. Although legally important and almost universally used, they are little more than a pro forma first step to trust building. *Transactional contracts* define the conditions of specific transactions, such as return policies, which are particularly important for building trust with consumers in used-goods marketplaces.

Smart contracts are computer programs that automate the execution of an agreement without third-party involvement. Created automatically from the standardized data buyers and sellers provide, they are fast, encrypted, and secure, so they ensure trust and transparency. Smart contracts may be particularly applicable to digital ecosystems. Ant Group's Trusple, an international trade and financial service platform, relies on smart contracts to automate the otherwise intensive and time-consuming processes that banks use to track and verify trading (particularly cross-border) orders. Such contracts also enable small and mid-sized enterprises to establish their creditworthiness and ease the financing process.

Relational contracts are flexible, principles-based (as opposed to rules-based) contracts in which parties define common goals, dependencies, or roles and obligations to the platform itself and among themselves. Relational contracts can be useful in establishing a general framework for collaboration, especially if the ecosystem is still expanding and evolving.

Incentives

Incentives prompt players to act according to the ecosystem requirements – not in direct ways but by setting conditions that are conducive to cooperation, as in game theory. A compensation model uses the prospect of value sharing to instill trust. Amazon Kindle's compensation instrument, for example, grants publishers the same payouts from e-books that they would get from print books, thus overcoming the trust concerns about cannibalization of their core business. Reputation premiums reward partners with a record of trustworthy behavior. For example, sellers on Taobao with a first-rate reputation can charge higher prices.

Commitment – in the form of coinvestment or cospecialization – is yet another incentive instrument.[1] SAP established a tiered partner network that confers extra benefits to higher-ranked partners. To obtain a higher ranking, partners must invest in the ecosystem. Doing so signals both their heightened commitment and their dedication to quality – which, in turn, enhance customer trust. HomeKit, Apple's smart home ecosystem, uses cospecialization to forge trust: Hardware manufacturers of accessories that connect to Apple devices are obligated to join the company's highly regulated MFi (made for iPhone/iPod/iPad) program to ensure quality.

Controls

While incentives influence by making specific behavior the rational choice, controls steer interactions directly and limit or impede unproductive behaviors, unacceptable inputs (for example, counterfeit items on a marketplace or nude photos on a social media site), or unintended consequences.

---

1 Cospecialization is a type of strategic alliance in which partners – such as a vendor and a client – bring their respective resources and expertise together to create value.

Formats, standards, and interfaces are common technology examples of input control instruments. For example, Spotify and Amazon's Kindle have forged trust with their partners (music studios and publishers, respectively) through their platforms' technical architecture and data format, which prevent piracy. Other ecosystems define input guidelines; Taobao, for example, determines which products are allowed on its platform; and social media platforms establish communication guidelines.

Process controls involve behavioral restrictions. Uber applies this instrument in two ways: automatically assigning the nearest driver to the customer and automatically picking the most efficient route to ensure that drivers don't take advantage of the customer.

Output controls include the frameworks and algorithms that mobile platforms like Android and Apple iOS use to check the quality of uploaded apps. For example, every app and update on Apple's App Store platform is approved by an Apple employee at the company's App Review division. YouTube's AI algorithm checks each video's music and removes any that violate copyright. Many social networks use editorial control instruments to monitor content. Facebook uses two methods to identify bad behavior: monitoring user complaints and, through AI algorithms, flagging content that violates ecosystem guidelines. Flagged content is ultimately judged by a human compliance team and is subject to an escalated punishment system; the company created an independent oversight board in May 2020 to review its more consequential and controversial content-blocking decisions.

Transparency

By making behaviors and performance visible to ecosystem participants, transparency instruments encourage them to act honestly and in desired ways, thus engendering trust among participants as well as newcomers. Transparency can be generated through reporting instruments that allow users to flag bad behavior – social media platforms such as Facebook, Twitter, and TikTok use these. Reputation-building measures, such as ratings and customer reviews, are especially useful for marketplaces (like Amazon) and gig economy ecosystems (like DoorDash and TaskRabbit) because they help reduce information asymmetry. The prospect of negative reviews curbs bad behavior and rewards those who fulfill or exceed their promise, and the credibility of user endorsements helps attract new participants.

An often-overlooked but powerful trust-building instrument is certification by the platform. Many ecosystems confer certification on members for their high quality, whether for products (think Carvana, the used car marketplace, or eBay), projects (as in Kickstarter, the crowdfunding platform), or merchants (Google's Trusted Store program).

Intermediation

Intermediaries shift trust out of the direct relationships between individual participants and make it a feature of the ecosystem. By providing a buffer, intermediaries give the transaction parties confidence that the other will live up to its end of the bargain. In one model, the platform (or orchestrator) inserts itself in the transaction, typically through an escrow model. Taobao and eBay use this model to ensure that goods are transferred only after the buyer has paid and that the seller is paid only after the transaction is completed. Some marketplaces even act as direct transaction partners: They buy the goods and later sell them, decoupling trust from providers and making it a simple relationship between the platform and the end customer.

Technology provides another powerful means of intermediation to elicit trust. Many ecosystems use algorithms to automate pricing or matching to ensure quality in interactions. Uber not only matches rides through a central algorithm but also uses algorithms to centrally create prices, using a dynamic pricing model that adjusts rates based on such variables as time, distance, traffic level, and current rider-to-driver demand. Blockchain is yet another technological instrument used for intermediation between users. Interestingly, although the whole point of distributed ledgers is to disintermediate, the platform, in this case, actually becomes the intermediary. De Beers' Tracr uses blockchain to connect the diamond industry on a common digital platform and establish the provenance, authenticity, and traceability of its diamonds throughout the value chain.

Mitigation

Mitigation instruments provide troubleshooting and conflict management as a last resort. Not only do they limit the damage in case of trust failures; their mere availability fosters trust upfront by offering protections that encourage parties to participate in the ecosystem. We discovered three types of mitigation instruments: conflict management tools, insurance policies, and guarantees. Many platforms, such as Uber and Airbnb, manage conflicts between partners centrally. Payment solutions like Visa also use central conflict management to arbitrate, as in the case of fraud. Other ecosystems use decentralized or distributed conflict management processes: at Reddit, moderators arbitrate the various forums; at Wikipedia, committees of editors resolve content disputes; and at Alibaba, a dispute mediation team reviews the complaint and makes a final determination to settle the matter. Insurance policies limit losses from adverse events; Airbnb, for instance, offers members insurance to cover property damages by guests. Finally, guarantees such as those provided in auction marketplaces and payment ecosystems ensure payback in the event of fraud.

Decoding Trust Formulas

Having identified seven classes of (and 22 individual) trust instruments, we asked the next questions: How prevalent are the instruments in the 45 successful ecosystems we studied? What patterns can be observed in those ecosystems? And are there particular combinations of instruments that seem to correlate with success?

Our in-depth analysis of each case revealed that most successful ecosystems use a broad set of instruments, both digital and nondigital, in a truly synergistic fashion. In each case, we gauged each instrument's relevance to trust creation – and thus its role in enticing cooperation and spawning the network effects that fueled accelerated growth and ultimately success. This was a crucial step because, by and large, most instruments are present in every ecosystem but are not necessarily decisive for building trust or fueling performance.

What were our most significant discoveries? Access, controls, and transparency are the most common classes of trust instruments; at least one of the three is present in almost 80% of the cases. Access is the most widely used (78% of cases), and controls are used by 67% of the cases. Transparency is the most predominant digital instrument (69%) and appears to be the glue that binds participants together in an ecosystem.

Digitization enables a broader deployment of instruments – instruments that in the nondigital past would have had limited application. This is especially true for transparency (think ratings and reviews) and intermediation (for instance, where the platform acts as a transaction partner). As a result, digitization has helped fuel growth. Without it, microlending platforms – whether nonprofits like Kiva or for-profits like Ant Financial – would never have been able to reach the scale they have achieved.

These findings raised the question: Are there distinct combinations of instruments that characterize different types of ecosystems? As we delved deeper to look for such patterns, we identified five more prominent ecosystem categories, or "clusters," that use distinct combinations of trust instruments according to the specific trust issues that they need to address: social networks, marketplaces, Internet of Things (IoT) ecosystems, financial ecosystems, and gig economy platforms.

To ensure complete objectivity, we began by looking for patterns agnostically, without regard to industry or business model. In a blind and mechanical fashion, without identifying the actual ecosystems, we grouped them into clusters based on similarly recurrent patterns of instrument relevance. Then, and only then, did we identify the actual ecosystems in each cluster to cross-check the consistency of emerging clusters.

To our surprise, we discovered that our mechanical grouping of ecosystems into clusters based on the relevance of similar trust instruments overwhelmingly matched reality. Figure 11.3 shows the "real-world clusters" that we arrived at in our hunt for patterns. Each of the 45 columns represents a single successful ecosystem case. For example, the eight columns under social networks represent eight successful ecosystems. Each cell corresponds to a class of trust instrument: dark green indicates a predominantly nondigital instrument; light green indicates a predominantly digitally enabled instrument. The highlighted cells indicate relevance, not simply presence.

For example, only three classes of instruments were relevant for social networks. Six of the eight ecosystems used predominantly nondigital access instruments, and all eight used predominantly digitally enabled control and transparency instruments.

For the sake of simplicity, we characterized instruments as predominantly digital or nondigital, based on the origin of the instrument. For example, for access, a background check with a fingerprint was classified as nondigital, whereas rating systems (transparency) are managed by an algorithm and were thus classified as digital. We use the qualifier "predominantly" for a few reasons. First, each class of instruments contains a mix: there are smart contracts (clearly digital) and traditional terms and conditions agreements, which are inherently nondigital (even if provided in digital format). Moreover, to an extent, everything today is digital, and at the same time, everything is human; most ecosystems are built on digital platforms that rely heavily on code, yet that code is written by a human with the inevitable human bias, deliberate or not.

Finally, most instruments are digitally enabled, and formerly nondigital elements (such as governance and policy-related instruments) are increasingly being digitized. Indeed, our classification reflects a point in time, but it's worth noting that, over time, the instruments (like the interactions themselves) will only become more digital. The remaining nondigital elements are typically the

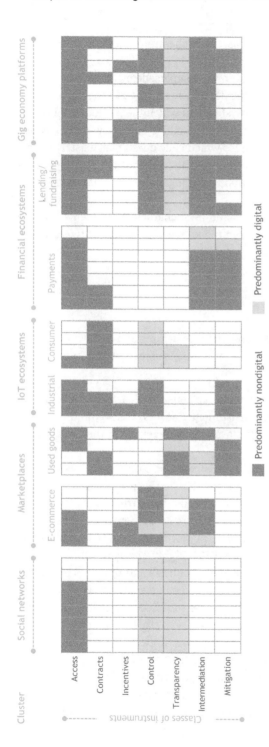

Source: BCG Henderson Institute
Note: Each column represents an individual ecosystem case, and each cell corresponds to a relevant class of trust instrument. For example, we studied eight social networks and they used only three types of instruments. Six used access instruments, and all eight used control and transparency instruments.

Figure 11.3: Real-World Trust Instrument Cluster Patterns.

"manned last mile" elements, such as the orchestrator's dispute escalation mechanisms for mitigation.

This is not to say that digital will ultimately supersede most human intervention. Digital has its limits, in three contexts: (1) where the ecosystem touches the physical world (as in gig economy ecosystems, in which the product itself comes through manned delivery); (2) where a judgment call is necessary; and (3) where the system encounters a new situation for which code doesn't yet exist. Nonetheless, this digital/nondigital spectrum reflects the true dual nature of business ecosystems. Knitting the digital and nondigital together in a synergistic way is what good design for trust is all about.

We describe the ecosystem clusters and their characteristics below, looking at the particular trust issues of each and the key instruments they typically use in combination to build trust.

Social Networks

In social networks, the quality of members' interactions and behavior are critical trust challenges. Because these platforms are inherently open, they cannot directly control what each participant does.

Key instruments: Successful social networks consistently leverage a combination of three classes of trust-based instruments: access, control, and transparency. The degree of influence each class exerts depends on the ecosystem's maturity level.

Consider Clubhouse, the recently launched audio-only social network. It strictly regulates access, allowing new members only through invitations by current members. This approach is designed to ensure trust in the quality of interactions while fostering growth. More mature social networks still regulate access, but mainly in a reactive way; most platforms kick out poorly behaving individuals. It's worth noting that, amid the highly charged political atmosphere of the past several years, the exclusion policies and practices of leading networks have been put to the test and have come under fire for what some say is bias or lack of transparency (or both) in their exclusion policies. This situation demonstrates that trust instruments must keep pace with a changing culture; in recent years, Facebook and Twitter, two of the world's biggest social networks, outgrew the policy guidelines that served them well in the sites' early days. It also shows that success today is no guarantee of future success.

As social networks grow, their entry requirements typically diminish in order to capture larger portions of the market. (Clubhouse has publicly vowed that it will eventually be open to all.) Mature social networks need instruments beyond access control to ensure the quality of interactions. Most use behavior-shaping instruments (such as input controls, curation protocols, and communication guidelines) to ensure that participants behave appropriately. Twitter, for example, clearly states what content is allowed and actively engages in fact-checking and blocking content that violates its guidelines. Here again, digital instruments such as algorithms can play to those ecosystems' strengths. Yet having an instrument in place doesn't necessarily mean that it is the right instrument or that it is effectively designed or deployed. Finally, transparency (usually through feedback and reputation instruments) makes behavior broadly observable and users accountable, enabling judgment calls from members on relational and systemic trust. Using instruments such as "likes" for specific content or for following specific members, social networks empower members to build their own trusted networks or feeds.

Marketplaces (E-Commerce and Used Goods)

Along with gig economy platforms, marketplaces use the greatest number of trust instruments.

E-Commerce

For e-commerce and digital marketplaces, the key trust concerns revolve around three issues: (1) whether the platform lives up to its value proposition, (2) whether providers deliver on their promise (in quality and timeliness, thus offsetting the inherent information asymmetry between seller and buyer), and (3) potential misbehavior (for example, counterfeiting) among sellers.

Key instruments: In traditional buyer-seller marketplaces, banning repeat offenders (sellers who fail to deliver on time or buyers who fail to pay) is effective. Access, along with transparency instruments in the form of user-based feedback (such as ratings) and platform-based measures (such as certification), implicitly serve to frame the incentives to promote cooperation and trust among participants. A large number of negative ratings on a product or seller will invariably limit sales. Conversely, high ratings can earn sellers "reputation premiums" – in effect, the ability to price their wares or services at a premium because they are more trustworthy. Some e-commerce giants, like Taobao and eBay, go one step further and certify especially trustworthy sellers, directly impacting their sales.

Because, practically speaking, e-commerce marketplaces cannot entirely prevent bad behavior, control instruments can help minimize adverse outcomes and boost trust. On many e-commerce marketplaces, counterfeit products are a real risk to legitimate sellers and customers. Deploying input control measures (such as traceability policies) against copycats is a commonly used and powerful tool.

When there is no foundation of trust between sellers and buyers (say, because an ecosystem is new), intermediation can be a powerful tool for enabling interactions. When Taobao was established in China, it entered the scene as an intermediary with an escrow model. Intermediation has become more widespread among subscription model marketplaces, such as e-book platforms and music streaming platforms like Spotify. Musicians trust Spotify because it effectively prevents piracy and secures payouts, and users trust the platform because it provides a broad offering at high quality for a reasonable price.

Used Goods

In used-goods marketplaces, the picture changes somewhat. Here, information asymmetry is even greater because a product's quality is a function not only of its original manufacture but also of its prior usage. In addition, because the primary relationship is now C2C and typically transactional (often only a one-off), trust between participants becomes harder to establish.

Key instruments: Used-goods marketplaces rely primarily on a set of five instruments: access, contracts (especially return policies), transparency, intermediation, and mitigation.

Access mainly involves barring bad actors. To appreciate the important role contracts play in this type of marketplace, consider Vroom and Carvana, two US-based used car retailers. Their return policies allow the customer to return the vehicle if the quality does not meet their standards. Both platforms provide transparency by inspecting every car listed on their platform, thus certifying quality and reducing information asymmetry. To further boost trust, both platforms serve as the active transaction partner – first buying and then selling the car. In this way, they make direct trust between players (relational trust) superfluous and trust in the platform (systemic trust) essential.

Others, like eBay, use traditional user ratings, which can yield hefty reputation premiums for five-star sellers. eBay's escrow model, in which payment is released to the seller only after the buyer receives the product, limits transaction risk. As in many used-goods marketplaces, these measures are not enough to ensure trust (especially when the goods in question are valuable or the potential for fraud or counterfeiting is high). Their final line of defense against trust erosion is mitigation by resolving conflicts or even compensating victims. To protect sellers from malicious bidders, LiveAuctioneers uses protection guarantees. These guarantees establish a dispute process that is triggered when a bidder fails to pay, allow sellers to contact the leading underbidder, and automatically suspend bidders with two or more disputes on their account.

IoT (Solution) Ecosystems

For IoT ecosystems, whether B2C (such as smart home systems) or B2B (like production-line devices), quality, of course, matters. But their main trust issue centers on data security. IoT devices capture and share vast amounts of often highly sensitive data, some of it destined for purposes unbeknownst to the customer or user. These can be private conversations or proprietary machine data culled in ambient data collection.

Trust in these ecosystems hinges largely on preventing misuse and maintaining security. How secure are the devices, and how safe is the stored data? Many of the devices are useless without the IoT connection, making trust issues a core concern of the service. Thus, the service's reliability is potentially addressed through product design rather than ecosystem design. These issues are relevant for both consumer and industrial IoT ecosystems.

Key instruments: Access, contracts, controls, and mitigation are the tools best suited for instilling trust in IoT ecosystems. The following two examples illustrate why.

HomeKit, Apple's smart home ecosystem, allows only trusted suppliers on the platform. The MFi program's enrollment verification process includes identity and legal entity status checks (access). It also clearly defines rights and obligations (especially those concerning data sharing) in nondisclosure agreements that providers sign upon joining. Controls also play an important role. Extensive input control (governing the kinds of products and applications allowed on the platform), as well as process control (determining how interactions and fulfillment are regulated), engender trust in the quality of the service and in data ownership structures. The smart home market leans toward more hands-off approaches than do B2B IoT solutions. Samsung's SmartThings, for example, doesn't regulate access but relies on precise use terms (contracts) and a thorough certification process (controls).

In the B2B arena, FieldView, a smart farming ecosystem, offers a good demonstration of trust instruments. Because its participant base is manageable in size, FieldView can afford to grant developers access on a case-by-case basis and allow the terms and conditions of its partnerships to be individually defined. Field-View determines who can access the platform and its data, letting farmers decide similarly on a case-by-case basis who can access their data. This instrument is defined in the terms and conditions of the ecosystem. The platform controls input and process via APIs and individual licensing agreements that regulate the solutions that software developers can offer and how data is shared. Whenever trust is threatened – as was the case in 2019 with FieldView's partnership with Tillable[2] – mitigation instruments kick in. At that time, farmers feared their data would be shared without their consent and potentially used against their interests. Field-View listened to its users and terminated the partnership before any breaches could occur.

Financial Ecosystems (Payment, Lending, and Fundraising Platforms)

For financial ecosystems, designed chiefly for transferring or raising money, fraud risk, losses, and security are the main trust issues.

Key instruments: Access – allowing only trustworthy participants – is just the first level of protection for minimizing fraud and losses. Payment platforms like Visa and Mastercard use credit scores to restrict membership and adjust payment limits. In all of the financial ecosystems we analyzed, fraudulent members are excluded. But exclusion has its limits, considering that it is tough, if not impossible, to identify bad behavior up front. The instruments of choice in such environments are intermediation and mitigation measures. PayPal, for instance, acts as the transaction partner (intermediating transactions), providing guarantees against fraud.

Because the range of potential interactions on lending or fundraising platforms is broader than on pure payment ecosystems – consider the greater amount of private data gathered – more can go wrong. So, beyond access, intermediation, and mitigation, these ecosystems need to tap other instruments. Kiva, the nonprofit microlending platform, and Kickstarter, the funding ecosystem, tightly control participants' input (the projects) and the process. For example, Kiva works only with financially excluded borrowers and is limited to projects that create social impact in their communities. Additionally, Kiva clearly defines how projects are approved, how funds are deployed, and how debtors are controlled. Both Kiva and Kickstarter also provide transparency to

---

2 "Climate FieldView terminates platform partnership agreement with Tillable," *Successful Farming*, February 15, 2020.

lenders in the form of certifications and recommendations that highlight especially trustworthy projects on the platform. Kiva, for example, features a five-star risk rating system for projects.

Gig Economy Platforms

Ecosystems that focus on services provided by gig economy workers face another set of trust issues: those centered on the provider's offering, qualifications, quality, and fulfillment performance.

Key instruments: Given their multiplicity of trust issues, gig economy platforms use the greatest number of instruments. These generally include access, controls, transparency, and intermediation.

Access restrictions are vitally important. If the wrong providers are on your platform, users will lose interest, and would-be users won't even show up, thereby critically constraining your growth prospects. Belay Solutions, a virtual staffing company serving the US, hires only US-based, highly skilled, and experienced professionals – regulating access to build trust in the quality of its solution.

Behavior-shaping instruments (controls) represent another way of ensuring that the quality of interactions is sufficiently high. Uber uses process controls to determine the entire value-delivery process – rider matching, pricing, payment, routing – thus shaping drivers' behavior. Airbnb clearly stipulates what tenants are allowed to do in their rented lodging.

Transparency is an important lever for many gig economy platforms because it reduces information asymmetry and makes past behavior relevant. HopSkipDrive uses driver ratings and safety statistics to generate trust in the platform's value proposition. Airbnb and Uber offer rating systems, not just for end customers to rate providers but also for providers to rate end customers; these systems identify participants from either side who should be barred. And intermediation, in which the orchestrator emerges as a transaction partner, is commonly used by gig economy platforms to shift trust away from individual interactions and toward the platform itself. Through an app, riders pay Uber directly, not their Uber driver; and Uber drivers need not worry about the rider lacking enough money, because Uber guarantees the transaction.

Developing the Right Trust Formula

As leaders look to embed trust into their ecosystems, the ecosystem cluster patterns we uncovered in our bottom-up analysis provide a useful initial framework. But there is no silver bullet or single formula – successful ecosystems combine multiple trust instruments. They should, therefore, also identify the specific trust challenges they face and pick the right instruments from the trust toolbox we've identified. Choosing at random, even if the instruments seem powerful, is ineffective. It's particularly important to consider the scope and diversity of an ecosystem's interactions; they will indicate the difficulty and complexity of any trust issues. In this way, they can guide the choice of the most appropriate instruments in the best (and most powerful) combination to foster trust in interactions, fuel cooperation, and ultimately boost the ecosystem's overall performance.

The following principles and practices gave the success stories in our study a strong foundation of trust.

- Ecosystem orchestrators must be prepared to combine trust instruments from different classes. But they should try to keep the number of trust instruments they deploy as low as possible to avoid complexity.
- Digital plays a crucial role in enabling systemic trust and, in some cases, the very existence of business ecosystems that would otherwise not be viable. However, our analysis shows that a digital-only approach can only go so far. Digital instruments must usually be combined with nondigital ones to build trust effectively.
- Ecosystems should address trust-related issues as early as possible so that these issues don't hamper growth. Trust-related issues can be viewed as weak signals of a vicious cycle of problem and erosion that can prove difficult to revert once fully established. Rethink the entire approach if you observe early signs of trust erosion in your ecosystem.
- Refine and reassess the combination of instruments deployed as your ecosystem scales and matures (as illustrated by our sample's successful social media platforms). Current effectiveness is no guarantee of future effectiveness.
- Utilize the trust instruments to design your ecosystem for repeated interaction. By using the toolbox, you can extend what political scientist Robert Axelrod referred to as "the shadow of the future" and make cooperative behavior rational – even in inherently challenging cases like HopSkipDrive, in which parents entrust strangers with their children's safety.

The broader the set of possible interactions, the more likely adverse events are. Generally speaking, this also means more instruments are needed. Ecosystem orchestrators must remember that the higher the stakes, the greater the potential losses – as the trust imperative grows, participants put even more stock in the trustworthiness of their transaction parties.

A good starting point is to clarify the problem to be solved and the associated trust issues. The ecosystem's life cycle stage should also figure into your instrument choices. As ecosystems gain scale and mature, their trust challenges often change. Actively monitoring the effectiveness of trust instruments over time – and adjusting them as needed – can help avert trust erosion before it becomes irreversible. Here, again, past success is not a guarantee of future success.

Critical Design Questions

Clearly, there are many important design decisions to weigh. Start by studying your ecosystem's expected trust-related issues and identify the trust instruments that will help address them. We distilled a selection of key questions and specific guidelines to help orchestrators in this effort.

What must an ecosystem do to convince participants of the quality of the experience? The most effective approaches for ensuring quality are regulating access and controlling supplier input (what partners can offer on the platform). Incentivizing providers to offer high-quality products or services and enhancing transparency are also effective.

When property is the offering – residences, in Airbnb's case, or cars, in Uber's case – the potential for property damage arises, either inadvertent, through sheer use, or through abuse by poorly behaving participants. The most effective measures for instilling confidence and trust and minimizing losses are transparency and banning parties who behave badly, both preventive measures, and compensating for any asset depreciation that occurs.

What if the transaction is susceptible to fraud? Fraud is a considerable problem in many ecosystems. It comes in many forms, but the most common are transactional or financial. Ecosystems have two basic approaches at their disposal in these instances: access and mitigation. They can strive to prevent bad outcomes by banning fraudulent parties or applying process controls, and if fraud occurs, they can provide compensation.

On platforms involving the exchange of funds, participants worry about whether they will receive payment. This question arises in situations where the seller does not trust the buyer to pay (in the case of upfront delivery) and instances where money is lent. What works best in such circumstances? Screening of potential participants (for example, through credit scores), closely monitoring inputs and processes on the platform (controls), establishing the platform as the transaction partner (intermediation), or offering compensation when an adverse event occurs.

What if misbehavior leads to uncooperative interactions? Successful ecosystems ensure that partners play by the rules by being selective and, more importantly, by banning partners who misbehave or fail to deliver (access). In such situations, control instruments are the best defense against future adverse events. Transparency also helps lower risk through its deterrent effect on would-be bad actors. Finally, ecosystems with problems that can be resolved through refund can rely on mitigation instruments to earn and sustain trust.

Asymmetry of information complicates trust building. The greater a party's information advantage, the easier it is to abuse it. In ecosystems with great information asymmetries, such as used-goods marketplaces, transparency tools lessen the information divide, and mitigation instruments ensure that the more knowledgeable party is held accountable for any misbehavior. Contracts are inherently imperfect because it is impossible to anticipate every kind of adversity that could arise or identify every possible contingency. Thus, most contracts contain a clause that designates intermediation through a neutral arbitrator to resolve any contractual conflicts.

What if participants question the ecosystem's security (virtual or physical)? As soon as sensitive data is involved, the risk of data misuse increases. Rigorous data governance instruments need to be in place to mitigate those risks. Successful ecosystems typically restrict access to trustworthy partners, define data usage and access rights in contracts, and closely control partners' behavior on the platform.

Many ecosystems penetrate participants' personal lives, either through social connection online or direct contact (in the case of personal services, such as ride hailing or home cleaning). The threat to a participant's personal security is, of course, one of the worst possible outcomes. Clearly, mitigation instruments are insufficient. Ecosystems must actively prevent bad behavior. Access instruments, along with control instruments that monitor platform users' behavior, are the most effective weapons in their trust arsenal.

What if participants mistrust the ecosystem orchestrator? It's not enough to build trust among participants, participants must have trust in the ecosystem orchestrator. Partners are free to engage in ecosystems and walk away from them at will. Orchestrators must internalize the fact that ecosystems compete on trust. Trust is, in effect, the lifeblood of ecosystems. An ecosystem's success is often built on the belief that the orchestrator will not misuse its platform dominance. We see this in the compact between independent software developers and large tech companies that own a platform (e.g., iOS for Apple, Windows for Microsoft). Software developers must trust that these companies will not take advantage of their dominance, that they won't change the rules for enterprise apps, and that they will honor their monetization models. Orchestrators can build this trust through contracts and transparency. But most importantly, they must consistently prove it through their behavior.

Embedding trust requires a mindset shift away from the naive belief that trust will spontaneously emerge among complete strangers. Trust cannot simply be treated as an after-the-fact consideration. As successful ecosystems demonstrate, trust must be front and center in designing ecosystems with the strength and resilience to thrive amid the challenges of the future. By fostering interaction and cooperation, trust not only helps ecosystems fulfill their value proposition but also becomes a source of competitive advantage.

The art and science of achieving this advantage reside in determining the right combination of trust instruments for an ecosystem's distinct needs and issues – in essence, designing ecosystems for systemic trust and making the enabling instruments observable and manageable in a true symbiotic fashion. The recommendations based on the patterns we've described represent the first step companies can take to understand trust and bolster both competitive advantage and resilience.

Section B: **Data in Business Ecosystems**

François Candelon, Massimo Russo, Rodolphe Charme
di Carlo, Hind El Bedraoui, and Tian Feng

Chapter 12
Simple Governance for Data Ecosystems

As big companies explore new revenue streams and business models based on data, they quickly run into a quandary. On the one hand, combining the data they control with data from other sources significantly increases the number and value of potential available use cases. On the other, that same act of data sharing opens up issues of trust and misuse, lost value, and unrealized opportunity. In many cases, the potential risks (which tend to be more readily identifiable) appear to outweigh the prospective rewards (which are often more distant and uncertain), and the companies proceed no further. This is unfortunate, understandable, and unnecessary.

Data sharing – particularly the exchange of the exploding quantities of data generated by the Internet of Things – has emerged as an important and high-value commercial activity. It can help advance new business models, drive innovation, and tackle some of society's most pressing challenges, such as making cities more efficient and livable. Data sharing is facilitated by data ecosystems comprising multiple parties within and outside of an individual company's industry. These ecosystems can overcome some major barriers to data sharing, including the unclear value of data at the point of generation and the need for collective intelligence to identify and match participants with opportunities for value creation. Broadly, data ecosystems are important vehicles for aligning companies around common goals while giving them the agility needed to innovate.

For the orchestrators of data ecosystems – which can be tech companies, large industrial incumbents, or innovative startups – the stakes are high: if other companies are not willing to share their data, the ecosystem dies on the vine. Still, many companies continue to hoard their data – to their own detriment and that of the ecosystem as a whole.

Simple and effective rules of governance can help break the data gridlock. But in the face of many possible design choices, companies don't always know where to start. A good first step is to understand that data sharing in an ecosystem is fundamentally an issue of cooperation, with rules guiding good behavior and setting the terms of engagement. BCG's *Smart Simplicity* framework, which is designed to help companies make sense of organizational complexity and encourage cooperation, can help.

https://doi.org/10.1515/9783110775167-012

The Sources of Data Gridlock

Our research and client experience show that problems with data sharing generally revolve around four issues: trust and privacy, transaction costs, competitive concerns, and worries over missed or lost financial opportunity (Figure 12.1).

Trust and privacy	Transaction costs	Competitive concerns	Lost financial opportunity
Fear of data misuse and concerns about privacy and security	Technological and procedural difficulties	Fear that surrender of strategic data will lead to loss of value or competitive advantage	Unrealized opportunity from not recognizing downstream value, misallocating value among participants, or neglecting opportunities to develop end-to-end data services

Source: BCG Henderson Institute

Figure 12.1: The Four Issues Revolving Around Data Sharing.

1. **Trust and Privacy.** This barrier is rooted in the fear that data will be mishandled, misused, or mis-shared. Poor technology, weak governance, and actual data breaches can all lead to data being used for purposes that were not agreed upon by the originator of the data and others in the ecosystem.
2. **Transaction Costs.** These costs underlie every data exchange, and problems can be both technological and procedural in nature. Technological impediments include poor connectivity, mismatched standards, and constraints on interoperability. Procedural barriers can involve mismatched skills, organizational complexity, or ambiguous rules. Technological advances such as 5G mobile connectivity, better industry standards, broker platforms, and data fusion tools are emerging to tackle the former. Sharing governance can tackle the latter. But as more heterogeneous IoT data comes online, new challenges are likely.
3. **Competitive Concerns.** The data landscape is still mostly unmapped, and new, unforeseen use cases appear every day. Companies rightly fear surrendering competitive advantage along with strategic data. Incumbent contributors to an ecosystem may worry that competitively sensitive information will be released to rivals. New digital entrants may worry about digital giants copying their tools or poaching their talent. All participants may worry about ecosystem orchestrators capturing a disproportionate portion of the value.

4. **Lost Financial Opportunity.** Another ramification of the unmapped landscape is the possibility that sharing data may cause financial opportunities
   to be overlooked. This could result from a failure to recognize data's downstream value, from misallocation of value among an ecosystem's participants, or from neglected opportunities to develop end-to-end data services
   internally. For example, vendors and customers can work together to coordinate logistics, rationalize inventory, and even codesign products, but the
   benefits and investments may not accrue evenly across the supply chain.

If the barriers to sharing are sufficiently high, they will cause data gridlock. A
2018 European Commission study found that of 129 companies surveyed, 60%
did not share data with other companies and 58% did not reuse data obtained
from other companies. When gridlock occurs, data ecosystems fail to thrive and
value creation is limited.

Overcoming Gridlock

Two successful European ventures demonstrate how to overcome the barriers
to data sharing and break out of gridlock. Their operations and data are now
global in scale.

HERE Technologies

Owned by a consortium of German auto OEMs and Tier 1 suppliers (including
Intel, Mitsubishi, and NTT, among others), HERE is the world's leading location
data and technology platform provider, supporting data sharing at scale through
both its core data offering and its marketplace platform. The company sources
data from thousands of independent contributors and partners, including the
OEMs themselves – which, as owners, are able to capture the residual value of
HERE's operations. The company provides recommended standards, pools data,
and provides scale and reach via aggregated data services, thus facilitating coordination and reducing the fear among the consortium's participants of any competitive disadvantage that might exist if a single company led the venture. HERE
Marketplace connects data sources (providers) with data consumers (buyers) and
supports the former in assessing the value of their data and capturing it through
potential use cases. The private marketplace's features reassure data providers
that they control access to and use of their data.

To facilitate data sharing, HERE provides an intuitive user experience and a suite of APIs and software development kits, as well as a set of data monetization services. Compliance with the EU's General Data Protection Regulation (GDPR) and a comprehensive privacy charter ensure approved and acceptable data use. The partner-vetting process and blockchain-based consent management system give data users and data contributors confidence that their personally identifiable information will be shared only with service providers they approve of and only once that approval is in place.

In addition to highlighting commercial use cases for data, HERE emphasizes the value of data sharing through public-service projects such as the EU Data Task Force, no-fee exchange of data shared under Creative Commons licensing, and its multiple customer- and partner-led COVID-19 response efforts.

Airbus Skywise

Launched in 2017, Airbus's Skywise open platform is an integrated service and data solution leveraging a data analytics software suite that helps airlines analyze aircraft data collected by sensors while planes are in flight and on the ground. Skywise now includes more than 100 airline partners – regional airlines, global giants, and industry rivals (Delta and United are both members) – that share data with the goal of improving operations.

Airbus maintains that each airline owns its data. In exchange for sharing, participants gain access to Skywise analytics insights and benchmarking data. The company also publishes success stories that illustrate the value of participation. To manage competitive concerns, Airbus ensures that only aggregated benchmarks are shared among contributors.

Because most of the sensor data is generated by Airbus planes and their flight data is similar, Airbus is able to transform data from different airlines into a standard format. GDPR compliance sets a baseline level of acceptable data use, and a publicized partner-vetting process provides transparency around data access.

Data Ecosystem Participants

In both of these examples, the companies involved overcame barriers to data sharing by setting up built-for-purpose ecosystems with clear rules of governance. Such ecosystems organize the data assets and customer connections of a group of business partners in order to deliver new products and services – both within and across traditional industry verticals.

Data ecosystems have three types of participant. Orchestrators (such as HERE and Airbus) set the rules, coordinate the activities of the other participants, aggregate their data and expertise, and deliver a range of products or services to the end customer. Contributors, which may be participants in multiple ecosystems, provide their data and services or build and sell applications with the help of the ecosystem's data. Enablers provide infrastructure for the ecosystem, including connectivity, security, and computing power.

Orchestrators cannot orchestrate unless they create the right context for breaking through the data-sharing gridlock and encouraging cooperation. Like employees who must decide whether it's worth their while to work together on a risky project, companies embarking on data sharing must assess the value, risk, and potential conflicts involved. This is where good governance can help.

Smart Simplicity Rules of Governance

BCG's Smart Simplicity approach promotes such cooperation within complex organizations. Instead of crafting rules one by one to target specific behaviors, Smart Simplicity explores the context underlying a system of behaviors by analyzing the motivations of individuals. It then uses six simple rules to change the context (Figure 12.2).

The first three rules help organizations create the conditions for individual autonomy and empowerment. The other three compel people to confront complexity and cooperate with others so that the overall performance of the organization – in this case, the data ecosystem – becomes as important to them as their own individual performance. Of course, there are additional rules that ecosystem orchestrators will need to consider regarding data ownership, access, and use, but those will vary by ecosystem.

Rule 1. Understand what people really do. To untangle the competitive and trust barriers within an ecosystem, orchestrators need to understand the goals, resources, and constraints of its participants. Such an understanding helps orchestrators design governance measures that address the underlying motivations of ecosystem participants, not just their behaviors.

Rule 2. Reinforce the integrators. In data ecosystems, the orchestrators and enablers often play the role of integrators – participants whose influence makes a difference in the work of others. Integrators bring others together and drive

Barriers addressed

#	Rule	Action	Trust and privacy	Transaction costs	Competitive concerns	Lost financial opportunity
1	Understand what people really do	· Map agents, goals, resources, and barriers	●	●	●	●
2	Reinforce the integrators	· Define standards · Create sharing pipeline and infrastructure		● ●		
3	Increase the total quantity of power	· Create 360 data use and sharing rules · Signal noncompetition · Define clear default rules · Define standards of good behavior	● ● ●	 ● 	● ● ● ●	
4	Increase reciprocity	· Define the mutual interest in sharing data · Publicize valuable use cases	● 		● 	● ●
5	Expand the shadow of the future	· Define value creation and sharing model			●	●
6	Reward those who cooperate	· Assign financial value to data shared · Create recognition system for data contributors				● ●

Source: BCG Henderson Institute

Figure 12.2: Smart Simplicity's Six Rules to Change the Context Underlying Data Sharing.

processes. They work at the nexus where constraints and requirements often meet. Defining standards by generating and sharing the same data formats, using the same protocols, and following the same reference architecture can lower barriers to data sharing. Organizations such as the International Data Spaces Association are exploring standards to make data sharing seamless. Creating pipelines and infrastructure (APIs, for example) that facilitate sharing can also reduce friction.

Rule 3. Increase the total quantity of power. Empowering people to make decisions without taking power away from others is a great way to make sure all participants feel they have a stake in the ecosystem's success. Orchestrators have several ways to do this. Access controls, 360-degree sharing rules, and rights management can build confidence that contributors' data will be used in the right ways, even as it moves out of the hands of the orchestrator. Providing transparency into the sources and uses of data, and giving contributors a role in deciding how their data will be used, can also help. A good example is the privacy settings on Apple's iPhone, which give users the ability to determine which applications can access which data streams.

Being explicit about the ecosystem's strategic positioning in the market and implementing noncompete agreements among participants can reduce competitive barriers and give contributors peace of mind about sharing sensitive data. Privacy-preserving analytical tools that protect the underlying data while others analyze it give participants further confidence that their data is secure.

Making clear the ecosystem's default position on such issues as data ownership and usage control promotes sharing and reduces concerns arising from ambiguity. Data ecosystems need clear standards of acceptable and unacceptable behavior. Data capture without consent, data sharing with competitors, and unauthorized resale to third parties should be clearly off-limits. Orchestrators can support monitoring and enforcement of these norms.

Rule 4. Increase reciprocity. The success of each participant in the ecosystem depends on the success of others. To drive this home, orchestrators should clearly define participants' common purpose and their mutual interest in sharing data. The clearer the purpose, especially in the absence of defined contractual terms, the more readily will the ecosystem's individual contributors move in the desired direction and avoid improper behavior. Orchestrators can also publicize successful use cases. At its annual LiveWorx conference, for example, IoT tech enabler PTC runs demonstrations of collaboration unlocked by its SaaS (software as a service) data-sharing tools.

Rule 5. Expand the shadow of the future. A good value creation and sharing model shows people how their success is furthered by contributing to the success of others. The same goes for fairly sharing the value that results, whether financial or some other benefit. For example, precision agriculture ecosystems often have a clear value proposition: share machinery data and we will give you the resources needed to improve your yields. Ecosystems that do not share value fairly soon find that they must rethink their model or fall apart.

Rule 6. Reward those who cooperate. There are at least two ways that orchestrators can create a recognition system for data contributors. One is to assign a financial value to the data shared; the other is to link some form of nonfinancial remuneration to data sharing. In some successful data ecosystems, sharing data is regarded as a good in and of itself, with the value created often linked to social as well as economic goals. New York University's GovLab has created a list of more than 200 data collaboratives that share data for public value. Similarly, companies such as Microsoft are promoting the idea of open data sharing. Orchestrators and contributors may be able to use their participation in data-sharing ecosystems to support their social-impact goals and reporting.

Ecosystems are emerging as promising vehicles for data sharing. Yet the cooperation necessary for their adoption at scale is still limited, hampered by issues of trust and privacy, transaction costs, competitive concerns, and worries over missed or lost financial opportunity. For data ecosystems to break out of data-sharing gridlock, they need to maximize value creation for all stakeholders while mitigating the risks and ensuring a safe space for exploration and learning. Smart, simple data governance measures, in partnership with technology, are key tools for enriching the data economy.

Massimo Russo and Tian Feng

Chapter 13
The New Tech Tools in Data Sharing

"There's gold in them thar hills," cried Yosemite Sam in the old Bugs Bunny cartoons, but he never got to enjoy it. "There's gold in them thar data," Sam might say today. But he'd be equally disappointed unless he was able to navigate the host of data-sharing challenges that come with the opportunities.

Here's Sam's conundrum in a nutshell. Data sharing, by definition, involves multiple parties that tend to coalesce around ecosystems. As these ecosystems grow, they share more types of data, and more detailed data, among the members of an expanding community. They also develop solutions that address an expanding range of use cases, some of which were totally unforeseen when the data was originally generated or shared. Each of these factors introduces its own set of risk-value tradeoffs. The extent of the tradeoffs depends on the specific data-sharing capabilities of the underlying platform.

The good news is that the technology companies that enable many ecosystems either have developed or are developing a host of technological solutions to facilitate data sharing by mitigating risk, enhancing value, and reducing the sources of friction that inhibit sharing. These solutions shift the tradeoff frontier between value, on the one hand, and risk and friction, on the other, in the direction of value. Forward-looking management teams should educate themselves on the issues at stake and the technology solutions coming into the marketplace.

Start with Your Needs and Goals

Before they delve into the details of complex technology solutions, management teams need to consider their data-sharing context (for example, their goals, prospective partners, and the potential pathways to value) and their priorities (orchestrating an ecosystem or contributing to one or more, for example). Three questions bear investigation.

1. **What sharing issues are raised by the underlying data needs, use cases, and scope?** Each industry and data-sharing ecosystem has its own challenges. For example, sharing patient data within a network of hospitals poses very different technology challenges than sharing carbon emissions data among companies in a particular industry or country. While both might have clear use cases, the former involves more private, and therefore

https://doi.org/10.1515/9783110775167-013

sensitive, data, which elevates concerns about security. At the same time, the relatively small number of companies sharing the data reduces risk and complexity. In a similar vein, companies working with personal data may need to protect individual data points, while companies sharing enterprise data may want to mask aggregated insights to maintain competitive advantage.

2. **Are good data governance procedures in place?** Good data governance practices ensure that technology is used appropriately and consistently. Common challenges such as data breaches often occur not because of technological shortfalls but because of user error. Management should consider data-sharing enablers and data governance as part of one strategic process. Some of the most effective tools, such as those for data management and classification, help companies establish good governance practices by identifying the right level of security for a given type of data. For example, data consent management and data access controls are automated ways of managing governance.

3. **Where do gaps in trust inhibit data sharing?** Trust is a prerequisite in many data exchanges, and a good number of data-sharing technologies function as trust substitutes or trust obviators. Among trust substitutes, technologies such as blockchain, ratings systems, execution environments, and application program interfaces (APIs) decrease risk by imposing controls or by creating transparency, introducing a technological intermediary in which all parties have confidence. Among trust obviators, technologies such as federated learning, edge processing, and private set intersections reduce the need for trust by creating alternatives to direct data sharing. To enhance sharing, it's important to identify trust gaps, determine whether you want to replace or reduce the need for trust, and then adopt the right technological solutions.

Available Technology Solutions

Cloud providers are integrating data-sharing capabilities into their product suites and investing in R&D that addresses new features such as data directories, trusted execution environments, and homomorphic encryption. They are also partnering with industry-specific ecosystem orchestrators to provide joint solutions.

Cloud providers are moving beyond infrastructure to enable broader data sharing. In 2018, for example, Microsoft teamed up with Oracle and SAP to kick off its Open Data Initiative, which focuses on interoperability among the three large platforms. Microsoft has also begun an Open Data Campaign to close the data divide and help smaller organizations get access to data needed for innovation in artificial intelligence (AI). Amazon Web Services (AWS) has begun a number of projects designed to promote open data, including the AWS Data Exchange and the Open Data Sponsorship Program. In addition to these large providers, specialty technology companies and startups are likewise investing in solutions that further data sharing.

Technology solutions today generally fall into three categories: (1) mitigating risks, (2) enhancing value, and (3) reducing friction. The following is a non-comprehensive list of solutions in each category.

1 Mitigating the Risks of Data Sharing

Potential financial, competitive, and brand risks associated with data disclosure inhibit data sharing. To address these risks, data platforms are embedding solutions to control use, limit data access, encrypt data, and create substitute or synthetic data (Figure 13.1).

Data Breaches. Here are some of the technological solutions designed to prevent data breaches and unauthorized access to sensitive or private data:
- Data modification techniques alter individual data elements or full data sets while maintaining data integrity. They provide increasing levels of protection but at a cost: loss of granularity of the underlying data. De-identification and masking strip personal identifier information and use encryption, allowing most of the data value to be preserved. More complex encryptions can increase security, but they also remove resolution of information from the data set.
- Secure data storage and transfer can help ensure that data stays safe both at rest and in transit. Cloud solutions such as Microsoft Azure and AWS have invested in significant platform security and interoperability.
- Distributed ledger technologies, such as blockchain, permit data to be stored and shared in a decentralized manner that makes it very difficult to tamper with. IOTA, for example, is a distributed ledger platform for IoT applications supported by industry players such as Bosch and Software AG.
- Secure computation enables analysis without revealing details of the underlying data. This can be done at a software level, with techniques such as secure multiparty computation (MPC) that allow potentially untrusting parties to jointly compute a function without revealing their private inputs. For example, with MPC, two parties can calculate the intersection of their respective encrypted data set while only revealing information about the intersection. Google, for one, is embedding MPC in its open-source Private Join and Compute tools.

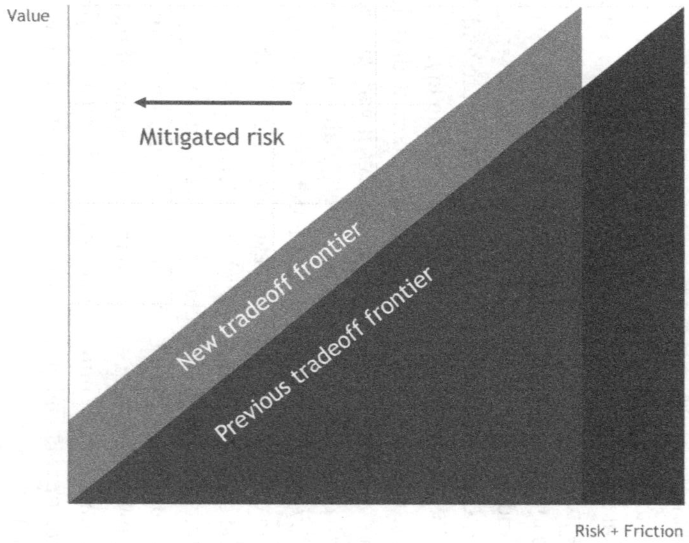

Challenges	Solutions	Examples
Data breaches	Secure data storage & transfer	• Secure cloud • Distributed ledger technologies
	Secure computation	• Secure multiparty computation • Trusted execution environments
	Data modifications	• Encryption • De-identification/masking/anonymity • Differential privacy
Data mis-sharing & misuse	Usage & access controls	• APIs • Secure database management • Self-destructing data
	Sharing substitutes	• Federated learning • Synthetic data
Data quality risks	Validation & authentification	• Distributed ledger technologies • Watermarking

Source: BCG Henderson Institute

Figure 13.1: Mitigation of Data Sharing Risks.

– Trusted execution environments (TEEs) are hardware modules separate from the operating system that allow for secure data processing within an encrypted private area on the chip. Startup Decentriq is partnering with Intel and Microsoft to explore confidential computing by means of TEEs. There is a significant opportunity for IoT equipment providers to integrate TEEs into their products.

Data Mis-Sharing and Misuse. Platforms are embedding a series of functions to control access to and distribution of data:
– APIs are the most widely adopted form of access control. For example, Alibaba's Data Middle Office uses APIs to provide a centralized data and analytics platform that acts as the single source of truth for the company's data. Startups such as Immuta are building fine-grained access controls in addition to smart-query and masking tools to ensure that sensitive data is used only by those with permission to do so.
– Federated learning allows AI algorithms to travel and train on distributed data that is retained by contributors. This technique has been used to train machine-learning algorithms to detect cancer in images that are retained in the databases of various hospital systems without revealing sensitive patient data.
– Synthetic data, a relatively new approach, mirrors the properties of an original data set without disclosing any private information. The data can then be shared with partners to train algorithms or test software. A platform called Mostly AI is designed to generate synthetic data sets.

Data Quality Risks. Before using data, it's critical to understand its provenance, reliability, and authenticity. Data watermarking, for example, can document the precise origin of data sourced from third parties, and any tampering will remove or distort the watermark. Adobe recently announced its Content Authenticity Initiative, which embeds an encrypted chain of metadata into digital media to reveal provenance and potential tampering.

2 Enhancing the Value of Data Sharing

Despite the oft-cited analogy, data is not a well-priced commodity like oil. Data has very different values depending on its uniqueness, the specific use case or problem it can help solve, and the degree to which customers are willing to pay for the solution. Valuing data is hard. Data platforms are creating tools to help assess and capture this value (Figure 13.2).

Challenges	Solutions	Examples
Value identification	• Data usage mapping	• AI • Data competitions
Value assessment	• Assessment tools	• AI • Data ratings
Value capture	• Usage tracking & control	• APIs • Smart contracts • Data watermarking
	• Payment systems	• Blockchain • Micropayments
	• Data organization	• Data containers • Data networks

Source: BCG Henderson Institute

Figure 13.2: Tools to Evaluate and Capture Data Value.

Value Identification. Some data marketplaces are employing AI to match data to potential use cases. For example, data broker Dawex is building AI solutions that match sellers and buyers of data. The company also provides a service to help evaluate data sets using factors such as volume, history, completeness, validity, and rarity. Data competitions are another way to help owners find use cases for their data.

Value Assessment. Once use cases have been identified, how can enterprises determine the value they should receive in exchange for sharing their data? While AI is traditionally viewed as a means of deriving insights from data, it can also be used to value the data itself. Collective and Augmented Intelligence Against COVID-19, a new coalition of researchers and nonprofits (including the Stanford Institute for Human-Centered Artificial Intelligence and UNESCO), are leveraging AI to sift through competing data sets in order to organize and evaluate the quality of available data. Other data validation tools, such as ratings, can likewise help with value assessment and are being applied in emerging blockchain data marketplaces.

Value Capture. As data travels from its point of origin to use, it can pass through multiple entities. Similar to raw materials that are transformed along a value chain into a usable product, data can be manipulated and combined – and its value enhanced. Functions such as micropayments, smart contracts, and subscription systems are being embedded into data platforms to capture value. Access control, permissions, and data-tracing solutions ensure that data is routed only for the intended use. New startups such as Digi.Me and Solid, an open-source technology developed in part by World Wide Web inventor Tim Berners-Lee, help consumers control and monetize their data through personal data container technologies. Solid, for example, stores data in "pods" in an interoperable format and provides users with the tools to control which organizations and applications can access their data. This type of technology could be applied to enterprise data as well.

3 Reducing Friction in Data Sharing

Data is often hidden behind enterprise walls, so it can be difficult to know what data exists. Solutions are emerging to search for potentially valuable data and then transfer and transform it into usable forms (Figure 13.3).

Dark Data. In a data-sharing ecosystem, there is a need to both discover unknown (or "dark") data behind enterprise walls and aggregate data from disparate

Challenges	Solutions	Examples
Dark data **Aggregation complexity**	• Discovery & aggregation tools	• Data curation/wrangling • Data directories • Data fusion tools • Master data management
Barriers to interoperability	• Interoperability support	• RESTful APIs • Semantic technologies • Standards
Barriers to transfer	• Transfer & streaming tools	• APIs • Edge/fog processing • Networking /communication technologies • Stream processing • Software development kits

Source: BCG Henderson Institute

Figure 13.3: Solutions to Reduce Friction in Data Sharing.

sources. Cross-enterprise data directories, such as those provided by marketplaces like Azure and AWS, can provide visibility into the types of data that exist. For example, Dawex is building a data marketplace technology that can search through a variety of data sources (across dimensions such as data types, attributes, and time series) provided by individual contributors.

Aggregation Complexity. Data from different sources will have different definitions, formats, and meanings. Companies such as Tamr and Trifacta are developing "data wrangling" and data curation tools to identify, clean, and interpret data so it can be easily understood and combined.

Barriers to Interoperability. Due to the prevalence of heterogenous data types and data sources, companies are investing in data standards and harmonized data models. For example, in mid-2020, Microsoft acquired ADRM Software, a data analytics company with a large set of industry data reference models that facilitate data aggregation and analysis for enterprises. Other reference architectures, such as LF Edge, the IDS Reference Architecture Model, and iSHARE, can enable secure and scalable peer-to-peer transactions. These initiatives are defining semantic metadata, which attaches context and meaning to a data set, and building registries to facilitate interpretation, aggregation, and analysis of data.

Barriers to Transfer. Fundamental to sharing is the ability to transfer data from its point of origin to its intended use with sufficient speed and without so much overhead that the data's value is compromised. Traditional tools such as APIs, streaming platforms (Apache Kafka, for example), connectivity solutions (5G), and cloud provider features like Azure Data Share have already led to many advances in this area.

There is gold in data sharing, which leads quickly to more efficiencies for companies, new services for customers, and new models and revenue streams. Data platform providers and ecosystem orchestrators are investing in solutions to push out the boundary of the risk-value-friction tradeoff in data sharing by enabling controlled access and analytics while protecting the underlying data. It's a complex marketplace that's taking shape, and corporate management teams with data-sharing interests or ambitions need to get up to speed.

Section C: **Industry Applications**

Ulrich Pidun, Niklas Knust, Julian Kawohl,
Evangelos Avramakis, and Andreas Klar

Chapter 14
The Untapped Potential of Ecosystems in Health Care

William Kissick, the father of the US Medicare program, once described the economics of health care systems as an iron triangle composed of three competing elements: access, quality, and cost containment. The core challenge: How do you make improvements to one of the elements without compromising the other two? Much of the focus has been on rising costs, which the traditional model of care delivery has tried to address with improvements in operational efficiency – delivering the same level of output with less effort and waste. However, this chase for efficiency has reached its limits. In recent decades, productivity improvement rates in health care in Europe and North America have lagged behind those of almost all other industries. It is time to pivot from a focus on efficiency to a focus on meaningful innovation, and business ecosystems in health care can play a major role in this paradigm shift.

Business ecosystems offer three important benefits. First, they can provide fast access to a broad range of external capabilities that may be too expensive or time-consuming to build internally. This is particularly relevant for companies that want to reap the benefits of open innovation, an area where ecosystems outperform pipeline models. Second, ecosystems can scale much faster than pipeline models. Their modular setup, with clearly defined interfaces, makes it easy to add partners and expand the network. And finally, ecosystems offer a large degree of flexibility and resilience. They can quickly adapt to changing consumer needs or technological innovation, which makes them particularly advantageous in unpredictable environments and during times of high uncertainty.

In business ecosystems, a dynamic group of largely independent partners work together to deliver integrated products or services. While the health care system meets all requirements of a business ecosystem, it is rarely managed as one. By learning from other industries and harnessing the innovation potential of the ecosystem model, health care could substantially improve all three dimensions of the iron triangle. Like Alibaba for retail, or Airbnb for travel, health care ecosystems could facilitate and improve access at scale for patients and consumers. Like smart farming or smart mining platforms, health care ecosystems could enable new solutions and major improvements in quality by enhancing

https://doi.org/10.1515/9783110775167-014

coordination and effectively using data across partners. Like cloud-computing platforms or e-commerce marketplaces, health care ecosystems could lower cost and tap the efficiency potential currently lost in the fragmented interplay of stakeholders, sectoral boundaries, and limited care coordination, which researchers estimate account for up to 25% of health care spending in Europe and the US. When designed and managed properly, business ecosystems allow health care organizations to break the painful tradeoff between access, quality, and cost.

Why Are There So Few Successful Health Care Ecosystems?

The ecosystem approach is not new to health care. Traditional health care payers, providers, and suppliers, as well as big tech companies, have attempted to establish ecosystems in order to deliver integrated or value-based health care. Some success stories exist, particularly among health maintenance organizations (HMOs), such as Kaiser Permanente, but the broader health care sector has not yet embraced the ecosystem concept.

There are a few reasons for this. First, innovation in care delivery is hampered by structural roadblocks that discourage the most important precondition of an ecosystem: cooperation between partners. In most developed economies, strict legal boundaries between the different health care segments fragment care delivery, and fee-for-service payment structures incentivize single treatments rather than holistic care. Stakeholders lack common outcome measures and shared goals.

Second, the health care sector is resistant to change. While the overall health care system is under considerable pressure from rising costs, many individual actors don't feel this pressure because their business models are still intact, creating a strong status-quo bias. Many of these actors are well organized and equipped with veto-like powers in political processes, making policy change difficult. Health policy plays an important role in defining common goals, providing a framework for cooperation, and driving long-term improvements. For ecosystem solutions to work, proactive changes in regulation are needed.

Finally, the strategic challenges of moving from a pipeline model to an ecosystem model are considerable, and few health care players have found the right approach.

Research conducted by the BCG Henderson Institute found that fewer than 15% of business ecosystems are sustainable in the long run – and six out of seven failures can be attributed to weaknesses in ecosystem design (see Chapter 4). To make the transition, business ecosystems must be designed and managed carefully from the outset.

Now Is the Time for Ecosystems in Health Care

Several trends are paving the way for a broader application of ecosystem models in health care. First, new competitors, many equipped with successful platforms and relevant experience in creating business ecosystems, are entering the market. Walmart has launched cost-efficient outpatient clinics, startups like mySugr and Omada Health are disrupting chronic care management, and tech players such as Google, Amazon, Microsoft, and Apple are offering health care solutions such as cloud services for health data and telemedicine. Second, patients are increasingly demanding levels of service and choice in health care that they are used to receiving in other areas of life – often delivered by ecosystems. Third, technology adoption has created new forms of access and interaction. Secure and cost-effective data-sharing solutions, for example, are increasingly available and enable new ecosystem applications. Fourth, we are starting to see momentum in regulatory changes. In Germany, for example, an enabling regulatory framework for telemedicine was recently instituted, digital therapeutics can now be prescribed by doctors, and systemwide electronic health records (EHRs) were launched in January 2021. Finally, while the COVID-19 pandemic has exposed many structural weaknesses of existing health care systems, it has also demonstrated the potential of digital ecosystems. Companies responding to the COVID crisis were required to rethink many existing rules, regulations, and routines, which enabled them to innovate and collaborate like never before. Virtually overnight, a contactless health care system became a necessity, fostering a plethora of new digital applications, including advances in telehealth, innovative distribution of medical supplies (via drones, for example), and coordinated care across broad geographical regions.

Of course, business ecosystems are not a panacea; for many business opportunities and situations a hierarchical supply chain or an open-market model will perform better (see Chapter 2). But ecosystems are the optimal governance model when a high level of modularity (offerings of different players can be flexibly combined) meets a significant need for coordination in order to align stakeholder activities. And these are exactly the conditions that we typically find in the health care sector. The entire health care system can be considered a large ecosystem made up of providers (hospitals, doctors, therapists, and others), payers (health insurers), suppliers (pharmaceutical and medtech companies, pharmacies, and others), and regulators. All of these partners offer complementary modules that need to be coordinated in order to provide coherent diagnostic, therapeutic, or care solutions for patients.

The Four Fundamental Value Propositions of Health Care Ecosystems

A clearly defined value proposition is vital to the success of a health care ecosystem. These value propositions will vary depending on the ecosystem's targeted disease scope (the number of indications and whether the focus will be on treatment, prevention, or both) and the targeted life area (health or beyond). Based on this framework, there are four fundamental approaches for creating a health care ecosystem (Figure 14.1).

Source: BCG Henderson Institute

Figure 14.1: Four Fundamental Approaches for Creating a Health Care Ecosystem.

1. **Optimize treatment of a disease.** Ecosystem strategies can focus on the treatment and prevention of specific indications, such as heart disease or cancer. This can be done through traditional disease-management programs as well as emerging solutions, such as optimizing COVID-19 treatment in hospitals. For example, the World Economic Forum launched the Atlanta Heart Failure Pilot in 2017. The pilot built an ecosystem of approximately 40 health care stakeholders and aimed to "make Atlanta a national leader in the heart failure survival rate by 2022 while significantly improving quality of life and reducing the average cost per capita."

2. **Improve life with a disease.** Ecosystem strategies can also move beyond the narrow health care focus and include other life areas such as nutrition, housing, mobility, or wellness in order to improve the lives of patients with a specific indication. Payers, care-management organizations, and startups are well-positioned to offer this value proposition. For example, mySugr, the Austrian diabetes-management startup (acquired by Roche in 2017), built an open ecosystem that brings together diabetes-focused partners like Novo Nordisk, specialized physicians, coaching, and other services to improve the lives of patients with diabetes. The company crisply captures its mission in the tagline: "make diabetes suck less."

3. **Enhance processes in health care.** Ecosystem strategies that can be leveraged to make health care processes more efficient and effective include EHRs and comprehensive telehealth offerings. Some solutions, like EHRs, need systemwide scale to be successful, while others focus on specific segments or services. Chicago-based primary-care provider Oak Street Health, for example, offers population health management for care-intensive seniors, dramatically improving patient outcomes by using advanced data analytics to gain deep customer insights and constantly expand its offerings.

4. **Facilitate a healthy lifestyle.** The broadest value proposition of a health care ecosystem is to span different life areas such as mobility or education to promote a healthy lifestyle – with or without a disease – including prevention and general health. Some traditional health care players have started to expand their offerings to address social determinants of health (SDH). RWJBarnabas Health, a US-based integrated-care provider, recently launched a tech-enabled SDH platform that includes assistance on housing, safety, nutrition, and access to transportation.

How to Put Health Care Ecosystems Into Practice

Health care companies that want to build or participate in a business ecosystem have much to gain, but they must first understand why some ecosystems work, and others do not. Based on our analysis of health care ecosystems around the world, we have found that the most successful, sustainable ecosystems embrace the following principles:

1. Focus on a big enough problem to solve.
2. Ensure that all essential partners are on board.
3. Select the right orchestrator.

4. Achieve critical mass by first increasing scale, not scope.
5. Create and harness data flywheel effects.

Focus on a Big Enough Problem to Solve

Many health care ecosystems have failed because they did not address a large enough problem. Establishing an ecosystem requires a considerable upfront investment to build the platform and incentivize partners to join. These investments can only be justified if the ecosystem, once fully established, creates sufficient value by addressing and solving a sizable problem.

Consider HealthSpot, a US telemedicine provider that allowed patients to video chat with doctors via walk-in kiosks equipped with videoconferencing tools and a suite of interactive medical devices. Despite significant funding of $44 million, and strong strategic partners, including Rite Aid (to pilot the kiosks at selected pharmacies) and Xerox (to provide IT infrastructure), Health-Spot, founded in 2010, shut down in 2016. A key reason for its demise was built right into its business model. In the US, access to care is broadly available, and an online doctor's visit does not remove a significant source of friction. Rather than creating value, HealthSpot just shifted value from one channel to another (offline to online), and from one doctor to another, in a zero-sum game.

But value propositions can be context dependent. In China, unlike the US, access to health care in rural areas is a major challenge, and this paved the way for integrated care offerings at scale, such as Ping An Good Doctor. Ping An reports that Good Doctor, which was founded in 2014, now facilitates more than 830,000 daily consultations and provides a network of 111,000 pharmacies, 1,800 in-house medical doctors, and approximately 10,000 external medical experts who can remotely diagnose more than 60% of common diseases.

Remote access to health care became an enormous problem that needed to be solved during the COVID-19 pandemic. In the US, online consultations increased from less than 0.01% of total ambulatory visits before the pandemic to nearly 70% in April 2020. By July 2020, the share of online visits dropped to 21%, according to analysis from Epic Health Research Network, and while it is unclear how big the share will be in the long run, many telehealth providers are profiting. In September 2020, Google-backed telehealth company Amwell raised $742 million in its IPO, with its stock price rising 28% in its first day of trading. As of September 2020, Amwell had provided 5.6 million consultations since its 2006 launch, with half of those coming in the six months from April through September 2020. Teladoc, a direct competitor, saw its share price jump from $84 in December 2019 to $208 in December 2020, an increase of approximately 150%.

Similarly, Grand Rounds identified a substantial friction in the health care system and developed an ecosystem solution with a clearly defined value proposition. When his son was diagnosed with a rare disease, Dr. Lawrence Hofmann, a professor at Stanford University Medical Center, reached out to his personal network to ensure the best possible care for his son. Hofmann knew that most people do not have the benefit of such a specialized network, and building on this idea, he helped found Grand Rounds in 2011. Grand Rounds offers not only a telemedicine solution but AI-based algorithms to match people with trusted specialists and top-rated medical facilities in their network when a second opinion is needed. In this way, the ecosystem creates value not only for the affected patient but also reduces health care costs overall by preventing expensive mistakes and identifying the most efficient treatments. Grand Rounds has since grown to become a care coordinator for large employers, with corporate clients that include Walmart and Home Depot. The company was last valued at $1.34 billion in a financing round in mid-2020 and recently announced a merger with the telehealth company Doctor on Demand.

Ensure That All Essential Partners are on Board

Once you have found a big enough problem to solve, the next challenge is to identify all essential partners needed to make an ecosystem work – and convince them to join the ecosystem. Start by creating a blueprint of your ecosystem that outlines the various activities, actors, and responsibilities, along with a clear view of the ways that information, goods or services, and money will flow through the ecosystem.

A blueprint can also uncover technological risks. Bold value propositions frequently require multiple innovations from different partners, and if just one of the components is not ready, the entire ecosystem may fail. Consider the example of remote robotic surgery, which promised access to state-of-the-art surgery everywhere. The technical proof of concept was established in 2001 when a group of surgeons in New York City used telesurgery to remove the gall bladder of a patient in France. Twenty years later, telesurgery is still rare. Innovations addressing latency (the lag between the operator and the remote system), reliability, and security have not been fully addressed. As a result, telesurgery has not taken off. But there is an important lesson here: timing matters. With recent advances in 5G, encryption, authentication, and robotics, telesurgery may finally be poised to bring high-level care to underserved populations.

Even if the technological problems are solved, convincing all participants to join and commit to the ecosystem can be a critical roadblock and a key reason for ecosystem failure. In health care, misaligned incentives are a chronic problem and the source of many inefficiencies. The German health care system has long struggled with systemwide adoption of digital infrastructure ("telematic infrastructure") because of low participation among health care providers. Neither positive incentives, such as investment subsidies, nor punitive measures, including fines of up to 2.5% of revenue, convinced a critical mass of providers to join, as many still perceived the net effects of adoption as negative.

To understand which players are ready, willing, and able to participate and invest in an ecosystem, you must first understand their specific incentives. Partners are more likely to commit if the following conditions are in place: participants can expect meaningful net benefits; there is a high competitive risk associated with not participating; limited investment is required; the probability and/or cost of failure is low; participants can build on existing capabilities rather than having to develop new ones.

An ecosystem can only be sustained if all required partners benefit. Strong incentives can be built into its design – and not just monetary incentives, but access to services or information. Consider the example of HERE Technologies. The mapping and location-data company has established mutually beneficial partnerships with transport and logistics companies, automakers, and traffic management centers. In exchange for receiving traffic or location data, HERE provides data and services to its partners, so all participants in the ecosystem benefit from the collaboration. Additionally, some partners are also paid for data sharing. By aligning all of the partners' goals, HERE has created a thriving business ecosystem (see also Chapter 12).

It's critical to convince health care providers and patients to participate in an ecosystem. Patients can be incentivized with free products, free services, or bonus programs. The situation is more complex for providers, who often face high investment costs and limited benefits, and orchestrators must think carefully about how to get them on board. The HMO Kaiser Permanente solved this dilemma by merging payer and provider, which has allowed it to ensure that providers participate and enabled the company to successfully implement EHRs at scale. More generally, health care players must find ways to encourage participation by establishing an aligned vision and generously sharing the benefits of the ecosystem.

Select the Right Orchestrator

In business ecosystems, an *orchestrator* offers a platform, defines the basic ecosystem governance, and encourages others to join (think of Google in its smart-home ecosystem). *Realizers* contribute complementary products or services (such as manufacturers of lighting, security, or entertainment devices in the smart-home ecosystem). *Enablers* supply more generic products or services to the ecosystem participants (such as manufacturers of sensors or displays).

Some health care ecosystems have failed because they had the wrong orchestrator. Two massive efforts to create EHRs offer a clear example of this. In 2007, Microsoft launched HealthVault, a web-based personal health record system. In 2008, Google launched Google Health, which was originally an attempt to create a repository of health records and data. Neither company managed to build a sustainable EHR ecosystem: Google Health was shut down in 2012, and Microsoft closed HealthVault in 2019. These big tech companies were not accepted as the orchestrator of an EHR ecosystem by providers and patients. Accordingly, many providers started to implement their own in-house EHRs, limited to their respective organizations, forgoing the full potential of the ecosystem model.

In any business ecosystem a successful orchestrator needs to meet four requirements. It must:

1. Serve as an essential member of the ecosystem and contribute key resources, such as access to users or a strong brand.
2. Occupy a central position in the ecosystem network, with strong connections to many other players, allowing for close coordination.
3. Stand to gain significantly from the ecosystem and thus have the incentive and ability to take on the required large up-front investments.
4. Be perceived as a fair or neutral partner by the other ecosystem members, not as a competitive threat.

The challenge in health care is that the natural orchestrator is not always obvious. That said, in some scenarios a particular organization is in a privileged position to take the orchestrator role, depending on the ecosystem's value proposition and the players' capabilities. For example, in ecosystems that focus on optimizing treatment of a disease or improving life with a disease, the point of care and medical expertise is critical; therefore, providers are in a good position to orchestrate these types of ecosystems. As geographic scope expands, larger health care players are often best positioned to become orchestrators, as we've seen with Novo Nordisk and its nationwide diabetes ecosystem in China.

If the ecosystem aims at improving processes in health care, it's more important for orchestrators to have a broad operational scope, putting health insurers and governments in a central position. In Europe, most systemwide EHR solutions are orchestrated by the government (as in Denmark and Estonia) or by payers (as in Germany). For more local applications, providers can take a central role, as we've seen with the integrated-care ecosystems of Kaiser Permanente and Mayo Clinic.

In ecosystems that aim to facilitate a healthy lifestyle, digital capabilities are frequently at the core of the value proposition, which means tech players are in a good position to take on the orchestrator role. In China, tech companies such as Tencent, Alibaba, and Baidu are demonstrating their ability to manage extensive health care ecosystems (both in terms of scale and scope).

Because they play such a crucial role in health care ecosystems, it's critical for orchestrators to be aware of and actively manage their potential shortcomings. For example, a tech company with limited experience in health care, or a health insurer with a track record of ruthless cost cutting at the expense of providers will first need to build trust with partners in order to be accepted as a fair ecosystem orchestrator.

However, it's not just the orchestrators that benefit from an ecosystem. In many cases, serving as a realizer or enabler can be highly attractive, because they typically have lower investment requirements and can select the most attractive ecosystem to join – or they can even hedge their bets by participating in more than one competing ecosystem. In particular, if they provide important components in an area that can become a bottleneck in the ecosystem, they are in a good position to claim a substantial share of the profits. Microsoft followed this path after the failure of its HealthVault platform by pivoting to an enabler role in digital health. In 2020 the company launched a health care cloud solution that combines Microsoft's existing services, like chatbots (which enabled more than 1,500 COVID-related bots), Teams (enabling provider-to-patient virtual visits), and Azure IoT (enabling remote health monitoring).

Achieve Critical Mass by First Increasing Scale, Not Scope

A key challenge during the launch phase is to achieve critical mass so the ecosystem can take off. To this end, the ecosystem must quickly increase its scale to achieve network effects, whereby additional partners and users make the ecosystem more valuable for existing participants, which in turn attracts further partners and users.

Increasing scale requires focus. A common failure is to broaden the scope of the ecosystem beyond its core value proposition before achieving critical mass. A number of health care ecosystems have fallen into this trap by adding too many services and products, only to find that they have diluted their value proposition, added complexity, and struggled to grow.

Consider Driver, a platform designed to match cancer patients with clinical trials. Instead of focusing on its core value proposition, Driver quickly broadened its scope. The company not only collected patients' medical records and tumor samples to be sequenced, but also opened two pathology labs (one in China, one in the US) and ran multiple apps for doctors and patients. Driver failed in 2018, just months after its launch, despite funding of $80 million. In an interview with MedCity News, co-founder William Polkinghorn concluded: "One of the biggest things we got wrong is we tried to do too much."

The scale and size of an ecosystem should not be measured by vanity metrics, such as the number of registered patients, but by the number of interactions or transactions, because this is how the ecosystem creates value for its participants. In many cases, it is not just about the quantity of members but about attracting the right members (just as an online booking platform like OpenTable must work with the most in-demand restaurants) in the right proportions (just as a ride-hailing ecosystem like Uber must balance the number of drivers and riders). Moreover, network effects are often local, so network density may be more important than network size.

In health care, ecosystems that are built on physical supplier networks, such as accountable care organizations or patient booking platforms, require local density. They can learn from the launch strategies of mobility and food-delivery platforms that built their network clusters country by country or even city by city. Other health care ecosystems, such as those focused on EHRs, can only demonstrate their strength when they operate across sectors and geographies and thus require supraregional or even system-wide density to take off. For more specialized health care ecosystems, such as the online patient network PatientsLikeMe, which connects patients with peers facing the same rare disease to share their experiences, relevant scale is defined as high penetration of the global population of patients with a specific indication.

Once the ecosystem has achieved critical mass, the scope can be broadened in a series of staged expansions. For example, LinkedIn was launched as a social network, allowing users to connect with other professionals based on simple profiles. Only after having achieved a leading market position did the company begin to add further services, such as a marketplace for online recruiting and a content-publishing platform.

Doctolib, an online and mobile booking platform, followed this path of strategic expansion to become one of the few health care unicorns in Europe. Founded in 2013, Doctolib focused on a clear and simple value proposition: launching a booking platform that helps patients find specialists and make appointments. With this clear goal, the platform aimed to quickly achieve scale by prioritizing local density. Doctolib conquered the French market, city by city, and became the leading booking platform for doctor appointments in the country. When the company expanded to Germany, it followed the same strategy of creating local clusters, starting in Berlin and expanding to other major cities. To promote network effects, Doctolib charged doctors for its services (€129 per month per physician), but not patients. Building on its leading position in France and Germany, Doctolib began to expand its service from primary care physicians to hospitals. At the same time, the scope of the platform was expanded step by step, with new solutions for doctor-patient communication, marketing offerings for providers, consulting services, digital referrals of patients, and telemedicine. Eight years after launch, the company is worth more than $1 billion.

Create and Harness Data Flywheel Effects

Data can be a key source of network effects in health care ecosystems. Sharing data among ecosystem participants can not only remove existing frictions and enable a seamless patient journey, but also enable new insights and innovation, such as preventive and predictive interventions, faster drug development, improved clinical decision making, and customized treatments. Take the example of Moderna. For years, the company has invested in data and artificial intelligence to improve its chances of success with drug development. During the coronavirus crisis, the company leveraged its digital and AI capabilities to gain an edge over many vaccine makers.

Data sharing can also amplify flywheel effects (Figure 14.2). As more users join the ecosystem, more and richer data are available, which enables deeper and better insights, which expands the value proposition of the ecosystem and encourages even more users to join. When the data flywheel gains speed, it can propel two additional flywheels in a health care ecosystem. A growing number of users will attract more partners to the ecosystem, which further increases the breadth and improves the quality of the offering and thus attracts more users. Such indirect network effects are well-known from ecosystems in other sectors (from video games to online food-delivery platforms) and can lead to a dominant market position. In addition, a growing number of users will also enable economies of scale by spreading the fixed costs of the ecosystem over more users while lowering unit costs, further increasing the attractiveness of the ecosystem for additional users and partners.

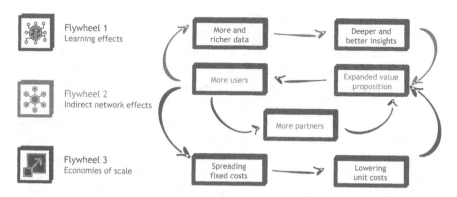

Source: BCG Henderson Institute

Figure 14.2: Data Sharing Can Amplify Flywheel Effects.

Ping An's Good Doctor exemplifies this flywheel effect. The platform was initially designed by 200 AI specialists using a data set of 400 million consultations. By integrating a range of online and offline services and digitizing most processes, Ping An was able to build a comprehensive ecosystem based on data analytics. The insights provided by Ping An's data set increase with every new user and every additional interaction on the platform, and the company uses this data to constantly improve its offerings. Its AI system has grown to incorporate 3,000 diseases and cover the entire consultation process. As a result, Ping An has doubled the efficiency of consultations, greatly reduced the risk of misdiagnosis or missed diagnosis, and constantly improved patients' experiences. The platform nearly doubled its number of registered users from approximately 193 million in 2017 to 346 million in 2020, according to company reports, and became the first AI health care system to reach the highest level of certification of the World Organization of Family Doctors (the world's largest family physician organization and a World Health Organization partner).

Of course, there are significant barriers to data sharing and analytics in health care. Existing data often lack precision and are difficult to analyze, data from different sources are not compatible, and integrating data analytics into existing workflows is complex and challenging for many incumbent health care players. At the same time, the stakes are high because health decisions can be life or death, and mistakes are costly. What's more, patients and regulators are rightfully concerned about data privacy and security.

To overcome these barriers, health care can learn from ecosystems in other sectors that face similar challenges. Two ingredients are essential. First, it's important to have an operating model that enables an effective data workflow among ecosystem participants, with clear data standards and application programming interfaces (APIs). Second, you need a data governance framework that strikes a balance between value creation and privacy risks by providing clear answers to the following three questions: (1) Who owns the data? (2) Who decides about access to the data? (3) Who can use the data for which applications? For example, in many EHR systems ownership lies with the patient who can make decisions about access and whether to share data with partners in the ecosystem. However, ownership and decision rights can also be separated, as in Google's smart home ecosystem, where the user owns the data, but Google broadly shares it with third parties, based on clearly defined rules and standards.

Beyond these concerns, effective data sharing requires a change of mindset. Providers, payers, and suppliers to the health care system need to stop guarding their data to protect their share of the pie and seek out innovative ways to share their (anonymized or aggregated) data in order to create new value and thus increase the overall size of the pie. The potential benefits are enormous. With over a quarter of US health care spending attributable to conditions related to modifiable risk factors, according to research published in the journal The Lancet Public Health, data-driven prevention alone could substantially improve the health of large parts of the population and reduce costs for the entire system.

Taking Action, Jointly and Individually

Payers, providers, and suppliers, as well as startups, tech companies, and regulators, all have a unique role to play in navigating, managing, and leading a successful ecosystem.

All stakeholders must act now to seize the opportunities ahead. Several trends are fueling the emergence of health care ecosystems, providing huge opportunities for new and enhanced value propositions. As new ecosystems emerge, the established roles in today's health care landscape will be unbundled, so it's critical to have a strategic vision of what the future might hold and what the roles in it might be. Don't wait for regulators to provide all required conditions and incentives. Embrace a collaborative mindset, build trust, and forge positive relationships with partners. Put yourself in the shoes of the other ecosystem participants and be sure every partner has an incentive to join and contribute.

Payers, providers, and suppliers must be proactive, not reactive. Too many incumbents have yet to develop an ecosystem strategy or establish clear positioning. New players threaten to disrupt the industry, and the time to build competitive advantage is now. Actively screen the market and expand the network to include new partners, such as startups and tech players, while leveraging a strong central position and deep expertise in the health care sector. Set up pilot projects focused on a clear value proposition for a specific population or region, then scale up. Organize this value proposition around the customer, not the service delivered. Invest in new capabilities to gain a competitive advantage by strengthening digital competencies, digitizing processes, building interoperable data lakes, and developing a data (and data-sharing) strategy.

Startups and tech companies should focus on cooperation rather than a "move fast and break things" approach. Health care is a sensitive and highly regulated sector, with many inherent challenges; it's important to learn the specifics of the industry and build on existing expertise. Clearly define the position you want to secure, whether it's as an enabler providing infrastructure or analytical services, a realizer offering specific solutions, or an orchestrator offering broad services or solutions. To thrive in this space, tech companies must deliver services that are interoperable, seamless, and modular. Trust is also key – and plays a crucial role in building relationships with patients as well as ecosystem partners (see Chapters 10 and 11).

Regulators should encourage pilot projects and use cases that enable ecosystems and new care delivery models, such as integrated, remote health offerings that provide telemedicine and digital therapeutics as not just standalone offerings, but as integrated, value-adding services. Over the long term, regulators should facilitate cooperation by enabling outcome-based or value-based payment structures and easing the boundaries between sectors. They should also encourage digitization to facilitate data sharing and data use cases.

Incumbent and new health care players that follow the five principles embraced by the most successful and sustainable next-generation health care ecosystems will do more than just optimize operational efficiency. They will finally overcome the traditional tradeoff of the iron triangle in health care by improving quality, enhancing access, and lowering costs – all at the same time.

Joël Hazan, Martin Reeves, and Pierre-François Marteau
Chapter 15
Solving the Cooperation Paradox in Urban Mobility

If you build it, the saying goes, they will come. But they have to be able to get there. In cities around the world, getting there is a challenge, fraught by growing traffic congestion and deteriorating public transit systems. All of this piles on travel time and impedes access to urban locations. But it's more than a source of frustration—the mobility problems that cities face threaten their economic viability, the environment, and society overall.

Traditional approaches to solving mobility problems—adding roads and transit lines—are not sustainable, primarily because of concerns related to climate change, public health, and funding. Hence the interest in new technology-powered forms of mobility: ride sharing, free-floating bikes, autonomous electric vehicles, digital mobility platforms, and more.

These technologies could be "congestion busters," prompting people to give up grueling commutes in single-occupancy private vehicles in favor of modes of transport that will offer swifter, easier, cleaner travel while decreasing the number of drivers and vehicles on the road. But when it comes to these new modes, most cities and transport authorities have effectively relinquished control by either allowing private actors to compete unfettered with traditional modes of transportation or letting mobility languish as they restrict innovation.

Waiting for the technology to sort itself out is not the way to proceed. It is incumbent on cities to be part of the mobility revolution and ensure that technologies are deployed in ways that are best for cities and the people who live and work in them. City governments need to, in a word, mobilize. They need to regain control of urban mobility by orchestrating the entire landscape of mobility providers and users.

Mobility Can Drive—or Derail—Wealth

The relationship of transportation and economic growth is well grounded in economic theory and empirical evidence. As Adam Smith explained in *The Wealth of Nations*, improvements in transportation systems increase the extent of a market, allowing the division of labor and unlocking economies of scale.

https://doi.org/10.1515/9783110775167-015

The development of the world's major cities illustrates this relationship. In New York City, for instance, the construction of the underground subway (financed by the city because no private players were willing to take on the risk) united the five boroughs and created what is now the world's second biggest city, as ranked by GDP. And in the Paris metropolitan area, the construction of the regional metro and the urban highway network in the 1960s and 1970s changed the shape of a territory, increasing the number of inhabitants from 5 million in 1900 to 12.2 million today.

As many economists (among them Jean Poulit and David Levinson) have demonstrated, in urban areas mobility drives wealth by fostering access. We define access as the number of valued destinations that inhabitants can easily reach within their daily travel time budget. Access is the effective size of the city. Given that daily travel time budgets everywhere have reached a steady state, increasing access relies on transportation speed—how quickly individuals can reach their workplaces and commercial destinations such as shops and restaurants—and the density of populations and destinations. Moving many people at a fast pace in dense areas is vital for cities; they don't want people or businesses, frustrated by congestion, unreliable public transit, and increased travel times, to leave.

Access increases productivity by allowing a better pairing between job demand and work supply. It is priced into land value—individuals and companies pay premiums for high-access locations. Our research, illustrated in Figure 15.1, shows the strong correlation between the areas where the wealthiest people choose to live and the areas with the greatest access to top jobs. Access also draws commerce to a city by attracting companies looking to benefit from a large pool of talented workers. Last but not least, access fosters social and economic inclusion by increasing exchanges between the different parts of a metropolitan area.

But urban mobility is at an impasse. Cities have not been able to increase access using traditional techniques (building new roads or extending transit lines). Worse, rising congestion (TomTom traffic data shows that from 2008 to 2016, congestion levels increased by 10 to 15 points in New York, Los Angeles, San Francisco, and other major US cities) along with the unsustainable levels of carbon and particle emissions and pressure on public-transport finances, threaten to decrease access. This presents clear challenges to the economy and the environment; it also sets the stage for troubling social outcomes in which mobility depends on income and magnifies income inequality.

Some might think that the solution to all these challenges lies in new technologies. Indeed, technology will be part of the eventual solution. But on its own it will not provide simple, quick fixes; in some cities, it is actually exacerbating near-term challenges. Cities have not yet figured out how to steer new technology opportunities toward desirable ends.

% of white-collar and "gray-matter" jobs[1] accessible within 30 minutes using the fastest mode of transportation

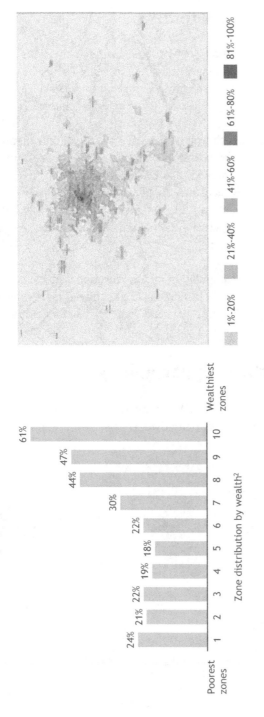

1%-20%   21%-40%   41%-60%   61%-80%   81%-100%

Poorest zones

1   2   3   4   5   6   7   8   9   10

24% 21% 22% 19% 18% 22% 30% 44% 47% 61%

Zone distribution by wealth[2]

Wealthiest zones

1. Jobs of "Cadres et professions intellectuelles supérieures" as defined by INSEE in 2015 2. Per decile, based on declared revenue per household in 2015

Note: Accessibility during the morning peak on a weekday in 2018 using public transport or private car. For reasons of simplification, we looked only at the most populated subzones, amounting to 90% of the total population of the Paris metropolitan area

Source: INSEE; Google Maps; TomTom; BCG analysis

Figure 15.1: Strong Correlation Between Where the Wealthiest People Live and Areas With Greatest Access to Top Jobs.

How We Measure Accessibility

Our objective was to measure access to opportunities within a city using a location-based approach. Our two main constraints: the measure should be easy to understand, and it should allow a meaningful comparison between cities around the world, regardless of the mobility modes available in individual cities.

We used two metrics:

1. **An Accessibility Index.** This shows the percentage of jobs in the metropolitan area that can be reached within 30 minutes from a given subzone using the fastest transportation mode at a peak travel hour.
2. **A Compactness Index.** This measures the percentage of jobs in the metropolitan area that can be reached within 30 minutes on average per inhabitant. It is the average of the accessibility indexes of all subzones weighted by the population of each subzone.

To compute the figures, we used population and job location data from offices for national statistics (such as INSEE in France). We simulated travel times by leveraging Google Maps for public-transit time and TomTom data for driving time.

An Untapped World of Opportunities

Urban mobility has never moved so fast. A combination of disruptive technologies and changes in the aspirations of city dwellers (shown in Figure 15.2) is

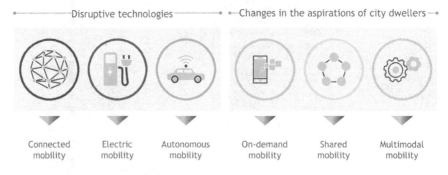

Source: BCG

Figure 15.2: Disruptive Technologies and Changing Aspirations of City Dwellers Are Setting Up a New World of Opportunities for Cities.

setting the stage for a revolution that could, if correctly managed, open up a new world of opportunities for cities.

From physical infrastructure to digital platforms, the mobility value chain is rapidly becoming more connected, emission-free, autonomous, shared, on-demand, and multimodal. Already, mobile apps have allowed the development of on-demand mobility services such as ride hailing and free-floating vehicles as well as real-time travel assistants; both types of innovation have started to change the way people move in cities. But much more is coming. Autonomous and electric vehicles, combined with the tremendous improvements in data generation, collection, and processing, could provide crucial elements of the solutions that cities are looking for.

If properly leveraged, disruptive technologies could—eventually—help cities pursue sustainable growth. What could the new urban mobility look like? Attractive possibilities exist in several areas:

- **Economic Performance.** Commuters could reclaim time and peace of mind by stepping out of their individual cars and relying instead on an integrated combination of new modes of transportation, such as ride sharing and free-floating vehicles. Maximizing the number of passengers per car would reduce congestion. With better access, opportunities for economic transactions—and therefore the wealth of a city—increase.
- **Environmental Sustainability.** Environmental benefits could be gained as a decrease in congestion reduces idle time per car, as electric vehicles replace gasoline-powered cars, and as new, lighter vehicles multiply.
- **Social Equity.** Cities could reinvigorate access through the thoughtful deployment of new modes of transportation that ensure inclusive access to all—across geographic areas of the city and income bands.
- **Funding.** Funding concerns could be alleviated as costly capital investments in new infrastructure are replaced with asset-light initiatives, thereby increasing the efficiency of existing public and private assets.

Mostly, though, cities have been standing aside, and as a result, the first wave of the urban mobility revolution has been somewhat chaotic. Public authorities lack the tools to work with the newcomers, and so regulatory progress is lagging, meaning that in many cases operators of new mobility modes either are able to operate unfettered or are unduly restricted. The uptake of ride-hailing services such as Uber, Didi, and Lyft has turned the old taxi industry upside down; such services are also directly competing with public transport through pooling and microtransit services. The development of free-floating services, such as some bike- and scooter-sharing models, has presented a new challenge to city officials, who are used to traditional sharing systems with docks or dedicated spaces and have no policies in place for new approaches. Further, cities now have to deal with a high number of mobility players, instead of the few well-known providers.

There have been some attempts to regulate new forms of mobility, but they have so far been scattershot rather than strategic (two acts in France that aimed to regulate ride-hailing services in just two years, for instance).

Cities' uncertainty about how to proceed might be explained by the fact that new mobility services have not yet begun to deliver on the above-mentioned attractive possibilities, despite massive investments from venture capital funds, tech giants, and car manufacturers. As of today, what matters most—the daily commute—has not changed. Ethnographic research that we conducted in the summer of 2018 in partnership with the French digital agency My Little Paris found that even though 75% of Parisians aged 25 to 45 have tried new mobility services, less than 6% rely on them for their daily commute.

New mobility services have also not been reducing congestion. For instance, a 2017 report from former US Department of Transportation official Bruce Schaller concluded that ride-hailing services had worsened traffic on the busiest streets of New York City, inspiring the recent decision to cap the number of for-hire vehicle licenses (used by drivers of Uber, Lyft, and their equivalents) there. Our research shows that without optimization mechanisms that consider all vehicles, autonomous vehicles are likely to further impede traffic flows in already congested situations.

All of the above findings, though they come somewhat early in the mobility revolution, strongly suggest that cities are not yet on the right track. In general, cities acknowledge that new mobility services can generate tremendous socio-economic value at a lower cost than investments in traditional infrastructure, but they are struggling mightily to understand how to unlock this potential.

The Imperative for Cities: Solve the "Cooperation Paradox"

Cities need to be part of the mobility revolution, for the sake of economic development, for their own financial viability, for the cause of fighting against climate change, and for the well-being of their residents. Indeed, without proactive moves on the part of cities, new mobility services could deliver more downsides than upsides, leaving cities ensnared in any of several potential mobility dystopias: paralyzed cities, for example, or cities dominated by private players that have commandeered public space and optimized mobility for their own narrow interests.

It is true that cities' interests conflict with those of new mobility providers. Cities want to achieve "asset moderation," a scenario that maximizes utilization of modes of transportation—ensuring, for instance, that each vehicle on the road carries as many passengers as possible. Many private players, on the other hand, want to pursue a model of "asset proliferation": more vehicles, roads, parking spaces, and hours of hired-vehicle time. These clashing goals create a cooperation paradox that needs to be resolved. But which stakeholders should cities work with to find solutions? It is hard to identify partners, though it's clear that cities can't rely on one player for all the right competencies.

The imperative for cities, then, is to become orchestrators of mobility.

By doing so, they will figure out the right balance of regulation and innovation. Traditional highly regulated models have value because they protect players and the public interest, but they can go too far and stifle innovation. On the flip side, an extreme laissez-faire approach allows innovation to flourish but also lets certain players act in ways that might not be wholly beneficial to the city. Cities can orchestrate the new mobility by taking six interlinked and sustained actions (see Figure 15.3 for an overview).

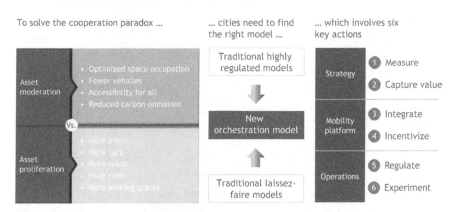

Source: BCG Henderson Institute Analysis

Figure 15.3: Cities Can Orchestrate the New Mobility by Taking Six Interlinked and Sustained Actions.

It's important to emphasize that cities will be orchestrating these activities, not performing them on their own or in a silo. Other stakeholders, such as the new mobility operators, will play important roles in carrying out these actions, negotiating with one another, and putting their findings to work.

Measure

What doesn't get measured doesn't get done.

To drive the urban mobility revolution, cities should start by putting in place the tools to understand its advantages and disadvantages in detail. They should equip themselves with a measurement framework that can help inform policies. This framework should be a common one, used by all cities, so that they can share their findings and insights.

This effort is not just an updating of existing measures. Indeed, traditionally, cities and transport authorities have assessed ease of movement rather than the interactions between movements and places. Today's in-depth socioeconomic analyses are limited to large infrastructure projects that cannot be easily adapted to asset-light initiatives. Current measurement systems also lack user centricity, which is needed to build a mobility offering that truly addresses the needs of residents instead of just optimizing each mode in a series of silos.

Cities need a way to monitor the socioeconomic value of asset-light initiatives, looking for signs of almost immediate implications as well as user satisfaction. Indicators should be available at both the urban and district levels to assess potential differences. They should also be de-averaged, by mobility service, to reveal the contribution of each service to the mix. This measurement will instruct pilots as well as policy decisions (Figure 15.4 shows examples of indicators to monitor).

Capture Value

Cities need to figure out where the value (economic, environmental, and societal) of the new mobility offerings goes and capture the fair share to be reinvested in balanced, integrated solutions; this is the great wealth-creating lever effect of urban mobility. It is essential to attain the right balance of funding sources for the mobility system overall. Three types of value sources are commonly used to fund mobility: general funding, user fees, and indirect, targeted funding such as development impact fees and land value taxes. The last category is particularly informed by insight into value—it tells authorities which private parties can derive value from the new mobility, particularly if they help to fund it.

This value capture plan will also help cities address urban mobility in the broader context of urban planning—to align planning and mobility decisions, ideally across a metropolitan area. It will force cities to consider actual interaction patterns rather than mere incremental shifts, and it will inform a shared goal of all stakeholders: improving sustainable accessibility for all in the city.

Category	Indicator	Description
Economic performance	Accessibility	Average number of jobs people can reach within 30 minutes at a peak hour of travel using the fastest mode of transportation
	Peak efficiency	Difference in accessibility between peak and nonpeak hours
	User satisfaction	Percentage of users satisfied with current offerings, overall and per mode of transportation
	Reliability	Continuity of accessibility at a peak hour during weekdays over the year
Environmental sustainability	Green accessibility	Average number of jobs people can reach within 30 minutes at a peak hour of travel by walking or biking
	Climate impact	Annual CO_2 emissions linked to urban mobility per capita
	Air quality	Average air quality index at the metropolitan level
	Asset utilization	Ratio of passenger-kilometers to vehicle-kilometers
Social equity	Public transit accessibility	Average number of jobs people can reach within 30 minutes at a peak hour of travel using public transit
	Geographic equity	Standard deviation of accessibility indexes per zone
	Affordability	Average cost of commuting as a percentage of average net hourly income
	Inclusiveness	Percentage of inhabitants not making a trip because of lack of access
Funding	Mobility budget	Total mobility spending across modes of transportation and infrastructure per year as a percentage of GDP
	User contribution	Percentage of the mobility budget coming from users (vs. general funding or indirect beneficiaries)
	Maintenance budget	Percentage of the mobility budget dedicated to the maintenance of existing infrastructure and vehicles
	Budget growth	Ratio of yearly mobility-spending growth to GDP growth

Source: BCG

Figure 15.4: Indicators Should Be Available at Both the Urban and District Level and They Should Be De-Averaged to Reveal the Contribution of Each Service to the Mix.

Integrate

Most transportation systems have been developed to address singular modes (car, public transit, or bike, for example) rather than to offer a comprehensive transportation approach that considers users' varied needs. In some cities, different modes and infrastructures are governed by different entities, limiting the ability to organize and synchronize the mobility ecosystem. Fragmented governance is posing a problem in the face of a convergence of mobility players and the desire to promote multiple modes. The rise of digital platforms that can integrate multiple modes of transport and multiple services (for example, booking, ticketing, and payment) gives cities a new opportunity to tackle this old issue.

Cities should integrate all mobility modes and services in a single platform to offer a seamless experience for users and to equip themselves with a powerful tool to supervise and orient flows. They should also use the platform to unify governance across modes of transportation and types of mobility infrastructure. In short, cities should pursue a smart and user-centric integration of public policy and new technology.

Incentivize

As mobility becomes integrated, authorities can begin to pilot a comprehensive social transportation policy. They could offer user-based incentives that emphasize particular modes, travel hours, and population categories. They could also incentivize mobility providers, which could be paid in exchange for an improvement in access or quality of service, for instance.

Based on the predefined measurement system, the incentives should focus on big-picture outcomes (an increase in travel speed, for instance, or a reduction of pollution) rather than contributing effects or inputs (like the percentage of on-time trains or the share of electric vehicles).

Regulate

It's clear that new forms of mobility call for new policies and regulations. The recent demise of the Autolib' electric-car venture in Paris is a signal that cities need to be nimbler in the way they deal with the private sector. Instead of following the tenets of traditional contracts, cities should limit their intervention. They should offer greater flexibility to private players (by, for instance, not requiring them to predefine transport routes).

When it comes to the new mobility, cities will benefit from balancing what is and is not regulated. New ecosystems need efficiency and guardrails, but they also must allow for diversity, initiative, and innovation. This requires positive partnerships and a great amount of trust between cities and private players, not reactive regulations.

Seattle's newly issued permitting system for free-floating bike sharing is a good example of the new form of regulation that cities should implement. The policy focuses public intervention on select steps of the value chain such as data sharing, parking, safety, and equity while maintaining the diversity and flexibility (regarding detailed pricing structure and user interfaces, for instance) of private operators.

Experiment

The mobility revolution is going to be rapid, and it is going to require major adaptations. Cities don't have time to wait for definitive solutions. They must learn by experimenting. Some experiments will fail. Given that, cities would benefit from sharing their experiences with other cities. And partnerships between cities and individual mobility players will be beneficial as well—more and more of these partnerships are being put in place, which is a good start for instructional experiments.

For instance, before implementing its permitting system for free-floating bike shares, Seattle used a "sandbox" approach, which included a pilot with LimeBike, ofo, and Spin in 2017 to better understand how to regulate and leverage this new mode of transportation.

Singapore, Dubai, Hong Kong, and London are regarded as exemplars of urban mobility. It is not a coincidence that these city-states (or close approximations thereof) have autonomous governing bodies that control the entire metropolitan area's transportation systems. They also have a clear understanding that transport and accessibility are the keys to success. Other cities can look to these standouts as models of best practices.

Indeed, looking to other cities and even joining forces with them will be a key advantage, given the magnitude of changes ahead.

Cities do share a common destination: a comprehensive mobility system that provides easy access and encourages participation in all sorts of commerce throughout the metropolitan area. The journey to that destination will vary as each city works, alongside stakeholders, through the six imperatives to find the best solutions for its future and the future of its residents.

Massimo Russo and Tian Feng

Chapter 16
The Risks and Rewards of Data Sharing for Smart Cities

Long before the arrival of COVID-19, cities around the world had started to reinvent themselves through "smart city" initiatives. Beset by growing populations, aging or insufficient infrastructure, and the rising cost and difficulty of meeting the needs of residents, cities were investing in technology to address environmental sustainability, traffic congestion, public transit, and public health, all while facing budgetary pressures.

The pandemic has intensified the need for intelligence and insight as cities struggle to assess the effectiveness of response measures and compliance in real time. Meanwhile, increasing reliance on e-commerce and the shift to remote working are stripping cities of two of their core functions – as places to shop and places to work. Public services are being strained by rapidly growing demand. New challenges, such as the rising volume of last-mile delivery trucks, are adding to the stress.

To develop innovative solutions to problems old and new, many cities are aggregating and sharing more and more data, establishing platforms to facilitate private-sector participation, and holding "hackathons" and other digital events to invite public help. But digital solutions carry their own complications. Technology-led innovation often depends on access to data from a wide variety of sources to derive correlations and insights. Questions regarding data ownership, amalgamation, compensation, and privacy can be flashing red lights.

Smart cities are on the leading edge of the trend toward greater data sharing. They are also complex generators and users of data. Companies, industries, governments, and others are following in their wake, sharing more data in order to foster innovation and address such macro-level challenges as public health and welfare, and climate change. Smart cities thus provide a constructive laboratory for studying the challenges and benefits of data sharing.

Why Cities Share Data

BCG examined some 75 smart-city applications that use data from a variety of sources, including connected equipment (that is, the Internet of Things, or IoT).

https://doi.org/10.1515/9783110775167-016

Nearly half the applications require data sourced from multiple industries or platforms (Figure 16.1). For example, a parking reservation app assembles garage occupancy data, historical traffic data, current weather data, and information on upcoming public events to determine real-time parking costs. We also looked at a broader set of potential future applications and found that an additional 40% will likewise require cross-industry data aggregation.

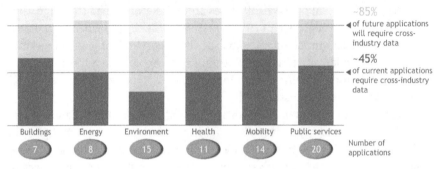

Source: BCG analysis

Figure 16.1: Smart-City Applications Use Data From a Variety of Sources.

Because today's smart solutions are often sponsored by individual municipal departments, many IoT-enabled applications rely on limited, siloed data. But given the potential value of applications that require aggregation across sources, it's no surprise that many cities are pursuing partnerships with tech providers to develop platforms and other initiatives that integrate data from multiple sources.

For example, Huawei is the chief architect of smart-city solutions in the city of Shenzhen's Longgang District, working with hundreds of partners to access data. Even a project with relatively limited scope – the LinkNYC program in New York, which replaced pay phones with Wi-Fi enabled kiosks – required three different companies to provide the necessary data, hardware, and network capabilities. Cities are becoming the managers of data platforms and the orchestrators of burgeoning digital ecosystems.

High-Impact Solutions Depend on Sharing Data

As smart cities turn to data and technology for high-impact solutions to high-value use cases, the need for data sharing will grow. Consider two examples: traffic management and elder care.

Current traffic applications use cameras, parking sensors, and telematics data to identify areas of high traffic density. In Austin (Texas), London, and San Francisco, the transportation team runs analytics that, respectively, optimize traffic signals, set dynamic tolling rates, and adjust smart-parking rates. In the future, cities may be able to maintain optimal mobility by adjusting tolls in real time according to actual traffic conditions. Instead of being extrapolated from historic data (as they are today), rates could be based on real-time traffic data using the locations of individual vehicles and their expected destinations (derived from their navigation systems). Drivers would decide whether to pay the toll to save ten minutes of travel time, for example, or take a detour to avoid it.

Elder care is a growing priority for cities with aging populations. Biometric data from wearables is already being used to monitor the status of high-risk patients and notify them or their physicians of health-related events. Citizen-centric pilots in cities such as Seoul are monitoring activity in the home with motion, electricity, and lighting sensors. Computers recognize changes in the daily patterns of seniors living alone and alert social workers in the event of a potential problem (such as when an individual is suddenly much less active than usual). In the future, wellness recommendations may be personalized according to an individual's condition and goals and combined with activity tracking as he or she ages.

How Cities Share Data Today

We reviewed the approaches to data management of 30 smart cities around the world and found a number of common practices (Figure 16.2). We also found that these cities need to address more than a few issues as they try to improve their current operations and develop new and better services that depend on data sharing. The issues fall into three categories: (1) how and when municipal departments share data, (2) how cities share data with private-sector vendors, and (3) how cities share data with the public.

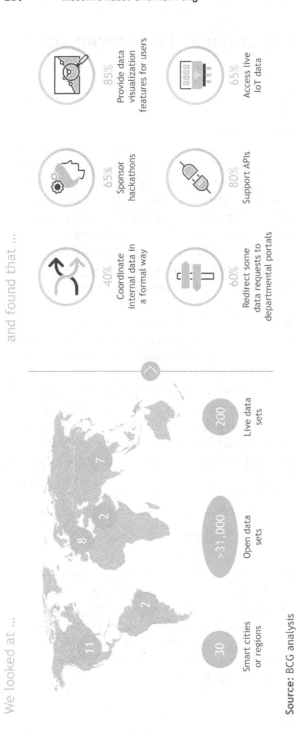

We looked at ...

and found that ...

85% Provide data visualization features for users

65% Access live IoT data

65% Sponsor hackathons

80% Support APIs

40% Coordinate internal data in a formal way

60% Redirect some data requests to departmental portals

200 Live data sets

>31,000 Open data sets

30 Smart cities or regions

Source: BCG analysis

Figure 16.2: Common Practices in the Approaches to Data Management of 30 Smart Cities.

Data Sharing By and Within City Governments

The siloed data repositories that municipal departments have built over the years limit cities' ability to develop an end-to-end view of how residents avail themselves of services and experience them. Moreover, cities have tended to pursue individual smart-city initiatives rather than citywide transformations. These initiatives typically lack an overarching strategy, reflecting both the fragmented nature of city agencies and legacy technologies. Cities need to overcome both organizational and technological siloes if they are to realize the full potential of smart cities.

Recognizing that citizen-centric solutions require more data sharing within government, cities are starting to invest in internal data exchanges. They are building open-data platforms and data directories that give all departments and agencies greater access to available data. Some 40% of the smart cities we reviewed have open-data platforms with integrated back-end databases that permit access by external applications, a prerequisite for easy data sharing and use. Another 15% have included the building of back-end connectivity as a priority in their digital strategic plans. For example, Portland (Oregon) and Seoul (South Korea) are constructing their own internal data repositories: Portland Urban Data Lake and Smart Seoul Data.

The sharing of some data is inherently problematic. Cities are rightly concerned about exposing personal and other sensitive information externally on open platforms or internally between departments. For example, should medical information be accessible to public agencies? Most people would say no. But what if such data, in aggregated form, could inform public policies designed to curb air pollution or reduce traffic emissions? In Kentucky, the city of Louisville used aggregated data from smart asthma inhalers to monitor the health impact of air pollution in real time. And when are the benefits of sharing data so great that investing in safeguards to anonymize it is justifiable?

Anonymization can be a shallow solution, however – and a potentially reversible one when multiple data sources are involved. Combining anonymized vehicle GPS and address data, for instance, can easily expose people's identity. Moreover, both anonymizing and aggregating data can mask important underlying patterns. As cities build data platforms, they will have to manage the tradeoff between innovative, valuable solutions and privacy risk through encryption, permissions, access restrictions, and other methods. And as more and more use cases continue to highlight those tradeoffs, cities will likely need to develop new or adjusted rules and guidelines about what can be shared, when, and with whom.

Data Sharing with Third Parties

Technology and other private-sector companies have long partnered with cities on specific programs. Given the scope of smart-city initiatives – with their ongoing service requirements, live data streams, and often bespoke applications – technology vendors are becoming critical partners in the collection, hosting, and management of data. The responses to Boston's 2017 smart-city request for information document, for example, included numerous proposals requiring comprehensive codesign. Likewise, the Connected Citizens Program of the navigation app Waze works with many cities, including New York, to provide real-time traffic data (such as user inputs on accidents or potholes) in exchange for data on road closures and public-works projects.

Cities also share data with private companies to nurture innovation. Many cities (and other governments) around the world host Startup in Residence programs that give startup companies the space, resources, and access to officials and data that they need to develop public-sector solutions. The City of Boston's Beta Blocks program aims to create a "clearing house, matching platform, or exchange" for civic experiments. The initial request for information generated more than 100 responses from potential partners worldwide.

Many of these partnerships involve data sharing, and the agreements vary widely in scope. Toronto struck a partnership with an Alphabet subsidiary, Sidewalk Labs, for a smart-city pilot in the city's Quayside neighborhood that made Sidewalk Labs responsible for all sensor data collection and analytics. The partnership sparked considerable public debate about data sharing and governance, and these issues contributed to the project's demise earlier this year. In other, narrower initiatives, such as LinkNYC and Kansas City's Smart and Connected City project, private-sector partners take ownership of the data generated. Cities need to consider whether to concede data rights to third parties and the potential for controversy regarding the sharing of residents' data with commercial entities.

Data Sharing with the Public

Cities initially developed public data-sharing platforms to improve government transparency. Now they are using open-data platforms, open-source methods, and competitions to encourage citizens to develop innovative solutions to urban problems. Cities are providing developer support and application programming interfaces (APIs) that enable citizens to access often live data directly so they can build solutions seamlessly on top of government data.

Almost two-thirds of the cities we reviewed are hosting events such as hackathons to support citizen engagement and innovation, and 80% offer data APIs. Singapore, for example, offers 14 APIs for users to access live data, Dubai has established an API and developer zone along with cloud hosting (for a fee), and Barcelona has developed an open-source data platform, Sentilo, that allows app developers to access a wide variety of sensor data.

City open-data platforms include features to manage data access and permissions, integrating functionality that provides varying degrees of access, control, and security. Amsterdam's API can be used by anyone, but access to certain data sets requires that users provide authentication and authorization. In Texas, the city of Austin requires a login to download certain data sets, with varying levels of permission. New York's transit API requires a free key registration so the city can track data use.

A few cities (and other government entities) are beginning to crowdsource citizen and enterprise data. Columbus (Ohio), San Francisco, Toronto, and all of Estonia are among the few that allow the public to upload their own data sets, which are then vetted by the government. In 2015, Copenhagen partnered with Hitachi to pilot a data exchange where the government and private-sector players can buy and sell data, but the project has yet to reach significant scale.

Real-time IoT data sets are just beginning to be integrated into open-data platforms. While 65% of the open-data platforms we surveyed featured some sort of rapidly updated sensor data, only a small number of live IoT data sets are available to the public, mainly in areas of high consumer interest such as public transportation, traffic, and the environment.

The Challenges of Broader Data Sharing

While cities are at different stages of maturity when it comes to data sharing, there is a broad trend toward more aggregation and sharing of data within city governments and with external parties. We see four big challenges that cities need to address.

1. **How to Break Down Data Silos.** In all the smart-city open-data platforms we observed, the city is the central collector, curator, processor, and host of a variety of data from different departments. But this approach, with each city creating its own bespoke data system, raises issues of expertise and scale. As data volumes increase, does every city really need to become a technology and data expert? Commercial technology partners can provide

ways to handle common needs and help more cities gain access to innovative solutions.

2. **How to Ensure Data Quality and Control.** Managing data quality and controlling access without unduly limiting innovation raise issues that are just coming to the fore. They apply to all manner of data sharing – within cities, with third parties, and with the public. Addressing these issues will likely require the development of national rules, regulations, and standards to avoid a complex tangle of individual municipal solutions. Technology providers are developing more sophisticated answers to questions of data access and control in order to encourage innovation while protecting privacy. The proliferation of COVID-19 contact-tracing solutions, and the challenges of adoption due to concerns about how the data could be used, provide a strikingly relevant illustration of the problem.

3. **How to Balance Innovation, Data Ownership Rights, and Value.** With increased data sharing, commercial relationships between cities and private-sector companies must address ownership rights. Who owns and controls what data? Who should profit from any insights generated by the data? What liabilities are associated with the use or misuse of data?

4. **How to Manage the Tradeoffs Between Data-Sharing Benefits and Privacy Concerns.** Cities are making tradeoffs between the value of innovation and the value of privacy. Singapore published data-sharing principles, for example, that emphasize the accessibility, co-creation, timeliness, and machine readability of data; the city also wants data to be "as raw as possible." However, more open and detailed data comes with privacy worries, and IoT sensor data can introduce additional concerns because of its sheer volume, real-time nature, and ubiquity. How can cities leverage governance and technology to balance the tradeoff between value and privacy? Various initiatives and organizations, such as New York University's GovLab and the UK's Open Data Institute, are pursuing data governance models and data collaboratives (in which participants exchange data for public value).

Cities are at the forefront in aggregating data to address large-scale challenges. As more cities seek to become "smart," they will face a growing conundrum. On the one hand, truly smart cities will develop more citizen-centric IoT solutions, and even solutions that address a single problem will involve more aggregation and sharing of data. Cities will become better equipped to address higher-value use cases such as public health and welfare. On the other hand, as more data is aggregated, the risk of misuse, privacy violations, and misappropriation of value will rise. Enterprises orchestrating ecosystems of partners face similar challenges in balancing innovation and risk.

Municipal leaders, corporate executives, government policymakers at all levels and their private-sector partners need to start considering how cities can create innovative solutions to complex and changing needs while limiting risks and protecting privacy. More than ever in the midst of a global pandemic, smart cities provide a real-life, real-time lab for all of us.

Wilderich Heising, Ulrich Pidun, Thomas Krüger,
Daniel Küpper, and Maximilian Schüssler

Chapter 17
Additive Manufacturing Needs a Business Ecosystem

When it comes to realizing the growth potential of additive manufacturing (AM), also known as 3D printing, industry players have been their own worst enemy. Although equipment providers, in particular, have enjoyed high margins by employing a razor-and-blades business model, intense competition within and across value chain segments has impeded end users' adoption of industrialized AM applications. As a result, despite high expectations, the industry remains a niche market.

The AM industry's natural business ecosystem has encouraged some companies to work together. But to unleash the potential of AM, industry players should go further and collaborate to advance the technology, identify new applications, and enable users to fully exploit its advantages. Research by the BCG Henderson Institute points to the concept of an actively managed business ecosystem as the best way to accomplish this goal.

Well-managed business ecosystems have important advantages over classic organizing structures, such as hierarchical supply chains and vertically integrated companies, that are typically used to create a product or service. For example, managed ecosystems are made up of multiple partners that can contribute their specific capabilities toward "co-innovating" and developing new products and services. Such ecosystems can also scale quickly because their modular structure makes it easy to add partners. And they are very flexible and resilient because they enable a greater variety of offerings and adapt more easily to changing customer requirements and technologies.

The AM industry can use these advantages and apply the lessons learned by other successful managed ecosystems in order to foster collaboration among independent companies.

https://doi.org/10.1515/9783110775167-017

The Ecosystem Offers a Solution to Unmet Expectations

Since the 1990s, AM has been heralded as the answer to some of the most pressing issues in the manufacturing industry. Many have recognized AM's potential to promote a step change in productivity by reducing tooling costs, cutting the lead time for machine setup, and trimming raw-material waste. They also have seen the endless possibilities for customization and design flexibility.

In fact, several years ago, analysts projected that the AM market would exceed $20 billion by 2020. However, the reality has fallen short of expectations. At the end of 2019, AM was still a niche market, with a value of approximately $12 billion.

Intense rivalry has hindered efforts to increase the adoption of AM. Traditional companies have expanded their role along the value chain, and new ones have entered the market. Even end users have integrated backward along the value chain – for example, in 2016, GE acquired Concept Laser and Arcam AB, two leading equipment providers for metal-based AM. As players are fighting for their share of the market, the AM industry is facing ongoing disruption.

Rather than seek advantage by undermining other industry participants, AM players should collaborate in an ecosystem. This ecosystem should be characterized by a specific value proposition (the desired solution) and by a clearly defined, albeit changing, group of partners with different roles (such as producer, supplier, orchestrator, or complementor). However, certain preconditions make an ecosystem work. It is best suited to a business environment that is both unpredictable and highly malleable. Specifically, offerings must be highly modular and require high levels of coordination to produce (see Chapter 2). Furthermore, because success requires joint problem solving, players need to have an incentive to participate.

In considering whether an industry meets the preconditions, the first issue to assess is which players and information, goods, and services are required for a coherent solution. In the case of AM, these players typically include:
- Suppliers of raw materials and formulations
- Providers of AM equipment
- Software companies that develop design and simulation software
- Service bureaus that print parts on demand

The AM industry can be mapped in a blueprint that connects these players along the flow of information and the flow of goods and services (Figure 17.1).

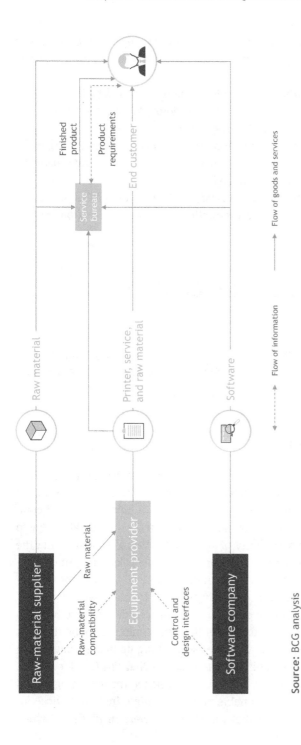

Raw-material supplier

Equipment provider

Software company

Raw material

Raw-material compatibility

Control and design interfaces

Raw material

Printer, service, and raw material

Software

Raw material

Finished product

Product requirements

End customer

Service bureau

Flow of goods and services

Flow of information

Source: BCG analysis

Figure 17.1: The AM Blueprint That Connects Players Along the Flow of Information and the Flow of Goods and Services.

This blueprint, along with an analysis of the underlying activities, indicates that AM fulfills all relevant preconditions for successfully applying an ecosystem model:

- **A High Level of Modularity.** The solution is best created by flexibly combining components that are provided by various players, and the integration of components entails low transaction costs.
- **A Significant Need for Coordination.** The required partners for a specific solution are not easy to identify and match because the interfaces between components are not fully standardized.
- **A Problem That's Better Solved Jointly.** Achieving objectives that maximize end-user benefits, such as production flexibility and customization, can't be done singlehandedly.

The Challenges to Creating an Effective AM Ecosystem

Although AM meets all the preconditions for a successful ecosystem, industry players must overcome a variety of challenges to enable strong and coherent collaboration.

Innovating Collectively

For an ecosystem to function properly, multiple players must contribute innovations that when combined can achieve a common objective. If players do not co-innovate effectively, the ecosystem will fail – even if only one critical component is missing. Assessing the potential for co-innovation is therefore key to evaluating an ecosystem's probability of success, as well as to identifying the components that need most attention to prevent bottlenecks. The primary objective should not be to win the race to market but to develop a set of innovations that provides a coherent and compelling offering for end users.

To understand the importance of co-innovation, consider the race between Nokia and Sony Ericsson to bring to market the first 3G mobile phone that was capable of video streaming. Nokia won the race, selling its first 3G handset in 2002. But, as described in the book *The Wide Lens: A New Strategy for Innovation*, other players in the ecosystem had not yet developed the technologies and services that were needed to fully enable video streaming, including those for digital rights management. Until these innovations were in place, 3G video streaming was not viable, rendering the new handsets largely useless other than for making phone calls.

Similarly, a lack of co-innovation has prevented AM players from developing large-scale compelling use cases for major industrial players. To promote significantly higher adoption, AM players must work together to eliminate AM bottlenecks relating to production speed, raw-material properties, and engineering and design capabilities. Companies must also work to improve software solutions that integrate planning, production control, and logistics. Industry players must collaborate to address these innovation challenges – a single company cannot do it alone.

Balancing Market Growth and Monetization

Before companies agree to participate in an ecosystem, they must see opportunities for joint value creation and be assured that they can capture their fair share of the value created. That makes establishing a value proposition and monetization mechanism essential for building and sustaining the ecosystem. Unlike most traditional product or service businesses, however, ecosystems should focus on establishing their value proposition for customers before putting too much emphasis on monetization. In other words, these ecosystems should seek to grow the market before distributing the value created.

Those ecosystems that focus on monetization too soon typically lose out to competing ecosystems. Consider the competition in China between eBay and Alibaba, two e-commerce ecosystems. EBay charged customers a transaction fee, whereas Alibaba offered a commission-free marketplace to promote rapid growth. Once Alibaba had captured a large user base, the company sought to monetize it through advertising and complementary product sales, and it prevailed over eBay.

Many providers of AM equipment, especially for plastic-based applications, have similarly focused too much on capturing value by increasing margins, rather than on creating value by increasing the size of the market. Equipment providers typically employ a razor-and-blades model in which they require end users to purchase raw materials from them, instead of allowing end users to select a raw-material supplier. Although this model fosters equipment providers' profitability, it has impeded the growth of the AM market. The absence of competitive pricing for materials has increased the cost of production for end users. It also has limited the possible use cases for AM because equipment providers offer a more limited portfolio of materials than would be available in an open ecosystem.

Achieving Demand-Side Economies of Scale

Like most traditional business models, many ecosystems promote supply-side economies of scale through declining fixed or variable costs. But unlike traditional models, ecosystems also have the potential to generate demand-side economies of scale (also known as network effects) – as more users participate in the ecosystem, it becomes more attractive to additional users as well.

Airbnb is an example of an ecosystem with substantial demand-side economies of scale (in addition to supply-side economies of scale from spreading the high fixed cost of technology and marketing across many landlords). As the number of landlords offering rooms increases, more potential tenants are attracted to the platform, which in turn attracts more room offerings, resulting in a positive feedback loop. The flywheel effect enables the ecosystem to capture most, if not all, of the market share.

The AM industry today has supply-side economies of scale, but players have not exploited the potential for demand-side economies of scale. For example, the industry could foster the faster expansion of software applications or the development of standards. This would help engineers understand how to design for AM manufacturing (a lack of knowledge is a major limiting factor for adoption today) and increase the breadth and attractiveness of potential applications for customers.

How to Design an AM Ecosystem

Designing an ecosystem is a complex undertaking – one that's more like conceiving of a residential district than planning a single house. By learning from successes and failures of ecosystems in other industries and making the right design choices, AM players will be able to address the challenges outlined above.

Select an Orchestrator to Take the Lead

To address the co-innovation challenges, as well as other coordination issues, an ecosystem needs a central entity that assumes a leadership role. This is the role of the orchestrator. The orchestrator builds the ecosystem, encourages others to join, defines standards and rules, and acts as the arbiter in cases of conflict. As the residual-claim holder of the ecosystem, the orchestrator must also make sure that all relevant players earn a decent profit. In return for its efforts, the orchestrator keeps the residual profit, which can be substantial if the ecosystem is successful.

Sometimes a company recognizes that an orchestrator is needed. For example, according to the book *Platform Leadership: How Intel, Microsoft, and Cisco Drive Industry Innovation*, Intel realized in the 1990s that its increasingly powerful microprocessors would have only limited benefits for users unless other component players in the PC system redesigned their products to be compatible with the chips. To orchestrate the ecosystem of component makers, the company created the Intel Architecture Lab. The lab sought to promote architectural improvements for PCs, stimulate and facilitate innovation on complementary products, and coordinate outside firms' innovations to drive the development of new system capabilities.

In many ecosystems, however, it is not clear which entity should be the orchestrator. The choice for the role can be narrowed by assessing the players according to these criteria:
- Is a company an essential member of the ecosystem, and does it control key resources?
- Does a player hold a central position and share strong interdependencies with other ecosystem participants?
- Is a company perceived as fair (or neutral) by other participants?
- Is a player likely to gain a large benefit, and can it shoulder large upfront investments?

Considering these criteria, equipment providers could be viewed as the natural candidates to fill the orchestrator role in the AM ecosystem. In addition to controlling essential resources (printers), equipment providers are centrally positioned with strong interdependencies to all other players, and they are likely to be perceived as fair or neutral. They also stand to gain large benefits from broad adoption. However, other players, such as raw-material suppliers, could also aim for the orchestrator role, provided that their estimated benefits are large enough to justify the investment and that they are able to position themselves as a fair or neutral player.

Recognizing the significant benefits of being an orchestrator, some industry participants have initiated intensive efforts to enhance coordination among all players. For example, the printer manufacturer EOS is seeking to improve the sharing of application know-how. It has also launched a consulting branch, called Additive Minds, to integrate multiple solutions into a single offering. Additionally, EOS has joined forces with Daimler and Premium Aerotec to develop custom-made and ready-to-use production lines for aluminum parts. The overall goal of these efforts is to promote greater adoption of AM in serial production through increased automation, the standardization of interfaces, and the use of software that connects automation with overarching software platforms, such as EOSConnect or Siemens NX.

Providing standardized interfaces for all ecosystem players provides another opportunity for a company to step up to the orchestrator's role. For example, Siemens has started the Additive Manufacturing Network to connect players via an online platform that offers streamlined collaboration, quoting, procurement, and order monitoring processes.

If none of the equipment providers are willing or able to take on the orchestrator role, raw-material suppliers have an opportunity. BASF, for example, has moved to obtain a strong foothold in the AM market by bundling its offerings within its Forward AM subsidiary. The company's full-service solution addresses many of end users' unmet needs, including optimizing part designs, simulating part and process properties, testing part behavior under load, finishing printed objects, and determining the most suitable 3D-printing process. The company continually adds capabilities by integrating service bureaus worldwide into its network.

By improving the coordination between the players, or in some cases taking responsibility to address some bottlenecks, an orchestrator can accelerate AM adoption and resolve many of the existing co-innovation challenges more rapidly than many players currently expect is possible.

Employ a More Open Governance Model

The governance model defines the rules and boundaries within which participants operate in an ecosystem (see Chapter 6). Implementing the right governance model at each stage of the ecosystem's development is critical to striking the appropriate balance between market growth and monetization.

Governance can be broken down into three basic issues:

- **Access.** Which players will be allowed to participate in the ecosystem? Which requirements do they have to fulfill in order to gain access to the platform and its resources?
- **Participation.** To what extent are ecosystem partners invited to shape the ecosystem? What is the scope, detail, and strictness of the rules governing this? Who decides how the value created is distributed among partners?
- **Commitment.** What levels of ecosystem-specific investments and "cospecialization" among partners are required? Is exclusivity demanded, or are partners allowed to join other competing ecosystems?

The choices relating to these governance issues depend on where the participants, under the leadership of the orchestrator, want the ecosystem to be on the continuum between fully closed and fully open. For example, a closed ecosystem, with restricted access, gives the orchestrator greater control over the development of the ecosystem and the behavior of participants, which ultimately helps to ensure the quality of the offering (Figure 17.2). It also facilitates monetization, such as by making it easier to charge participants for access. In contrast, an open ecosystem, with looser restrictions on access and behavior, fosters faster growth and increases the speed of innovation.

The right balance between a closed and open design may change as the life cycle progresses. For example, Google initially designed an open ecosystem for its Android mobile operating system in order to promote growth that would allow Android to catch up with Apple's iOS. To incentivize developers to join, Google shared jointly created value with them by taking a commission on app sales that was lower than the one Apple charged. After Android achieved a leading market position, Google increased its control of the ecosystem – such as by exercising approval rights over changes to the operating system and increasing its commission on app sales.

For AM, a relatively closed ecosystem seems to be better suited to the industry's needs, at least initially. In the early stages of ecosystem formation, AM players need to make deliberate choices on design, control participation, and manage downside risks effectively. Indeed, 3D Systems, EOS, and Stratasys have followed a relatively closed model for their AM ecosystems. However, this approach has led to higher prices for the end user and limited experimentation with new materials, ultimately resulting in a slower adoption of AM solutions.

In our view, the AM industry will soon be ready to take the next step in its development. Players should focus on fueling growth and innovation, tapping the creativity of a broader set of players, and growing the pie.

Some entrants to the AM industry, such as HP, have used a more open or semiopen platform model and not compromised on quality. For example, in HP's ecosystem, material suppliers qualify their materials via a process that is transparent to end users as well as to other material suppliers. This enables the ecosystem to build a broader material database and gives end users the opportunity to source materials at the lowest available price and with the best-suited properties for the application. The ecosystem also has an innovation platform that software companies and other innovators can use to advance the development of software across a variety of applications.

An open ecosystem model needs to be supported by industry standards. For example, a consortium of large equipment providers and software developers have established an improved 3D-printing file format called 3MF. The format

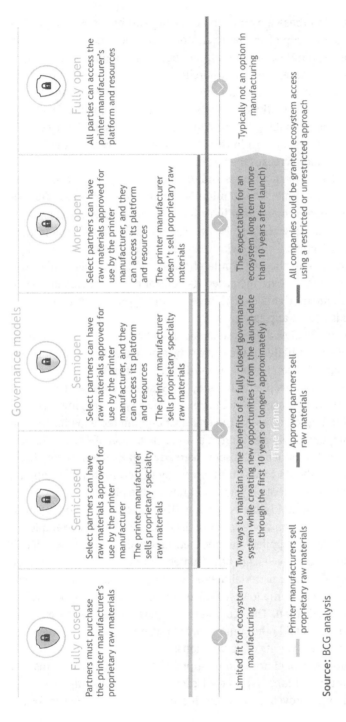

Source: BCG analysis

Figure 17.2: The Choices Relating to Governance Issues Depend on Where the Participants Want the Ecosystem to Be on the Continuum Between Fully Closed and Fully Open.

makes the design-to-print process easier and more intuitive. AM adoption can also be fueled by using open application programming interfaces (APIs) and expanding the use of data.

Experiment with Innovative Monetization Strategies

In defining an ecosystem's monetization strategy, participants must balance competing objectives: maximizing the size of the total pie, ensuring fair value distribution, and anticipating scale effects that kick in when the ecosystem matures. The appropriate balance depends on the answers to three questions:
1. What should the ecosystem charge for?
2. Whom should the ecosystem charge?
3. How much should it charge?

In general, an ecosystem should design a monetization strategy that encourages and incentivizes participation, thus fostering network effects. Moreover, the ecosystem should use monetization to overcome AM bottlenecks by subsidizing R&D investment, for example. The ecosystem should also encourage innovation by offering better terms for new products, including by providing support for development. For example, in its role as orchestrator, a printer manufacturer could cofund the development of advanced materials, thereby encouraging innovation by raw-material suppliers.

In an AM ecosystem, as in other solution ecosystems, participants capture value by selling a product or service. In addition to capturing margin, participants can set their prices to promote further growth and scaling of the ecosystem. If possible, participants should also establish control points – products, services, or technical features that are essential to the overall solution – so that they can be monetized as the ecosystem matures.

For example, although Apple has historically been a product-focused company, it has built an ecosystem with a variety of monetization models that support a variety of revenue streams, including revenue from app commissions and subscription services. The models are generally designed to support further usage or growth of the ecosystem, while ensuring that Apple retains control of monetization opportunities.

To create additional value and encourage adoption, the AM ecosystem could experiment with more innovative approaches that other manufacturing-heavy industries have employed. These include:
- **Pay per Use.** The pay-per-use model has been a hot topic in the manufacturing industry in recent years, and adoption is increasing. For example, a laser

manufacturer charges customers for the number of items produced using its equipment, instead of selling customers the production equipment. And an elevator company charges customers on the basis of their usage of its products. Such models lock in customers and generate steady cash flows. They also provide a way for companies to bring innovative machinery to the market, because customers only pay if the equipment delivers the impact promised by the innovation.

- **Data Sharing.** Equipment providers could offer customers reduced prices for machinery if they share the data that they generate by using the equipment. The provider could then sell the data to other parties interested in aggregated insights on the goods produced or processes used. By sharing data across companies, manufacturers can unlock additional value and accelerate innovation.

EOS pursues a mixed monetization approach. The majority of its revenue is from traditional printer sales and leasing as well as raw-material sales. In addition, the company offers full-service packages, which include personnel to operate the printers at the customer's site. EOS offers these packages mainly to customers that are new to AM. On the basis of the experience gained on these projects, the company created software solutions and platforms that let customers and partners apply pay-per-use models (for example, paying per laser- or machine-hour or per printed part).

One cautionary note: although new monetization models can provide additional revenue for some ecosystem partners and increase the adoption of AM by industrial companies, the models can have a negative impact on other ecosystem players (as does the razor-and-blades model). Thus, before implementing new monetization models, players should consider the potential negative consequences for their partners in the ecosystem.

Ultimately, each player should ask this key question: "How can my company make the best use of the ecosystem to earn money?" The answer to this question should focus on a joint approach that increases the size of the pie, not on maximizing one's own share of the pie at the expense of partners.

Solve the Chicken-or-Egg Problem During Launch

Solving the chicken-or-egg problem of creating a critical mass of both partners and customers during the launch is among the most difficult challenges ecosystems face as they seek to promote both supply- and demand-side economies of scale.

The traditional approach to product development calls for building a full version of a product and then testing it in a small pilot market, improving it, and rolling it out across the broader market. In contrast, as described in *The Wide Lens: A New Strategy for Innovation*, most successful ecosystems start by launching a minimum viable ecosystem (MVE) with limited scope that seeks to achieve full scale by quickly establishing a dense network of partners and customers. Over time, the ecosystem then can expand its scope and value proposition in a series of staged expansions.

For example, like other companies that make smart-home solutions, Amazon employed an MVE approach when it launched Alexa and focused on voice recognition, although it also included some early smart-light applications. The Alexa ecosystem then sequentially added more and more use cases, and Amazon now features more than 100,000 applications that can be downloaded in its store.

A successful launch requires not only a large enough number of participants but also the right participants in the right proportions. The challenge is that the breadth of suppliers affects the number of customers attracted to the ecosystem, and vice versa. Thus, the selection of early members and the sequence of attracting members can have a big impact on the ecosystem's success.

Achieving critical mass – on both the supply and demand sides – has been a slow process in the AM industry. For example, Stratasys, one of the largest equipment providers, took more than 20 years to reach sales exceeding $660 million. To foster the growth of the ecosystem, AM players can choose among a broad set of proven options. For example:

- **Start with a well-functioning customer application and then add others.** This approach is often used to introduce complex business-to-business solutions that use the Internet of Things. For example, Formlabs, a printer startup, initially focused on the consumer segment with simple products, but it soon expanded its offerings to professional users. It now emphasizes significantly more advanced products (such as industrial printers and materials and resins) for medical applications. GE uses key applications to showcase its AM offerings while adding applications that use more advanced technology. The most prominent example is its fuel nozzle tip for the jet engine. The company's superior design allows it to produce more efficient turbines.
- **Develop or acquire products to complement the core offering.** In the smart-home market, Amazon and Google have invested heavily in physical products that complement their voice technology. AM players have employed this approach – most notably, photopolymer printer manufacturers have developed their own photo resin materials. For example, Carbon, Inc., developed proprietary raw materials to boost its technology, and Markforged developed fiber-reinforced filaments for its thermoplastic extrusion printers.

- **Provide free or subsidized tools or services.** For example, Google's tools for search engine optimization create value for advertisers by allowing them to more effectively and efficiently use Google search (the company's core service). BASF gives its conventional-manufacturing customers free software to simulate properties of injection molded parts. The software runs optimally only when used with BASF's engineering plastics. A similar approach could be followed for printed parts. As an early example, Stratasys supports designers and engineers in its GrabCAD community by giving them free access to a computer-aided design library.
- **Demonstrate commitment to the ecosystem and partners by making large upfront investments.** For example, Xbox used this approach when entering the video game console market. By making credible commitments to the project, it convinced developers to create games exclusively for Xbox. HP employed a similar approach when entering the 3D-printing market. The company boldly positioned its technology as a replacement for injection molding and said it would use an open platform for raw materials. Industry participants considered both claims to be disruptive, which created strong traction for HP and helped to establish its brand in AM.

Taking Actions Jointly and Individually

To realize the growth potential of an AM ecosystem, the partners need to take actions collectively and individually.

All partners need to adopt an ecosystem perspective in order to understand interdependencies that lead to co-innovation challenges and to develop joint solutions. In developing solutions, it is critical to consider the tradeoffs between gaining advantages from increased adoption and potentially taking market share from partners in the ecosystem. To drive adoption of the solutions, ecosystem partners should create industry-wide standards. They should also experiment with new monetization models and innovative launch strategies.

Raw-material suppliers have an opportunity to increase the scope of their role in the ecosystem. This includes offering a wide variety of materials through multiple channels, taking a leadership role in the formulation and certification of new materials, supporting the development of a material database, and offering printing services. To be successful, suppliers need to clearly prioritize their focus application areas, better understand end-user needs (for example, through collaborations with service bureaus), and increasingly expand their offering (for example, by providing free support software).

Equipment providers that are considering launching an ecosystem should follow a three-step approach to taking on the orchestrator role, promoting standards, and fostering connections among ecosystem partners. First, the equipment providers should establish a semi-open raw-material platform that gives material suppliers access to the ecosystem, and they should use the platform to increase the range of applications and reduce material prices, thereby promoting adoption. If the existing AM equipment providers fail to open their systems, new entrants (such as HP) will have an opportunity to conquer the market with their more open approaches. Second, equipment providers should define industry standards and norms on the basis of the ecosystem's technology. Standards and norms facilitate part design and the approval and certification process and promote adoption among engineers in users' industries. Third, equipment providers should use standardized and open APIs and other interfaces to facilitate the integration and use of the ecosystem's equipment in end-to-end production processes.

Software companies should encourage other ecosystem participants to employ a more open approach and to pursue standardization with respect to design as well as process-stability solutions. APIs will be essential to enable connections in the ecosystem and with end customers. Software companies should also seek to drive adoption by integrating their software into manufacturing execution systems. In addition, these participants have an opportunity to support less-experienced end customers by establishing their software platform as the single point of entry to the ecosystem. Finally, software companies are well positioned to evaluate and harness the potential of data sharing among players.

Service bureaus should support customers in navigating the AM ecosystem and exploit resulting business opportunities (for example, by offering value-added services and training for AM engineers). Through these efforts, service bureaus can avoid being commoditized as an outsourced labor force. To succeed in the emerging AM ecosystems, service bureaus should take advantage of their proximity to customers to understand unmet needs; offer value-added services – including virtual services (such as software and design platforms) and physical services (such as educating users, screening parts to identify future applications for customers, and optimizing designs); and team up with material and equipment players to optimize materials and printers.

Although AM offers great potential, it has yet to deliver on the promise of industrialized applications. By adopting a managed business ecosystem approach that is based on the success factors of other industry ecosystems, companies may finally be able to achieve the long-awaited step change in the AM industry's development.

Massimo Russo and Gary Wang

Chapter 18
Orchestrating the Value in IoT Platform-Based Business Models

In the modern industrial age, the principal model for organizing economic activity has been linear value chains running from component supplier to OEM to end customer. The Internet of Things (IoT) presents a new opportunity for value creation – and a risk for those who ignore it.

The opportunity: Industry incumbents that aggregate data from their own products or their customers' business processes can establish an IoT platform or ecosystem business that serves a single- or multi-industry user base. Other companies can contribute data, products, and services to make the platform more valuable. Platforms and ecosystems have the potential to dramatically alter linear value chains by breaching industry barriers and establishing new value pools.

The risk: Incumbents that do not participate in the new IoT models could become mere suppliers of commodity hardware and see their customer relationships erode.

Here's how we think a major transformation in the B2B industrial economy will play out.

Defining Platforms and Ecosystems

In business, experts generally recognize two platform types: innovation and transaction.[1]

Innovation platforms, such as the developer platforms from Amazon Web Services, Facebook, and Salesforce, enable other companies to create complementary services or products using the resources of the platform. For example, independent software vendors can use the AWS cloud computing infrastructure to build their own applications.

---

1 A distinction drawn from *The Business of Platforms: Strategy in the Age of Digital Competition, Innovation, and Power* by Michael Cusumano, Annabelle Gawer, and David Yoffie.

https://doi.org/10.1515/9783110775167-018

Transaction platforms enable multiple parties to exchange goods, services, software, or data in exchange for money. Such marketplaces as Airbnb, Uber, and the iOS and Android smartphone app stores are classic examples.

To be successful, innovation platforms must provide a broad ecosystem of players with the tools they need to build complementary services or products. Transaction platforms must reduce the transaction costs between two parties. In many cases, companies create a hybrid model that combines both types of platform. Salesforce, for example, offers a combined app development platform and a marketplace for third parties to sell their enterprise apps.

The value of data in B2B is difficult to extract; companies need both the domain expertise to develop new data-driven solutions and the customer relationships required to monetize them. This complexity means that digital ecosystems, such as those built around IoT platforms, are insufficient for capturing the value of data on their own. New, built-for-purpose data ecosystems are required to organize the collective data assets, capabilities, and customer connections of a group of business partners to deliver new products and services – both within and across traditional industry verticals. While digital ecosystems provide the underlying platforms, data ecosystems enable B2B companies in asset-heavy industries to generate additional revenues and build enduring competitive advantage with their IoT data (Figure 18.1).

IoT Demand and Supply

Two primary drivers for IoT ecosystem formation, both powerful forces, are taking shape. Customers seeking to lower implementation costs and scale up solutions in their own businesses are creating demand-side pull. Meanwhile (and partly in response), supply-side industry incumbents are partnering with technology companies to deliver industry-specific platforms, push standards, and aggregate use cases into broader solutions. Both forces are fueled by network effects, which strengthen the size and quality of ecosystems; data aggregation, which enables companies to turn data into competitive advantage; and data models, which ease the replication of IoT solutions across multiple customers.

Demand-Side Pull

For enterprise customers struggling to implement IoT solutions, it's a heavy lift. They need to build their own customized solutions or integrate solutions from

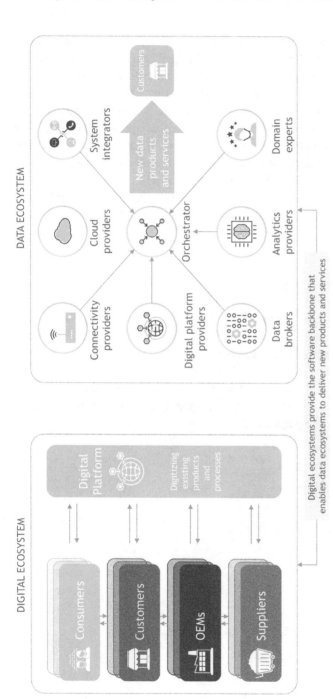

Source: BCG Henderson Institute

Figure 18.1: Digital and Data Ecosystems.

multiple suppliers. Both paths involve a host of tasks and plenty of participants. For example, a company must implement an IoT platform to aggregate machine data and provide the IoT application development environment. The same company has to work with a telecommunications or network equipment provider to connect its equipment and transmit data to the cloud. A systems integrator is required to integrate the IoT platform with other enterprise applications. And cybersecurity providers are needed to secure the entire IoT architecture, from the deployed sensors and equipment to the network and cloud environment.

It becomes very clear very quickly that implementing IoT solutions at scale can be more efficiently addressed by an ecosystem approach that makes the requisite solutions readily available, lowers integration costs, enables data aggregation, and delivers a secure infrastructure.

Supply-Side Partnering

To meet this demand, technology firms and leading industrial companies have been partnering to build ecosystems that take advantage of each other's core capabilities. These partnerships address multiple objectives: establishing common data and technology standards, developing IoT solutions based on industry templates, enabling independent software vendors to develop additional solutions, mounting joint go-to-market programs, and driving IoT adoption within a specific industry (Figure 18.2).

Partnership objective	Number of partnerships	Example tech company	Example incumbent	Description
Codevelopment	20	IBM	ABB	Codevelopment of ABB IoT solutions for utilities, transport, industry, infrastructure verticals
Joint go-to-market campaigns	4	Microsoft	Avnet	Joint GTM to drive adoption of IoT platform
Promote common data and technology standards	7	Cisco	Rockwell Automation	Promotion of common networking standards for industrial environments
Drive adoption of IoT across the value chain	3	Amazon	Ford (via Autonomic[1])	Drive adoption of IoT across mobility players (e.g., fleet management, ride hailing)

1. Autonomic (owned by Ford) is building a transportation mobility cloud platform
Note: Analysis of 37 IoT tech/industrial company partnerships between 2016 and 2019; many partnerships had multiple objectives
Source: BCG Henderson Institute

Figure 18.2: Supply-Side Partnership Frameworks.

Take the example of Microsoft, which is working with OEMs in multiple industrial segments, including elevators (Schindler, ThyssenKrupp) and industrial automation (Honeywell, Schneider Electric, and ABB), to establish IoT platforms specific to industry verticals. In each instance, the industry incumbent brands its own platform (for example, Honeywell Forge, Schneider Electric EcoStruxure). The industrial OEM then draws on Microsoft's technological capabilities and codevelops solutions using the tech giant's investment in cloud infrastructure and tools.

In another example, Airbus has partnered with Palantir to build Skywise, an IoT platform that aims to improve the operations of airlines. As more such partnerships are formed, the suppliers to the large OEMs face increasing pressure to join the OEMs' platforms. For example, Volkswagen plans to encourage its supplier base to join the Volkswagen Industrial Cloud, an IoT platform formed with Amazon Web Services (AWS) for the automaker's more than 120 factories. The ecosystems that set data standards (one of the goals of the Volkswagen Cloud) will be able to aggregate data and apply analytics at scale to address a variety of use cases and unlock the value of machine data.

The Factors Shaping IoT Value Pools

In the early days of enterprise software, companies developed custom code to automate business processes. Over time, third-party software companies offered less expensive and more capable enterprise applications, such as ERP (enterprise resource planning), MRP (manufacturing resource planning), SCM (supply chain management), and CRM (customer relationship management). We expect a similar pattern of development with the emergence of IoT applications that target the use cases unlocked by machine data. Several structural factors will shape the value pools and ecosystems of IoT application providers (Figure 18.3).

Use Cases Benefiting from Network Effects

A substantial number of high-value use cases, in a single industry or spanning a group of industries, that benefit from network effects can constitute the basis for a platform marketplace connecting buyers and sellers. For example, Zira, an industrial IoT startup, has created a marketplace of customers and equipment suppliers with a platform that triggers automatic work orders for maintenance and repair in response to equipment data indicating machine failure. As more

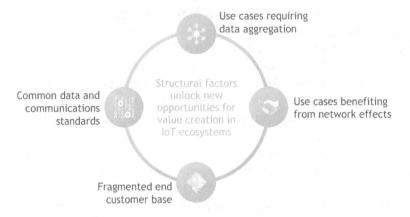

Figure 18.3: Structural Factors Shaping Value Pools and Ecosystems of IoT Application Providers.

customers connect a wider variety of equipment to the marketplace, Zira and its suppliers can offer new services such as asset sharing and benchmarking of equipment reliability. Once a robust market of suppliers and buyers is established, third parties can offer innovative services and solutions and Zira can make it easier for these participants to develop new services by providing data and other development services.

Use Cases Requiring Data Aggregation

There are entire categories of use cases that require aggregation of data from multiple parties. For example, operational benchmarking (such as when a company benchmarks its maintenance strategy against those of its peers) will be most valuable if the data set is large, comparable, and as comprehensive as possible with respect to the operational dimensions it includes. Companies that aggregate data from multiple sources benefit from both network effects and economies of scale as they amortize the fixed costs of defining data standards and application programming interfaces (APIs). Third-party data-as-a-service providers can help overcome such challenges as collection cost, data that is perishable or time-sensitive, data that is controlled by multiple companies, and the need for anonymization.

In many refineries and factories, multiple components and assets work together to improve throughput; the dependencies along the production process require aggregation of data from devices and sensors belonging to multiple suppliers. Honeywell's INspire program has recruited multiple oil and gas component suppliers to share data with the Honeywell Forge platform to deliver software solutions, data, and algorithms that optimize entire processes in an oil refinery.

The Need for Standards

Data and communication standards lower integration and aggregation costs and enable solutions to scale across customers and suppliers. For example, the Society of Automotive Engineers established the J1939 data standard for transmitting vehicle data from all commercial trucks in the US, regardless of manufacturer. This enabled fleet management companies to offer plug-and-play telematics hardware and software that tracks location, fault codes, fuel levels, and other truck data. Without this common standard, each fleet management company would have had to develop software to translate proprietary data from different truck models. Standards also exhibit direct network effects: once adoption of the standard reaches a tipping point, it becomes uneconomical for companies to develop solutions incompatible with the standard or to promote alternative standards.

Fragmented Customer Base

A highly fragmented customer base will benefit from data aggregation, network effects, and reuse of solutions. Customers are unlikely to have the resources needed to build their own IoT-based solutions and will seek to join third-party platforms. The aggregating demand and data from customers helps solutions providers lower their customer acquisition and integration costs.

Participating in Platforms

The combination of these factors drives platform competition toward three potential outcomes. In each, the value pools are divided differently:
- A winner-take-most dynamic, similar to platform competition in B2C, where a dominant platform and ecosystem emerges
- A competitive oligopoly where a few (two or three) platforms and ecosystems directly compete with similar solutions

- A complementary oligopoly where the platforms and ecosystems offered address different, complementary use cases and have the potential to interoperate

In all cases, however, the ecosystems will comprise companies that play three distinct roles (Figure 18.4). Orchestrators will own the platform and establish the ecosystem. These companies will typically be incumbents with a strong right to win. Contributors will develop and sell specific solutions on the platform. Enablers will provide infrastructure or common platform services but will not be unique to a given vertical.

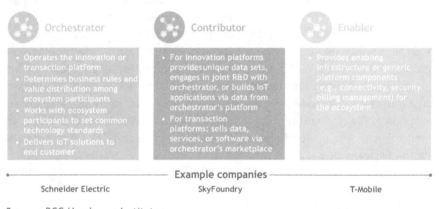

<table>
<thead>
<tr><th>Orchestrator</th><th>Contributor</th><th>Enabler</th></tr>
</thead>
<tbody>
<tr>
<td>• Operates the innovation or transaction platform
• Determines business rules and value distribution among ecosystem participants
• Works with ecosystem participants to set common technology standards
• Delivers IoT solutions to end customer</td>
<td>• For innovation platforms provides unique data sets, engages in joint R&D with orchestrator, or builds IoT applications via data from orchestrator's platform
• For transaction platforms: sells data, services, or software via orchestrator's marketplace</td>
<td>• Provides enabling infrastructure or generic platform components (e.g., connectivity, security, billing management) for the ecosystem</td>
</tr>
</tbody>
</table>

Example companies

| Schneider Electric | SkyFoundry | T-Mobile |

Source: BCG Henderson Institute

Figure 18.4: The Three Distinct Roles in IoT Ecosystems.

The BCG Henderson Institute studied a broad set of ecosystems and discovered that only a minority (about 15%) of orchestrators achieve the critical mass necessary to succeed (Chapter 3). To be a successful orchestrator requires investment, commitment, and continual renewal of the value proposition. The majority of companies will therefore be contributors, a role that can have a very attractive risk-reward profile of its own because solutions can be developed and sold across multiple ecosystems to maximize reach and revenue growth (Chapter 8). Here's our analysis of the specific moves required to build winning positions in each of the three roles.

Orchestrators and Contributors. Orchestrators orchestrate. They have the resources and capability to invest and operate a platform. They recruit contributors and enablers (by partnering with technology companies, for example). They define the governance model and value sharing rules, establish the legal framework surrounding data and intellectual property, set the standards (for data, communication, APIs, and the like), and provide common tools to make it easy to develop new solutions.

Contributors increase the value of the ecosystem by bringing unique data sets or intellectual property, engaging in codevelopment with the orchestrator, or building solutions on the orchestrator's platform. Contributors can sell their solutions via the orchestrator's platform, generating network effects for the ecosystem by increasing its value to customers. For example, SkyFoundry, a connected-building startup, offers a set of white-label building-specific data and analytics solutions to its building automation OEM partners, each of which has its own platform. SkyFoundry's solution is offered on multiple, competing ecosystems. SkyFoundry is better off joining the ecosystems orchestrated by major building automation OEMs because the OEMs have oligopolistic market share (and thus access to building data), deep relationships with building owners and operators, and, in some cases, the ability to "close the loop" by automating control of building equipment. By joining these ecosystems, SkyFoundry can access a bigger customer base and differentiate the value proposition of its OEM partners' connected-building platform and software suites.

Enablers. Enablers are companies that provide the generic underlying technology capabilities (such as cybersecurity, connectivity, and billing functionality) for an IoT ecosystem. While enablers can differentiate themselves from one another on the basis of features and functionality, they offer common solutions because the same underlying technology needs apply across industry verticals.

Paths to Ecosystem Orchestration

For business leaders with the ambition to become orchestrators, there are three potential paths, each with a different starting point, for attracting customers and contributors and building critical mass (Figure 18.5).

Innovation Platforms

Some orchestrators begin by launching an innovation platform. If companies are incumbents with a strong right to win, they will have large equipment data sets (from their installed base of customers) and can create APIs and software development kits to enable third parties to build complementary solutions that widen the scope of addressable use cases.

Starting points and commonly required capabilities

Source: BCG Henderson Institute

Figure 18.5: The Three Paths to Becoming an IoT Ecosystem Orchestrator.

Given the inherent complexity and heterogeneity of equipment and data, creating the necessary data standards can be challenging. Almost every industrial customer – a trucking company, a manufacturer, a farmer, or a building owner – operates a set of assets supplied by multiple OEMs. A successful orchestrator must cooperate with multiple equipment OEMs to create data standards and interfaces that enable integration and interoperability to drive innovation.

Transaction Platforms

If there is a preponderance of IoT use cases that exhibit network effects, orchestrators can start with a transaction platform to establish a marketplace that connects buyers and sellers of data, software, or equipment and spare parts. Most OEM incumbents already offer parts and equipment through online marketplaces or their dealer network. IoT data unlocks insights into a customer's operations and equipment health to enable better inventory planning and potentially more customized marketing offers. With a deeper understanding of customer operations, based on customer transaction data, OEMs can recruit third parties to sell complementary goods and services. Farmers Business Network (FBN), for instance, expanded its e-commerce marketplace from seeds to chemicals and spare parts. Alternatively, OEMs can create asset sharing marketplaces, leveraging equipment data (such as location and usage) to enable customers to monetize higher equipment utilization by renting their asset to others.

As a transaction platform scales up, it may evolve into an innovation platform as it aggregates data, making it possible for independent software vendors to build and market new solutions. For example, Avnet, a distributor of electronic components for equipment manufacturers, has partnered with Microsoft Azure to launch a platform that offers advisory services, APIs and software development kits, prebuilt IoT applications, embedded software, and a program to accelerate the adoption of IoT solutions by customers. Avnet has moved from a strictly transactional platform to enabling innovation and the reuse of solutions in an innovation platform.

Over time, orchestrators' platforms tend to evolve toward providing both innovation and transaction functionality, which enables third parties to build and monetize IoT solutions. Orchestrators can leverage the transaction data generated by the platform's marketplace to gain a deeper understanding of which products and services are gaining traction and use that insight to inform future decisions. A key question for orchestrators to ask is: Which solutions do we develop ourselves and which do we look to contributors to develop? Over time, orchestrators building innovation platforms can adopt an "embrace, extend, extinguish" strategy in which they initially support a third-party solution but then build a competing application and integrate the solution into their own proprietary offering. This approach, however, carries the inherent risk of alienating contributors and sending them to competing platforms.

Data Aggregation

Another starting place is aggregating data, which creates the option of building either a transaction platform or an innovation platform. Otonomo began as a startup, aggregating connected-car data from a variety of OEMs in order to address data-driven use cases for insurance companies, municipalities, and other customers. Then it created a set of APIs, developer documentation, and such value-added services as data anonymization to enable customers to build apps using Otonomo's aggregated data set. In precision agriculture, Farmers Business Network has pursued a similar approach, initially aggregating data from farmers and offering benchmarking services. It then created a transaction platform that aggregates demand from its members and suppliers. FBN has been able to apply machine learning techniques at scale across its aggregated data set to recommend which seeds to plant to optimize yield. Farmers can buy the necessary seeds and other materials through the FBN marketplace.

Winning Strategies for Contributors

Not all companies have the ability or requisite investment appetite to be an eco-system orchestrator. But they may still have valuable IoT-enabled solutions to offer. For these companies, becoming a contributor is a viable path to capturing a piece of the IoT value pool. Moreover, contributors can participate in multiple IoT ecosystems, but they need to consider how to de-risk their relationships with orchestrators to avoid two potential pitfalls: product commoditization and orchestrator lock-in. Several strategies can help.

The first is to specialize in truly differentiated capabilities (such as IP and data) that cannot easily be replicated by the orchestrator. Senseye, a startup providing predictive maintenance analytics for rotating equipment, leaves the data integration and device management to its orchestrator's platform and instead focuses on developing better-quality predictive algorithms that use proprietary machine learning approaches.

Second, contributors should pay close attention to an orchestrator's announced product roadmap and be wary of investing in use cases that are close to those that the orchestrator is itself targeting. For example, numerous industrial IoT platforms have released application suites and services that target asset and process optimization in manufacturing. While the platform vendors are addressing only a limited set of use cases today, we can expect that they will expand their offers over time. Contributors with similar solutions could find that the orchestrators absorb their offers in future platform functionality.

Third, contributors need to sustain investment in innovation. SkyFoundry focuses its efforts on product development and leverages orchestrators' platforms for distribution. In industries with fragmented customer bases, long sales cycles, and complex value chains, using a platform as a distribution channel can reduce contributors' go-to-market costs.

Contributors within the same industry can also collaborate to build their own innovation platform and then resell the solutions through multiple orchestrator transaction platforms. For example, several European machine tool manufacturers (such as Karl Mayer, Engel, and Dürr) formed a joint venture, Adamos, with technology provider Software AG. The machine tool manufacturers used the platform to develop a set of IoT applications that they sell through multiple other platforms, including their own application marketplace.

Platform and ecosystem coopetition will ultimately become the norm in industrial IoT, with new value pools emerging from clusters of use cases and new categories of software that address these cases. The question for top management is this: Does your company have a clear strategy to win, either as an orchestrator or a contributor?

Section D: **Ecosystems and Sustainability**

David Zuluaga Martínez, Martin Reeves, and Ulrich Pidun
Chapter 19
Ecosystems for Ecosystems

Human societies have an outstanding ability to solve complex collective action problems, and for the last 400 years they have done so primarily through the mechanism of the nation-state. However, states have found it especially challenging to tackle collective action problems that are global in scale.

The COVID-19 pandemic made it clear both how much power states have to act and how difficult it is for them to act in concert when challenges transcend national borders. COVAX, the international effort to ensure equitable access to COVID-19 vaccines, had shipped over 365 million doses to some of the world's poorest countries.[1] Yet vaccine nationalism remains conspicuous, with affluent countries stockpiling vaccines even as research shows that they would be better off sharing them "to lower disease burdens in countries with less access, reduce the cost of having to be constantly vigilant for case imports, and minimize virus evolution."[2]

State-led collective action on a global scale is even more constrained in response to complex challenges on longer timescales – which is precisely the case with climate change, arguably the greatest known existential threat humanity faces. We know that environmental degradation will have devastating consequences, but because harm materializes progressively over the course of decades rather than days or weeks, we have been less willing to take decisive action.[3] The trajectory of state-led climate efforts proves as much. The Intergovernmental Panel on Climate Change (IPCC) issued its first report in 1990, but it took seven years to create the first legally binding agreement to reduce greenhouse gas emissions, the Kyoto Protocol. Seven more years passed before the Kyoto Protocol could enter into force. Over that 14-year period, annual global greenhouse gas emissions increased by 23%.[4]

---

1 Gavi: The Vaccine Alliance. Figures as of October 15, 2021.
2 C. Wagner, C. Saad-Roy, S. Morris et al. "Vaccine nationalism and the dynamics of control of SARS-CoV-2." *Science*, 373, no. 6562, September 24, 2021.
3 P. Slovic, "Perception of Risk." *Science*, Vol. 236, Issue 4699, April 17, 1987. Cited in E.U. Weber, "Climate Change Demands Behavioral Change: What Are the Challenges?" *Social Research: An International Quarterly*, 82: 561–581.
4 Climate Watch. Accessed on October 7, 2021. BCG analysis.

https://doi.org/10.1515/9783110775167-019

While there is no question that states must play a central role in climate action, we need to mobilize every resource available – including the power of private enterprise.

We think there is reason to be optimistic about the business community's ability to act collectively to tackle climate change. But rather than being content with individual company 'net-zero' pledges and efforts, we should leverage the sophisticated coordination mechanisms that enable thousands of independent companies to participate in today's business ecosystems. The governance model behind today's largest, technology-enabled business ecosystems can be a powerful tool for global climate action. The few orchestrators at the heart of those ecosystems have the ability and the strategic opportunity to mobilize thousands of businesses across the world in ways that few (if any) other existing coordination mechanisms can match. This will not solve all of our problems, but could meaningfully accelerate the current pace of progress.

Why We Need Collective Business Action

Many businesses are already taking action on climate change at an individual level. At least one-fifth of the world's 2,000 largest public corporations have adopted some kind of net-zero greenhouse gas (GHG) emissions commitment.[5] However, there are strong reasons to believe that individual efforts of this kind will fall short of what's needed given the magnitude and complexity of the challenge we face.

For starters, CO_2 emissions have continued to rise despite the growing number of climate agreements and pledges. Additionally, even if we did manage to deliver on all the pledges and targets that governments and businesses have committed to, global temperature is expected to increase well above the goal set by the Paris Agreement (Figure 19.1).

To complicate matters further, we lack clear, shared standards for how countries and businesses should pursue their net-zero ambitions, and a robust scorekeeping system to assess and track climate action plans. Of the 43% of Russell 1000 companies that have disclosed a commitment to reducing emissions, only 9% have set commitments that meet the Science Based Target Initiative (SBTi) scenario to limit global warming to only 2 degrees above pre-industrial levels by

5 The Energy & Climate Intelligence Unit and Oxford Net Zero. "Taking Stock: A global assessment of net zero targets," March 2021.

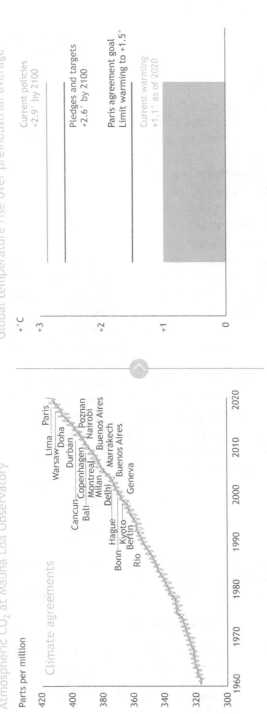

Figure 19.1: Global Temperature Is Expected to Increase Well Above the Goal Set by the Paris Agreement.

Note: Current policies and pledges and targets are projections. In each scenario, the temperature shown is the most likely in a range of possible outcomes.

Sources: Scripps Institution of Oceanography; National Oceanic and Atmospheric Administration; UC San Diego; Earth System Research Laboratories; Climate Action Tracker; Council on Foreign Relations

2100.[6] As a recent study at Imperial College London puts it, "choosing different gases, different timing for net-zero emissions, and different methods of aggregating emissions can have very different outcomes."[7]

The problem of translating lofty pledges into concrete plans that can be evaluated, measured, and compared is further complicated by the fact that individual companies may have non-additive climate effects. Net-zero strategies defined by individual businesses could even have detrimental aggregate outcomes in some cases. For example, companies pledging net-zero emissions very often adopt "offset" strategies that rely on carbon trading. Highly carbon-intensive businesses could thereby become net-zero in a technical, accounting sense – without any actual reduction in the overall amount of carbon that is released into the atmosphere. The "offset" strategy is constrained by the economics of carbon trading: it will only work until the price of carbon matches or exceeds the cost a business is willing to incur to honor its net-zero pledge. As the price of carbon rises, it is hard to tell whether individual businesses that have adopted the "offset" strategy will be driven to transform their business models – or just renege on their environmental commitments.

Even when businesses do change the ways in which they operate to curb emissions, they may nullify their own contributions if they fail to act in concert with others. For example, it is estimated that a 10% reduction in vehicle weight could result in 6–8% fuel economy improvements. One way to achieve that is by replacing cast iron and traditional steel with lighter materials like aluminum.[8] But because aluminum production continues to rely heavily on fossil fuel energy sources, the increase in emissions associated with higher aluminum demand could in some cases offset the beneficial effect of reduced fossil fuel consumption associated with vehicle weight.[9] As noted by the IPCC's 2014 report, mitigation strategies to reduce GHG emissions require a "life cycle perspective" that cuts across the activities of individual businesses.[10]

6 L. Thornton and S. Cabral, "More Corporate Climate Commitments Are Essential to Limiting the Effects of Global Warming." *Just Capital*, September 2021.

7 J. Rogelj et al. "Net-zero emissions targets are vague: three ways to fix it." *Nature* 591, 365–368; 2021.

8 Office of Energy Efficiency & Renewable Energy, energy.gov, "Lightweight Materials for Cars and Trucks."

9 G. Saevarsdottir, H. Kvande, and B.J. Welch, "Aluminum Production in the Times of Climate Change: The Global Challenge to Reduce Carbon Footprint and Prevent Carbon Leakage." *The Journal of the Minerals, Metals, and Materials Society* 72, no. 1, November 2019; IPCC, Climate Change 2014: Mitigation of Climate Change. Cambridge University Press, 2014, p. 764.

10 IPCC, idem.

As things stand, states have made progress toward setting global emissions targets, but those targets are vague, progress is difficult to measure, and enforcement is virtually impossible. Some, especially large, businesses have committed to contribute their share – but in the aggregate these individual efforts could easily be insufficient. What is required is collective business action of the sort that the business ecosystems of the digital age are uniquely positioned to enable, especially through the agency and activism of their orchestrators.

The Power of Orchestrators

Ecosystems are a way for independent businesses to organize in order to realize a collective value proposition. The lesson to be learned from the expansion and proliferation of business ecosystems is that independent enterprises can, under certain conditions, successfully coordinate a very complex set of actors and activities to create value without relying on command-and-control hierarchies.

While business ecosystems are diverse, their governance structures exhibit some key commonalities. Ecosystems are modular in that their components – the multiple businesses that contribute to them – are independent yet function as an integrated whole, at least for purposes of delivering a joint solution. Most importantly, ecosystems are held together by orchestrators who, despite having considerable power over the structure and workings of the ecosystems, nevertheless do not deploy hierarchical control of activities, as in the case of most individual enterprises and vertical supply chains.

Orchestrators are the central nodes of coordination that make an ecosystem's collective value creation possible. They typically build the ecosystem and its coordinating platforms, encourage others to join, define standards and rules, and act as arbiters in cases of conflict. Some of today's most successful ecosystems are built around orchestrator-owned digital platforms, as in the cases of Alibaba, Amazon, Apple, Tencent, Facebook, or Yandex. Because of their place at the heart of ecosystems that can synthesize hundreds and even thousands of contributors, orchestrators wield extraordinary influence; they have the power to shape behaviors across far-reaching networks of partners, often on a global scale.

Our analyses suggest that over the last 20 years, ecosystem orchestrators have grown considerably in size, reach, and power. Among the S&P 100, the number of ecosystem orchestrators has grown from 3 to 22. More importantly, those 22 orchestrators account for 40% of the total market value of the S&P 100. The rise of ecosystems shows also in the share of new "unicorns" associated with them: 23% of the new unicorns between 2015 and 2021 have based their business model on orchestrating a business ecosystem.

These facts illustrate the considerable (and growing) share of economic activity concentrated around ecosystems and therefore the extraordinary reach and coordinating power of their orchestrators. With thousands of contributors of all sizes that rely partially or wholly on ecosystems, orchestrators have become critical nodes in some of the world's largest and most complex coordination systems.

How Ecosystems Can Simplify the Challenge

Business ecosystems can enable ambitious climate action essentially because they simplify the collective action problem we face. Instead of having to coordinate across thousands of enterprises globally, action by a handful of powerful orchestrators can have outsized effects because it can directly shape the decisions of their ecosystems' contributors.

Consider the case of Amazon, which according to Marketplace Pulse has approximately 1.5 million active sellers.[11] Any norms or standards Amazon chooses to adopt as orchestrator of the global retail ecosystem that runs on its digital platform could shape the behaviors of hundreds of thousands of businesses globally. And the same holds for other orchestrators. When dealing with a problem at the scale of climate change, such drastic reduction in the number of key players whose decisions can be pivotal amounts to a transformation of the situation, turning a virtually impossible *consensus gentium* into the feasible adoption of shared norms and practices by a few, disproportionately powerful actors.

One important virtue of business ecosystems is the sheer diversity of contributors who can come to act collectively through the influence of orchestrators. More specifically, ecosystems reach large numbers of small- and medium-sized enterprises – those that are less likely to make public net-zero pledges or indeed take any unilateral climate action. Yet the "long tail" of small and medium-sized enterprises (SMEs) all over the world is critical to truly addressing climate change collectively – SMEs account for 90% of all businesses, 50% of employment, and over 40% of GDP globally.[12]

---

11 Marketplace Pulse, "Number of Sellers on Amazon Marketplace." Accessed on October 7, 2021.

12 The World Bank. "Small and Medium Enterprises (SMEs) Finance: Improving SMEs' access to finance and finding innovative solutions to unlock sources of capital." Accessed on October 7, 2021.

In a sense, ecosystems can realize the idea of "climate clubs" proposed by Nobel Laureate William D. Nordhaus. Collective action around climate change is especially difficult because of the free-rider problem: Those who undertake costly mitigating action create benefits from which no one can be excluded, and so those who do nothing can ride for free. To solve the free-rider problem, Nordhaus has proposed that countries should create "club regions" such that "the 'dues' to the club are expensive [emissions] abatement, while the 'penalties' for non-membership are tariffs on exports to the club region."[13] Business ecosystems could do something very similar, especially when they rely on digital platforms. Access to the platform can be immensely beneficial to individual businesses, but orchestrators could structure it so that contributors pay their dues in terms of adherence to rigorous environmental norms, while exclusion from or higher cost of access to the platform could function as penalties for non-members. Orchestrators have the power to replicate in the business world the collective action dynamics of what Nordhaus has described as "the best hope for effective coordination" to contain global warming.

Business ecosystems also have another important qualifying characteristic: the ability to unlock experimentation and innovation toward new solutions. An important aspect of the climate challenge problem is that we do not currently know all of the eventual solutions but rather need to iterate our way toward them. Climate change is as much a challenge of innovation as of execution. Any governance mechanism, therefore, needs to be evolvable in nature. Individual ecosystems can deploy their modular structures to explore, adapt, and iterate on solutions; through digital platforms, learning can be fast and easily spread around for contributor networks to continuously rebalance their approaches to a common problem. As multiple ecosystems do the same, there is the additional benefit of multiple, parallel experimentation.

Furthermore, the robust digital technologies that power most of today's largest ecosystems can go a long way toward filling the complex "scorekeeping gap" of environmental mitigation. As noted above, today's net-zero pledges are virtually impossible to evaluate and compare, in part because there are no robust standards on the scope and metrics for emissions reduction plans and no continuous flow of consistent data. Digital tools can make the difference in terms of setting clear standards, aggregating progress data, and thereby presenting an accurate picture of progress that also creates transparency over and within an ecosystem.

---

13 W.D. Nordhaus, "Climate Change: The Ultimate Challenge for Economics." Nobel Lecture in Economic Science, Stockholm University (December 2018).

How Ecosystem Orchestrators Can Make a Difference

To reap the benefits of ecosystem-enabled collective action on climate change, orchestrators will have to adopt rigorous GHG emission standards as integral to the governing norms of their ecosystems. They can thereby mobilize the thousands of contributors in whose interest it is to retain access to the ecosystem. While many orchestrators – including Amazon – are already mobilizing businesses in their own supply chains, we are talking here about something more ambitious because the vast set of contributors to Amazon's ecosystem reaches well beyond the confines of their own operations.

So how could this work? We think there are a few concrete steps orchestrators could take.

- **Assess ecosystem-level climate impact.** Orchestrators should think about all the upstream and downstream activities associated with either their business or their contributors' businesses. Where are the most salient environmental impacts and risks? What clusters or types of contributors may be responsible for the highest rates of energy use or GHG emissions? What is the total footprint of the ecosystem? It is already standard practice among some of the world's largest businesses to track environmental impact across their supply chains: Apple, for instance, reports a total carbon footprint of 22.6 metric tons of CO_2, of which 71% is associated with the entire product manufacturing value chain, which encompasses its suppliers.[14] The addressable scope of an orchestrator's footprint can be expanded to include the broader network of ecosystem contributors.
- **Map and understand the network of contributors.** Orchestrators could in parallel develop a clear map of their business partners to identify the contributors and processes that account for the most salient climate impacts and determine where they are. How strong are the relationships with the agents involved? Are they one-off transactions or enduring partnerships? Where is the greatest potential for footprint reduction in terms of size, substitutability, technology adoption, and willingness?
- **Collaboratively set rigorous targets for the ecosystem.** Engage the key players – including large contributors – to agree on what the ecosystem should collectively achieve in terms of climate action. Targets should be bold and backed by hard scientific evidence. Organizations like the Science Based Targets Initiative (SBTi) have the expertise to support orchestrators

---

14 Apple, Environmental Progress Report, Fiscal Year 2020.

in their efforts to set the right ambitions for an ecosystem and give those goals concreteness (for example, a precise definition of what constitutes net-zero emissions).

– **Leverage coordination power.** Orchestrators have the power to steer an ecosystem toward decision-making principles that incorporate a rigorous dimension of sustainability. For instance, they can require contributors to adopt certain standards or practices, 'advantage' those who more proactively adopt sustainable solutions, and even serve as advisors or knowledge-sharing nodes for contributors to share and learn from best practices across the ecosystem. This can be especially effective in reaching the long tail of SMEs that are harder to engage directly. Consider, for instance, Alphabet's decision to make available the cloud technology solution that helped reduce energy utilization for cooling data centers by 30%.[15] Given the high environmental impact of cooling and heating commercial businesses, widespread access to this technology could enable businesses of all sizes in Alphabet's ecosystem – and potentially beyond – to reduce their own emissions.

Orchestrators could also make transparent to consumers the environmental footprint of different companies and products, thereby creating a new adaptive mechanism for reducing emissions.

– **Keep action plans adaptable across contributors and over time.** Individual ecosystem contributors face very different realities. For example, they may differ considerably in the extent of dependence on fossil fuels, access to clean energy sources, or feasibility of sustainable alternatives to existing business processes. To make collective targets reasonable and achievable, orchestrators need to foster the development of context-specific, science-based action plans for key contributors and empower agents across the ecosystem to design solutions within the bounds set by the ecosystem's shared parameters. This decentralization of action while retaining norm-setting influence at the core can make the ecosystem both powerful and adaptable.

– **Design shared and actionable monitoring and reporting standards.** Orchestrators, especially those that lead digital ecosystems, can harness the power of technology to create transparency and accountability. Technology can help build trust by gathering and communicating accurate information about the ecosystem's environmental impact, system-wide as well as at company-level. It is important, however, that technology not be used merely

---

15 S. Pichai, "Our third decade of climate action: Realizing a carbon-free future." September 14, 2020. Accessed on October 7, 2021.

with a compliance mindset, but instead with a strong action and impact bias: agents across the ecosystem should learn from the decentralized experimentation and real-time efficacy of environmental efforts across the network.

Why Orchestrators Should Act Now

The existential urgency of climate change should be sufficient reason for orchestrators to take action, leveraging their position at the core of today's ecosystems for the good of everyone. But there are also strong strategic reasons why orchestrators should do so – and do it now.

As we have noted elsewhere, one of the key principles of corporate longevity and resilience is "embeddedness," or the alignment of a company's goals and activities with those of the broader systems within which they operate. An enterprise is not poised for long-term success, even survival, if it works up against the goals and aspirations of society at large. Indeed, there are strong signals that some of the world's largest digital ecosystem orchestrators are increasingly at risk in this regard. Regulatory pressure aimed at curbing the power of digital ecosystem orchestrators over contributors is on the rise:

- A US judge ruled in September 2021 that Apple could no longer force its developers to use its payment system in apps.
- Amazon has come under increasing scrutiny for the terms on which it transacts with its ecosystem contributors (third-party sellers on its retail platform), becoming the target of an ongoing investigation by the EU competition commissioner.
- Alibaba was recently fined $2.8 billion by Chinese regulators on grounds that it unduly prevented merchants (contributors to its e-retail ecosystem) from selling on other platforms.

The regulatory pressure on digital ecosystem orchestrators is part of a broader challenge to the legitimacy of globalization and technology. Between 2010 and 2019 the share of people in the US who believed that tech companies had a positive impact on society decreased from 68% to 50%.[16] Although citizens continue to hold technology companies in high regard, their trust and respect appear to be slipping.

---

16 "A Policymaker's Guide to the 'Techlash' – What It Is and Why It's a Threat to Growth and Progress," *Information Technology & Innovation Foundation* (itif.org), October 28, 2019.

In this context, turning ecosystems into active instruments for climate action can be a powerful reaffirmation of corporate purpose in line with societal expectations and goals. Moreover, technology can be robustly deployed for good, making sustainability pledges tangible and measurable for thousands of enterprises. Orchestrators can draw on what they already know how to do – build and sustain business ecosystems – to make substantial contributions in the effort to combat climate change, thereby renewing their 'social license to operate.'

Creating environmental transparency can help orchestrators manage some of the risks they face today. But in so doing, they can also unlock a source of competitive advantage for the future. Orchestrators stand to gain by offering a moral choice to consumers on something they care deeply about and will only care more about over time.

Climate change is so urgent a challenge that we cannot afford to not try everything that could be of use. While governments continue to mobilize, business ecosystems can become important complementary mechanisms for collective environmental action. Ecosystem orchestrators are uniquely positioned to bring this about. In short, they have the power to rebuild trust in the extraordinary problem-solving power of business.

David Young, Ulrich Pidun, Balázs Zoletnik, and Simon Beck
Chapter 20
When a Business Ecosystem Is the Answer to Sustainability Challenges

The success of ecosystems is a hot topic these days – and rightly so. Apple, for example, has built a powerful business ecosystem of app developers and software players around its iOS operating system. Amazon has similarly built a robust business ecosystem including brick-and-mortar and online retailers. And Visa has built a robust business ecosystem around its payment platform. But what if the power of business ecosystems could be taken a bit further? What if business ecosystems could be leveraged to help save the planet?

That's not as far-fetched as it may sound. As companies around the world remake their business models to advance their sustainability and boost their business advantage, many are finding that they need to drive change beyond the boundaries of their business. Creating changes in the wider system in which a company operates demands collective action. In some cases, that change is best driven through the creation of a business ecosystem.

Business ecosystems are complex and often more difficult to develop than alternative approaches to collective action, including partnerships or joint ventures, as well as broad-based corporate-led sustainability alliances. So how do companies determine when a business ecosystem is the best option for a specific sustainability challenge? On the basis of BCG Henderson Institute's continuing research into sustainable business model innovation (SBM-I) and business ecosystems, we have identified six barriers that often inhibit a company's ability to address a sustainability challenge, either in their own operations or for their customers, and where business ecosystems could provide a solution:

1. Fragmented demand
2. Fragmented supply
3. Matching challenge
4. Lack of trust
5. Insufficient co-innovation
6. Lack of close coordination across industries

Companies looking to tackle sustainability challenges that exhibit at least one of these barriers should consider creating a business ecosystem to drive collective action toward an ecosystem with enhanced sustainability performance.

https://doi.org/10.1515/9783110775167-020

The Sustainability Imperative

Our research on more than 115 sustainable business model innovations finds that companies on their own frequently run into constraints within the wider system. That, in turn, limits their ability to achieve greater environmental or societal benefits in a way that is economically or operationally feasible for the business.

Consider the challenge of reducing plastic waste, for example. Major consumer-facing brands are making significant commitments to reduce the use of virgin polyethylene terephthalate (PET), in part by using recycled PET (rPET). But companies looking to switch to rPET face yet another challenge: by 2025, according to BCG estimates, roughly 45% of demand for rPET will be unmet due to limited supply. Filling that gap will require a portfolio of ecosystem interventions that include R&D into such alternatives as biodegradables, the scaling of emerging solutions, and coordinated approaches to expand recycling infrastructure.

This is where collective action can be particularly helpful in removing the constraints that limit the adoption of more sustainable business practices. There are three primary methods for engaging in collective action to remove system sustainability constraints:

1. **Sustainability Partnerships or Joint Ventures.** These arrangements involve formalized agreements among organizations to advance a specific sustainability-related product, service, or initiative. Royal DSM, for example, has partnered with several public, private, and social-sector players – including the government of Rwanda, international development banks, and NGOs – to set up Africa Improved Foods, which will increase access to affordable and nutritious foods. Such partnerships tend to be built by and around a single core business and its own value chain to deliver an SBM-I.

2. **Broad-Based, Corporate-Led Sustainability Alliances.** These alliances are a form of collective action that involves more than two entities with a focus on establishing joint standards, policies, or approaches that advance sustainability. Corporate-led sustainability alliances operating today include One Planet Business for Biodiversity, which focuses on cultivating and restoring biodiversity; the Global Platform for Sustainable Natural Rubber, which aims to make the natural rubber value chain fair, equitable, and environmentally sound; and the Consumer Goods Forum, which focuses on addressing such issues as environmental sustainability and the opportunity to develop products that contribute to global health and well-being.

3. **Sustainability Business Ecosystems.** This is a very specific type of collective action that is often highly focused on addressing a particular market need – and is more than just a kind of loose affiliation, which the word

"ecosystem" often evokes. And the approach has been gaining traction. Too Good To Go, for example, has built a business ecosystem to reduce food waste through a marketplace connecting customers with restaurants and stores that have surplus food.

Understanding Business Ecosystems

The term "ecosystem" is widely used in business but often carries a meaning that differs from the one we intend in this chapter. For example, some might describe London's financial center – with large investment banks, small financial players, and the network of companies and employees that support them – as an ecosystem. Silicon Valley – with its large network of established companies, startups, and leading research institutions – might also be labeled as such. But neither fits the bill of a business ecosystem under our definition.

That's because a true business ecosystem is not simply a means for connection or collaboration. Rather, it is a collection of independent businesses, orchestrated by a business at the center, that come together to address a specific need in the market. Most important, the solution that is developed by the business ecosystem creates value for every participant. And to make things a bit more complicated, business ecosystems can also incorporate the other two forms of collective action: partnerships and alliances.

Business ecosystems play an increasingly vital role in sustainability efforts. In our study of more than 115 SBM-Is, we found that roughly 30 of them built business ecosystems as a core part of their SBM-I. Notably, many were what we call sustainability front-runners: SBM-Is that most successfully push the boundaries of competition and reimagine their businesses in order to create more robust competitive advantage from sustainability.

In general, business ecosystems are the right choice to address a sustainability challenge that requires combining complementary solutions from different businesses in a highly coordinated fashion. To succeed, the business ecosystem must yield economic benefits for all players along with creating unique value to the end customer. While complex to build, business ecosystems offer the ability to easily access capabilities, scale fast, and achieve flexibility and resilience. In addition, business ecosystems can sometimes be a good interim solution to business sustainability challenges that stem from the absence of clear standards and universal regulation. For example, several players in the world of smart homes – including Samsung (SmartThings), Apple (HomeKit), and Amazon (Alexa) – are expanding their own connected ecosystems while, at the same time, setting up an alliance to work on establishing an industry-unifying, royalty-free connectivity standard called Matter.

Our research has found that sustainability business ecosystems tend to focus on addressing a few specific sustainability challenges and currently tend to be concentrated in a few industries, including financial services, education, and health care. However, business ecosystems remain a relatively untapped opportunity in many other industries.

When Business Ecosystems Make Sense

To determine whether a business ecosystem model is the right solution to a sustainability challenge, companies should assess the nature of the problem they are trying to solve. We have identified ways that a business ecosystem approach may offer a viable solution to the six barriers to addressing sustainability challenges listed at the beginning of this chapter. These barriers are not mutually exclusive; in fact, most sustainability challenges where business ecosystems are successfully deployed exhibit several of them (Figure 20.1).

Fragmented demand	Fragmented supply	Matching challenge
Business ecosystems can quickly aggregate demand, including among small-scale customers, to make supply and innovation economically viable	Business ecosystems can improve supplier practices and aggregate fragmented or small-scale distributed supply to support market depth and liquidity	Business ecosystems can help create markets with sufficient depth to ensure buyers can find and access sustainable products and sustainability services
Lack of trust	Insufficient co-innovation	Lack of close coordination across industries
Business ecosystems can reinforce the trust that a product is produced or sourced sustainably through verification, certification, and tracing	Business ecosystems can incentivize and link the innovation activities of many players to create a sustainability solution, often targeting common infrastructure challenges	Business ecosystems can drive close coordination across players, value chains, and industries to provide customers with coherent solutions

Source: BCG Henderson Institute

Figure 20.1: Ways Business Ecosystems Can Address Six Sustainability Barriers.

Fragmented Demand

Some sustainability challenges are difficult to address because of an inability to aggregate demand so that an SBM-I reaches sufficient scale. This is critical in situations where demand is highly fragmented (often across many small-scale customers), making the economics of serving those customers unattractive. Expanding financial inclusion or access to health or education for rural populations and underserved communities often requires addressing challenges with disaggregated subscale demand.

Consider insurance startup BIMA, for example. The company uses mobile technology to bring vital health and insurance products to more than 35 million customers in 10 countries: seven in Asia and three in Africa. BIMA's platform integrates offerings from various companies (telecom providers, mobile money providers, and insurance underwriters) and provides a seamless, user-friendly experience from registration to claims processing with no paperwork involved. To aggregate demand, BIMA employs 3,000 agents to educate and build trust among customers, three-quarters of whom, typically, are accessing insurance services for the first time. Those agents then direct interested customers to BIMA's multiple channels – including an app, a call center, and social media – to make their purchase.

Fragmented Supply

Supply of certain inputs to a sustainable offering, typically some sort of commodity, can also be a constraint – particularly when supply is highly fragmented (often across many small-scale suppliers). In such instances, transaction costs for customers are prohibitively high. As a result, supply needs to be aggregated before customers can find sufficient market depth to meet their demand or sufficient liquidity in the market exists to enable consistent transactions.

The need for aggregated sustainably produced supply is often an issue for companies that are aiming to improve the practices of small-scale producers throughout their supply chain, particularly in sustainable agriculture. Supply aggregation is also likely to be valuable in the renewable energy sector where energy generation need not be done only at utility scale.

For example, Singapore energy company Sembcorp launched its renewable energy certificate (REC) aggregator platform in 2020 to enable companies to purchase certified renewable energy (from Sembcorp and other suppliers) in lieu of paying government carbon taxes. The platform creates liquidity and flexibility by aggregating sources of RECs and will allow more large energy users to manage their energy portfolios across different sources and geographies and to achieve their renewable energy targets.

Matching Challenge

Companies attempting to market new sustainable products or services can find that high search costs prevent them from transacting with potential customers. In such instances, the challenge is less about scaling supply or demand and more about creating transparency about the offering and consolidating distinct products or services to enable sufficient depth for matching to occur. Sustainability challenges with this barrier include those related to improving resource efficiency, such as increasing the utilization of shipping containers or car sharing, and to providing access to recruitment and job opportunities for underrepresented groups. This barrier can also often be found in challenges in the circular economy, where certain products – such as excess or imperfect foods and second-hand items – require little or no adaptation to make them valuable to other users.

Poshmark plays that market-making role in the fashion industry, facilitating circularity and shopping for second-hand goods. The company – which went public in 2021 and now has more than 80 million registered users in Australia, Canada, India, and the US – has developed a platform for buying and selling items, mainly clothing, in a variety of categories. The platform aims to combine the human connection of a physical shopping experience with the scale, reach, ease, and selection benefits of e-commerce, leveraging a variety of social tools and features designed to drive engagement, including sharing, liking, following, commenting, and real-time virtual-shopping events, such as "Posh Parties."

Lack of Trust

In some cases, a lack of trust among parties is the major barrier for successful SBM-I, and a business ecosystem can help address this challenge. Trust can be created through verification, certification, and tracing applications (see Chapters 10 and 11). This is particularly important when what matters most to a buyer is how a product was made and what materials went into its production – so, for example, a buyer may choose a sustainably made product over an identical one that was made in a less environmentally friendly way. This could involve certifying that a certain amount of sustainable content (for example, the amount of nonvirgin PET in a bottle) or a product (for example, cotton) has been produced in a sustainable manner. This is also critical in the carbon offset market, where concerns about the underlying quality of offsets have increased in recent years.

The sustainability action platform rePurpose Global, founded in 2016, takes aim at the trust challenge. The platform enables individuals and businesses to offset their plastic footprints through the purchase of so-called plastic credits. These credits are created through the verified removal of low-value plastics from the land and plastics from the ocean, along with investment in recycling facilities in underdeveloped areas and new innovations for plastic alternatives. The platform also provides advisory services to clients to address the root causes of plastic use. It removes roughly 11 million pounds of plastic waste each year and provides fair employment for more than 9,500 waste workers through partner organizations in Colombia, India, Indonesia, and Kenya.

Insufficient Co-Innovation

Frequently, distributed players, in tandem, need to innovate their products or services in order for a coherent solution set for a sustainability challenge to emerge. Business ecosystems can drive co-innovation among fragmented players, including those in different industries or parts of the value chain, to create a solution to a specific problem. The need for coordination in sustainability often relates to the underlying common infrastructure for a product or service for which clear operational standards are required. Consider the heavy transportation industry, for example. Battery-powered electric vehicles that require a long time to recharge are ill-suited to an industry in which an idle truck is a drag on profitability. Innovations that rely on natural gas, particularly renewable natural gas or blue and green hydrogen, are being developed to decarbonize the heavy transportation industry. But without coordination, truck manufacturers, fuel distributors, and logistics companies are unlikely to adopt any kind of solution quickly.

Business ecosystems can also create the conditions for distributed innovation without a focus on a specific sustainability solution. Here, the business ecosystem provides the underlying platform that supports the exchange of ideas and data involving multiple players. Microsoft's AI for Good initiative, for example, offers an AI platform for innovation ecosystems that includes cloud computing services, AI tools, and technical support as well as cash awards to facilitate collaboration among key public and private stakeholders to address sustainability challenges.

We believe that there are several SBM-Is that could explore creating a sustainability business ecosystem to address the need for distributed innovation. Consider Salesforce's Sustainability Cloud platform, for example, which provides clients with data on their greenhouse gas emissions and energy usage. By opening its platform to external solution providers, Salesforce can offer them the opportunity to leverage the underlying data platform to create differentiated solutions for energy and emission management for Sustainability Cloud's clients across different industries.

Lack of Close Coordination Across Industries

Some sustainability challenges are difficult to address without continuous coordination among different types of stakeholders. Such coordination is especially required in situations where a coherent solution for customers is needed – such as, for example, in health care, where multiple care providers need to be coordinated for each patient. And coordination can be particularly important in circular economy solutions. That's because multiple players often have a role in a product's life cycle and therefore must make adaptations to their own products and processes to ensure that circularity can be achieved. Companies involved in the production, use, recycling, and second-life applications of plastic packaging, for example, must coordinate across the entire circular life cycle, including the collection of waste products from often fragmented end users.

Cityblock Health, a 2017 spinout from Sidewalk Labs (an Alphabet company focused on urban innovation), has cultivated the development of a business ecosystem that addresses the need for close coordination in health care. Cityblock, working with ecosystem participants – including primary care providers, behavioral health specialists, social workers, and community partners that address social needs, such as transportation, housing, and food – provides health care to Medicaid and lower-income Medicare beneficiaries. Cityblock's proprietary care management platform, Commons, provides a 360-degree view of a patient's health, enabling care teams to make recommendations on the basis of a holistic understanding of the patient and support coordination among experts. This tech-enabled community care model has proven to be cost-effective, resulting in a 15% reduction in emergency room visits and a 20% reduction in inpatient hospital stays. Cityblock currently serves 90,000 members in Connecticut, Massachusetts, New York, North Carolina, and Washington, DC.

Business ecosystems are an emerging model for tackling sustainability issues confronting society. While such ecosystems add complexity, they also provide access to critical capabilities and resources and the ability to scale rapidly.

To understand if a business ecosystem is the right way to organize to address a sustainability issue, companies must start by identifying the core barrier limiting their progress. In instances where the sustainability challenge exhibits at least one of the barriers outlined above, the development of a business ecosystem may unlock critical constraints and help companies address daunting societal challenges while creating competitive advantage.

François Candelon, Harald Rubner, Hans-Paul Bürkner,
Ulrich Pidun, Balázs Zoletnik, and Anna Schwarz
Chapter 21
How Public-Private Ecosystems Can Help Solve Societal Problems

Rwanda is Africa's most densely populated nation, with 13 million people living in a land-locked country that is smaller than Switzerland. Nevertheless, the agriculture sector accounts for more than one quarter of the country's GDP, and some 70% of Rwandans participate in the farming business. As such, agriculture is viewed as central to the future of the country. "Its value goes beyond providing our basic human need for food," says Agnes Kalibata, a former Rwandan agriculture minister, "it grows our economies and, more importantly, it changes society."[1]

For this reason, the Rwandan government invests heavily in the agriculture sector. But until recently, the investment did not have the hoped-for impact because of a lack of collaboration and coordination among the agricultural ministry, companies, and farmers. Things started to improve five years ago, when the government launched the Smart Nkunganire System (SNS), a public-private partnership (PPP) between the Rwanda Agriculture and Animal Resources Development Board and BK Techouse, a subsidiary of the BK Group, the country's largest commercial bank.

The initial product of this alliance was a digital supply chain management platform that gave farmers better access to the country's agricultural inputs subsidy program, which provides seeds, fertilizers, pesticides, farming machinery, and other inputs for a reduced price. The hope was that this would increase the productivity of Rwanda's 1.2 million smallholder farmers.[2]

Shortly after its launch, however, the PPP evolved into something we call a public-private ecosystem (PPE), which we define as a dynamic network comprising a government or other public body and an evolving and ever-changing group of largely independent economic participants. The government invited more than 1,000 small agriculture dealerships, along with some 30 small fertilizer and seed companies, to join the digital platform.

1 A. Kalibata, "Agriculture Is the Key to a Prosperous Africa," *Financial Times*, December 6, 2017.
2 "Smart Nkunganire System to Enhance Access to Agriculture Inputs," Rwanda Ministry of Agriculture and Animal Resources website, accessed on December 6, 2021.

https://doi.org/10.1515/9783110775167-021

Since then, the ecosystem has expanded even further, and it now also connects farmers and participating companies with banks and other providers of financial services. For example, the Bank of Kigali has created a universal digital wallet called IKOFI designed to provide farmers with a pathway to financial inclusion. Already, more than 250,000 farmers have registered for the service.[3] In the future, the ecosystem may become a one-stop shop where farmers can access a wide range of services that boost their – and, ultimately, Rwanda's – fortunes.[4]

By bringing different sections of society together, Rwanda's SNS powerfully demonstrates just how far the country has come in recent years. And we think that PPEs can serve as a model for all governments and businesses – in developed and developing countries – as they try to solve some of today's great societal problems. Food scarcity, poverty, unemployment and underemployment, inequality, environmental pollution, and climate change – these and other challenges are just too big for governments to solve on their own. In our view, they need to tap the expertise of business leaders by engaging with them in a collaborative, creative, nontraditional way.

Governments Need to Rethink How They Engage with the Private Sector

Traditionally, governments have engaged with the private sector in three main ways (Figure 21.1). One is through specific regulation, by issuing decrees – official orders with the force of law that are directed toward companies within a single industry. In Germany, for example, waste disposal companies are required to recycle 50% of the garbage they collect in order to win and retain a license to operate.

Another way is through framework legislation – by imposing rules, through general regulation or legislation, on a broad set of companies. Across Europe, for example, the General Data Protection Regulation imposes strict rules on how all companies can collect and use the personal data of millions of citizens.

A third way governments engage with the private sector is through PPPs, where a government invites one or more companies to collaborate on a specific project. Before evolving into a PPE, the Rwandan SNS was a classic PPP.

---

3 GSM Association, "Digital Agriculture Maps: 2020 State of the Sector in Low and Middle-Income Countries," September 2020, p. 49.
4 "BK Techouse Partners with Bill & Melinda Gates Foundation to Enhance 'Smart Nkunganire System'," IGIHE, March 4, 2021.

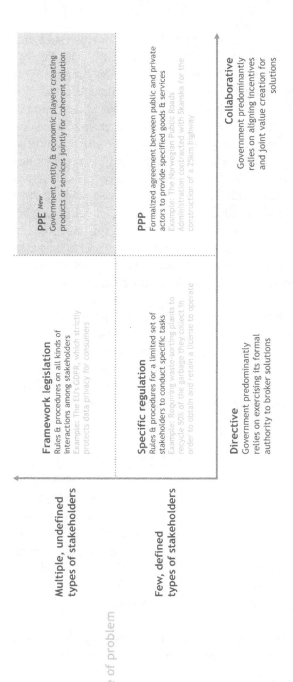

Framework legislation
Rules & procedures on all kinds of interactions among stakeholders
Example: The EU's GDPR, which strictly protects data privacy for consumers

PPE *New*
Government entity & economic players creating products or services jointly for coherent solution

Specific regulation
Rules & procedures for a limited set of stakeholders to conduct specific tasks
Example: Requiring waste-sorting plants to recycle 50% of the garbage they collect in order to obtain and retain a license to operate

PPP
Formalized agreement between public and private actors to provide specified goods & services
Example: The Norwegian Public Roads Administration contracted with Skanska for the construction of a 25km highway

Directive
Government predominantly relies on exercising its formal authority to broker solutions

Collaborative
Government predominantly relies on aligning incentives and joint value creation for solutions

Multiple, undefined types of stakeholders

Few, defined types of stakeholders

Scope of problem

Governance of stakeholders

Note: GDPR = General Data Protection Regulation; PPE = public-private ecosystem; PPP = public-private partnership.
Source: BCG Henderson Institute

Figure 21.1: Governments Have Engaged With the Private Sector in Three Main Ways.

These traditional ways of engaging with the private sector have their strengths. Top-down and directive legislation offers efficient and effective ways for government to tackle defined problems with specific solutions. By contrast, PPPs are effective for solving problems with clearly defined solutions because they help governments and businesses resolve questions relating to risk, capital, and the lack of capabilities and resources. But traditional ways of engaging with the private sector have their limitations, too. If they are strictly enforced (as they usually are), specific and framework legislation can have unintended consequences: companies pursuing their own self-interest may choose to follow the letter of the law but not, necessarily, the spirit of the law. Similarly, if PPPs are struck among a small number of companies (as they usually are), they become a kind of closed shop, and the opportunity to find the very best solution may be lost. Also, if the scope of PPPs is defined within a fixed and limited contractual framework (as it usually is), then their innovative potential may be reduced even further: PPPs have a reputation for delivering efficiency rather than sparking creative solutions.

Fortunately, there is a fourth way: public-private ecosystems. Designed well, they can overcome some of the limitations of the traditional ways of engaging with the private sector. They put companies on an equal footing with governments (in fact, some PPEs are orchestrated by companies rather than by governments) and they create a collaborative space where the energy and entrepreneurial ingenuity needed to solve society's biggest problems can run free.

The Transformative Potential of PPEs

Originally, the word "ecosystem," as coined by the British botanist Arthur Tansley in the 1930s, described a community of organisms in the natural world that collaborate and compete with one another, evolve together, adapt to new challenges, and exploit new opportunities. The word was first applied to the business world by James Moore, a strategist, in the early 1990s.[5] Since then, driven by the enormous success of tech firms and thousands of startups building their businesses according to this model, the concept has developed into a distinct discipline within the realm of business strategy.

Business ecosystems – including Amazon's marketplace, Apple's iOS, and Meta's Facebook – are able to facilitate the creation of highly modular solutions.

---

5 J.F. Moore, "Predators and Prey: A New Ecology of Competition," *Harvard Business Review*, May–June 1993.

This is because they offer four critical benefits: access to a broad range of capabilities, the ability to scale quickly, significant flexibility, and great resilience.

The business ecosystems created by the Big Tech companies demonstrate the transformative potential of the model. And they can serve as good blueprints for governments that want to work out how best to engage with business in order to tackle some of the biggest social, political, economic, and other public problems. As uniquely collaborative environments, business ecosystems offer participants the space to create products or services that together constitute new solutions to those challenges.

PPEs can help solve the problem of insufficient scale on the demand side and the supply side – for example, by supporting local farmers in aggregating their produce and matching it to larger resellers. They can also foster collaboration across sectors by establishing trust and facilitating coordination. And they can help overcome co-innovation challenges by encouraging various participants to innovate simultaneously and by providing a platform for effective coordination.

PPEs Have Already Helped Solve Big Societal Problems

Currently, PPEs remain an underused way for governments to collaborate with the private sector. Nevertheless, there are some good examples for governments to consider in addition to the Rwandan government's SNS.

One example is the Slovenian digital procurement platform initiative that links farmers with schools and other public institutions. The goal for the digital platform was twofold: to improve the nutrition of school children and public-sector workers and to improve access to the local produce of Slovenian farms. Within four months of its launch, the platform had registered 114 farmers, food producers, and cooperatives, along with 754 public institutions; and it had made available for purchase more than 2,200 locally farmed products. The effort was a great success: some 60% of schools increased their consumption of local produce. Since then, the platform has become a full-fledged ecosystem.

Another example is the so-called digital sandbox ecosystem established by the City of London and the Financial Conduct Authority in the UK. Providing innovative companies with a digital testing environment, this ecosystem was initially launched to encourage solutions to problems caused by COVID-19. In the first 11-week pilot, some 94 companies applied to join the ecosystem, and 28 were selected to participate. They were offered specific data to help them solve three problems:

1. Detecting and preventing fraud and scams amid a sharp rise in phishing emails
2. Supporting vulnerable citizens, especially older people who were more susceptible to COVID-19 and who found it difficult to perform basic financial activities
3. Improving access to finance for the small and midsize companies that were hardest hit by the economic downturn resulting from widespread lockdowns

The results were encouraging: the sandbox ecosystem accelerated product development times for some 84% of participants, led to improvements in the design of financial products, and helped companies refine their early-stage business models. One product in particular, which is still in the developmental stage, shows great promise: it gives unbanked people, such as the homeless, easier access to benefit payments.

But unquestionably, the best-known PPEs are those orchestrated by the various advanced research project agencies of the US government. The most famous of these is the Defense Advanced Research Project Agency (DARPA), which is responsible for creating breakthrough technologies and capabilities for national security. Since its founding in 1958, DARPA has orchestrated an ecosystem of innovators – including companies, universities, and government bodies – that normally compete against one another. It has also invested in fundamental research that led to the invention of the internet, the personal computer, GPS, drones, and Moderna's COVID-19 vaccine. In other words, DARPA has, as The Economist noted, "shaped the modern world."[6]

Politicians, policymakers, and other government decision makers face a daunting task: to find solutions to massive, multigenerational problems that will improve the lives and livelihoods of their citizens. That job was tough enough before the pandemic; now, it is doubly difficult. What should they do? To solve these problems, governments should look to tap the expertise, ingenuity, and resources of the private sector by engaging with companies in public-private ecosystems. Similarly, companies should try using this collaborative approach to increase the leverage of their own social impact and sustainability initiatives.

By working together in this way, governments and companies may not only solve immediate societal problems but also change society – or even, as DARPA has done, shape the world.

6 "A Growing Number of Governments Hope to Clone America's DARPA," The Economist, June 5, 2021.

List of Figures

1.1   Comparing Different Production Structures with Ecosystems —— 5
2.1   The Two Basic Types of Business Ecosystem —— 16
2.2   Rubric for Choosing a Governance Model —— 19
3.1   The Four Typical Paths of Business Ecosystems —— 29
3.2   Strategies and Success Rates for the Three Critical Windows in the Ecosystem Life Cycle —— 30
4.1   Seven Fundamental Failure Modes of Business Ecosystems —— 38
4.2   When Do Business Ecosystems Fail? —— 44
4.3   Ecosystem Design Vulnerability Checklist —— 46
5.1   The Four Phases of Business Ecosystem Growth —— 49
6.1   Five Building Blocks of the Ecosystem Governance Framework —— 66
6.2   The Option Space of Ecosystem Governance Models —— 75
6.3   General Characteristics of Good Ecosystem Governance —— 76
8.1   Orchestrators, Complementors, and Suppliers Comprise Business Ecosystems —— 91
8.2   Ecosystem Contributors Increasingly Achieving Unicorn Status —— 92
8.3   Imperatives to Succeed in Being an Ecosystem Complementor or Supplier —— 103
9.1   Step-by-Step Framework to Develop a Company's Ecosystem Strategy —— 105
9.2   The Three Flywheels of Successful Business Ecosystem Design —— 111
9.3   Two Categories and Eight Vectors of Ecosystem Evolution —— 120
10.1   Failed Ecosystems and Business Stage Where Trust Was a Factor in the Failure —— 130
10.2   Elements of a Trust-Building Framework —— 132
11.1   Trust Spells the Difference Between Ecosystem Success and Failure —— 141
11.2   The Seven Classes of Trust Instruments —— 142
11.3   Real-World Trust Instrument Cluster Patterns —— 149
12.1   The Four Issues Revolving Around Data Sharing —— 164
12.2   Smart Simplicity's Six Rules to Change the Context Underlying Data Sharing —— 168
13.1   Mitigation of Data Sharing Risks —— 174
13.2   Tools to Evaluate and Capture Data Value —— 176
13.3   Solutions to Reduce Friction in Data Sharing —— 178
14.1   Four Fundamental Approaches for Creating a Health Care Ecosystem —— 186
14.2   Data Sharing Can Amplify Flywheel Effects —— 195
15.1   Strong Correlation Between Where the Wealthiest People Live and Areas With Greatest Access to Top Jobs —— 201
15.2   Disruptive Technologies and Changing Aspirations of City Dwellers Are Setting Up a New World of Opportunities for Cities —— 202
15.3   Cities Can Orchestrate the New Mobility by Taking Six Interlinked and Sustained Actions —— 205
15.4   Indicators Should Be Available at Both the Urban and District Level and They Should Be De-Averaged to Reveal the Contribution of Each Service to the Mix —— 207
16.1   Smart-City Applications Use Data From a Variety of Sources —— 212

https://doi.org/10.1515/9783110775167-022

16.2 Common Practices in the Approaches to Data Management of 30 Smart Cities —— 214
17.1 The AM Blueprint That Connects Players Along the Flow of Information and the Flow of Goods and Services —— 223
17.2 The Choices Relating to Governance Issues Depend on Where the Participants Want the Ecosystem to Be on the Continuum Between Fully Closed and Fully Open —— 230
18.1 Digital and Data Ecosystems —— 239
18.2 Supply-Side Partnership Frameworks —— 240
18.3 Structural Factors Shaping Value Pools and Ecosystems of IoT Application Providers —— 242
18.4 The Three Distinct Roles in IoT Ecosystems —— 244
18.5 The Three Paths to Becoming an IoT Ecosystem Orchestrator —— 246
19.1 Global Temperature Is Expected to Increase Well Above the Goal Set by the Paris Agreement —— 253
20.1 Ways Business Ecosystems Can Address Six Sustainability Barriers —— 266
21.1 Governments Have Engaged With the Private Sector in Three Main Ways —— 273

Index

additive manufacturing XIV, 14, 17, 35, 221
antitrust 33, 64
application programming interface (API) 15, 69, 72, 196, 216, 231, 242
artificial intelligence (AI) 11, 73, 145, 173, 175, 177, 189, 194–195, 269

backlash 42, 64–65, 79, 112, 133
bias 24, 27, 84, 148, 150, 184, 260
big tech XIII, 184, 191
blockchain 22, 73, 136, 146, 166, 172–173, 177
business model innovation XIV, 21, 263–264

carryover 42, 57
chicken-or-egg problem 23, 25, 37, 41–42, 44, 111, 232
churn 131
circular economy 268, 270
climate change 199, 204, 211, 251–252, 256–258, 260–261, 272
cloud 34, 92–93, 98–99, 185, 192, 241
coevolution 4, 7, 10–11, 20
co-innovation 16, 95, 224–226, 228, 234, 263, 269, 275
collective action 251, 256–258, 263–265
commoditization 97, 100, 118, 248
compliance 42, 83, 145, 166, 211, 260
conflict management 70–71, 146
control
– input control 72, 85, 145, 151–153
– output control 71–72, 77, 85, 94
– process control 72, 80, 84, 153, 155, 157
cooperative 110, 134, 141, 156
coopetition 97, 248
coring 116
critical mass 37, 41–42, 44, 111, 129, 188, 190, 192–193, 232–233, 244–245
culture 67–68, 86, 94, 101, 137, 143, 150
curation 18, 73, 83, 114, 151, 179
cybersecurity 240, 245

data security 63, 153
decision rights 40, 51, 67, 70, 77, 81, 86, 94, 117, 196

design 36–37, 44–45, 135, 153, 184
disintermediation 21, 42, 117

electronic health record (EHR) 73, 185, 191, 196
evolution 20, 24, 33–34, 44–45, 50, 58–59, 79, 93, 119, 251
expansion 22, 25, 57–58, 193, 226, 255
exponential 115, 139

failure 36, 39, 47, 83, 101, 127, 190
first mover 31–32
flywheel 41, 111, 188, 194–195, 226
fork 24, 117

gig economy 68, 80, 139, 145, 148, 150–151, 155
governance XIV, 24, 40, 65, 67, 73–74, 76–77, 79, 81, 97, 112, 128, 190

increasing returns 18, 53, 115
intermediation 22, 146–147, 152, 154–155, 158
Internet of Things (IoT) 148, 163, 211, 233, 237

launch strategy 41, 44, 68
life cycle
– evolution phase 44–45, 50, 58–59
– launch phase 44, 48, 50–53, 59, 94, 192
– maturity phase 44–45, 50, 55–56, 58
– scale phase 44, 50, 53–54, 94, 129

mindset 36, 159, 196, 260
minimum viable ecosystem (MVE) 41, 233
mission 67, 71, 80, 187
modularity 19–22, 35, 108, 185
monetization 116
multihoming 37, 42–43, 95–96, 117–118

network effects 17, 37, 94, 111, 194, 243

openness 7–8, 40, 44, 51, 110
open-source 70, 80, 143, 173, 177, 216–217

https://doi.org/10.1515/9783110775167-023

path dependence 77, 114
PC system 20–21, 227
public-private ecosystem (PPE) XIV, 271, 274,
    276
public-private partnership (PPP) 271–272

red flag 48, 50, 52, 60–61, 94, 117
reputation 31, 65, 144, 151–152, 274
resilience 23–25, 159, 183, 260, 265, 275
role 109
– complementor 14, 77, 99, 102, 117, 222
– contributor 90–91, 93, 102, 109, 115
– enabler 169, 192, 197
– orchestrator 90–91, 109, 191–192,
    227–228, 235
– supplier 90, 96

smart cities XIV, 213, 215, 218–219
smart contract 143, 148, 177
smart home 14, 17, 35, 144, 153, 196, 265
Smart Simplicity 163, 167–168

software development kit (SDK) 72, 166,
    245, 247
strategy XIV, 10, 34, 105, 121, 196
subsidization 41–42, 54, 74, 111, 116, 231,
    234

take rate 59, 74
transaction cost 21, 38, 164, 170, 224, 238,
    267
transaction fee 18, 24, 116, 225
trust 135, 140, 151–152, 156, 159

unicorn 89, 92–93, 98, 102, 105

value capture 24–25, 36, 74, 77, 85, 99, 116,
    206
value distribution 36, 58, 65, 74, 80, 116,
    231

winner-take-all 37, 42–43, 94, 113, 115, 119

9 783110 775044